14 Days

W9-AXC-033

THEY SURVIVED

A Study of the Will To Live

by Wilfrid Noyce

Foreword by Sir Vivian Fuchs

Illustrated

A S *On July 24, 1962, Wilfrid Noyce fell to his death while descending Mount Garmo in the Pamirs of the Soviet Union. During his eventful life he had won fame as a brilliant mountaineer and as a highly successful writer. Wilfrid Noyce spent much of his life in the shadow of possible sudden death and was deeply interested in the characteristics that enabled certain men and women to survive in situations of exceptional hardship and danger. Just before leaving on his last expedition to the Pamirs, he finished the writing of* They Survived, *a vivid, imaginative, yet authentic study of great cases of survival and of the psychological and spiritual powers which made them possible.*

(continued on back flap)

BOOKS BY

WILFRID NOYCE

MOUNTAINEERING

Mountains and Men
Scholar Mountaineers
British Crags and Climbers
(edited with E. C. Pyatt)
South Col
Snowdon Biography
(edited and written with
G. Winthrop Young and G. Sutton)
Climbing the Fish's Tail
To the Unknown Mountain

POETRY

Michael Angelo
Poems

BIOGRAPHY

Samson: The Life and Writings of Menlove Edwards
(with G. Sutton)

NOVEL

The Gods are Angry

GENERAL

The Springs of Adventure
They Survived

Wilfrid Noyce

They Survived

A STUDY OF THE WILL TO LIVE

1963

E. P. DUTTON & CO., INC.

NEW YORK

First published in the U. S. A., 1963 by E. P. Dutton & Co., Inc.

FIRST EDITION

Excerpts from *Alone* by Richard E. Byrd reprinted by permis-
sion of G. P. Putnam's Sons. Copyright 1938 by Richard E.
Byrd.
Line drawing of the accident on Haramosh and photos of Tony
Streather and John Emery from *The Last Blue Mountain* by
Ralph Barker. Copyright © 1959 by Ralph Barker. Reprinted
by permission of Doubleday & Company, Inc.
Quotation from *The Waste Land* by T. S. Eliot in *Collected
Poems of T. S. Eliot* reprinted by permission of Harcourt,
Brace & World, Inc.
Material from *K 2: The Savage Mountain* by Charles Houston
and Robert Bates reprinted with permission of McGraw-Hill
Book Company, Inc. Copyright © 1954 by Charles Houston
and Robert Bates.

Library of Congress Catalog Card Number: 63-8928

To
Those Who Endured,
That
We May Learn To Endure Also

Foreword

by Sir Vivian Fuchs

The character of an individual is complex indeed, but basically it is the product of the qualities with which he is born and his environmental experience. This fascinating selection of almost incredible stories of survival makes one wonder at the toughness of the human mind and body.

It has been said that many brave deeds have only been performed because of a lack of imagination, or indeed the intelligence to appreciate a situation. Yet the difference between man and beast is the ability to think, and to reason from previous knowledge. In a dangerous situation the power to reason can be an aid, but, when there is nothing to be done, the human must have great mental stability, as well as the physical endurance of an animal. Passive resignation is not enough and the conscious will must be invoked to aid the body to survive.

One may read these accounts and be astonished at the unexpected reserves of strength which they reveal. Besides invoking admiration, they are a reminder that in every one of us there are similar reserves of strength if only we can learn how to call upon them.

Preface

I have called this book quite simply *They Survived*. I say at once – it would be readily perceived if I did not – that I am no scientist, nor indeed any sort of -ist. Books like *The Science of Survival* (by L. Ron Hubbard of the Hubbard Dianoetic Foundation) attack the broad canvas of human existence in terms of dynamics and categories into which all our functions can be pigeon-holed. I have neither skill nor wish to do this. I could no more pigeon-hole dynamics than fly, and I am foolishly frightened by charts and lists. Here I am concerned only with the extreme physical situations in which some people have found themselves, and I adumbrate certain qualities of mind as having brought those people through. In the last chapter a brief attempt is made to link these 'survivors' together and to ask whether their qualities are those which will help men and women of this twentieth century to survive as individuals, as a community and as a species. I have based the book on a very few, carefully chosen stories, the truth of which I have taken pains to check.

Nevertheless, I have been drawn into fields of which I know little or nothing. Here I have turned for help to the experts: to the physiologist, the doctor, the psychologist, the priest. Invariably help was given with a generosity that astounded me, not only by the experts but by the 'survivors' themselves. I would like first to thank many who responded to letters in the papers requesting stories, and on whose experience I have drawn even when they are not specifically mentioned. And I would like publicly to express my thanks to the following:

Dr R. Asher; the Rev R. Born; Mrs R. A. Butler; F. Spencer Chapman; J. Church; J. Duncan; Dr F. Ellis; Dr J. A. G. Emery; Mrs D. Grose-Hodge; Captain B. R. Hanauer; R. A. Hodgkin; Dr C. S. Houston; J. W. Lambert, Assistant Editor of the *Sunday Times*; Mrs H. W. Leakey; E. C. B. Lee, Secretary of the Naval Life-Saving

Committee; P. Mason; D. N. Paton (photographic work); Mrs M. Piriou; Mademoiselle M. Renault; Mrs R. F. Russell; J. M. Scott; the Scott Polar Research Institute (permission to use photographs and other help); Dr C. Seward; J. Sillito; Mrs A. Spence; Major H. R. A. Streather; A. S. Till; Dr Judith Waterlow; Dr J. A. Waycott; Major C. G. Wylie (photograph); the Wiener Library.

I acknowledge gladly my debt to all those whose writing has helped me. A list of books to which I refer is given at the end. For more extensive quotations and pictures I here express my thanks to authors and publishers of the following works: *The Last Blue Mountain* by Ralph Barker (Chatto and Windus Ltd and Doubleday & Company); *K2: The Savage Mountain* by Charles Houston and Robert Bates (William Collins, Sons & Co., Ltd. and McGraw-Hill Book Co., Inc.); *Raft of Despair* by Ensio Tiira (Hutchinson & Co. and E. P. Dutton & Co., Inc.); *Tibet's Great Yogi Milarepa*, edited by W. Y. Evans-Wentz (Oxford University Press); *Alone* by Richard Byrd (Putnam & Co., Ltd. and G. P. Putnam's Sons); *The Informed Heart* by Bruno Bettelheim (Thames and Hudson Ltd and The Free Press of Glencoe); *La Grande Misère* by Maisie Renault (Chavane); *Collected Poems* by T. S. Eliot (Faber & Faber and Harcourt, Brace & World, Inc.). I also take the opportunity to thank my own publishers, William Heinemann of London and E. P. Dutton of New York, for their continued interest and support, and J. Michie of Heinemann for the personal trouble he has taken with my text.

WILFRID NOYCE
Hindhead, January 1962

Contents

Illustrations

Maps and Plans   *page*

I

Environment Makes the Man

'HE'S LUCKY TO HAVE SURVIVED.'

The words, spoken I do not know by whom, floated towards me across a black river, red and black with pain. I could see white shapes of people dimly, as through a film, from my right eye. The glare of electric light hurt me. My jaws gaped to enclose a great stone sausage, my left cheek felt as if a hammer had been pounding it for some time. But I was lucky to have survived.

I was nineteen and had been rock-climbing in the Lake District, from the house of a friend. On the very severe long pitch of Mickledore Grooves, on the East Buttress of Scafell, there had been a turf ledge at a point where the leader is about a hundred feet above his second man. Nowadays the leader can be protected with rope slings or 'running belays' left over convenient knobs on the way, but in 1937 these had not yet come into fashion. It had rained slightly, and, though I still do not remember the accident at all, I know that the ledge came away under me so that I fell through air to a point a hundred feet below the second man. On the way I must have received one blow on the face from the side, another from below. The rope stretched a further twenty feet. My second, Menlove Edwards, was physically as strong a man as I have known. He held me on the rope over his shoulder – or rather two ropes, for one had not been enough and we had tied two lengths together. His hands were torn a little.

An emergency operation saved my life, though I knew nothing about that. The face, in the wrong shape, was together again. Plastic surgery was to follow, but not yet. A long business.

Lucky? Yes, partly that. Lucky that the ropes did not break (one strand held), that Menlove was so strong, that there were helpers near, that one of the finest surgeons could reach me from Scotland. I was also supremely fit, having returned from five weeks in the Alps. And I was cocksure of my own fitness, so that, when I came round, the thought of death never so much as approached me. Nor did I ever doubt, not only that I would recover completely, but that I would climb again; in a different way, perhaps, but as surely as before.

It was not the least of my luck, as I realise now, twenty-four years after the accident, that this was a survival situation with which the I of those days could grapple: short and sharp, a purely physical shock, and after that shock all the forces on my side, everybody, beginning with the most understanding of parents, seeing me through. The mental cruelty, added to long-drawn-out physical suffering, of a concentration camp would have killed me then as it would now, even though it might not have exposed me to as great a single blow, measured simply in biological terms, as the one that struck me that day.

Each of us seems to be born with certain faculties which help us to survive in certain situations. Sometimes these are obvious qualities: stubbornness in everyday life, tenacity, the fighting spirit and so on. Often, however, they lie submerged, waiting to be dug from the depths by the particular situation. In these cases we may not know at all why a certain person survives, nor may he. Some 'miraculous' survivals against all expectations have been noted by doctors in babies of under a year old, the qualities they would show in life seemingly quite undeveloped. Again, a person may not consciously want to survive at all, and yet do so. A woman whom I know, whose husband had recently died, lived on after a very bad car crash, in which her youngest and dearest son was killed with his wife. Mrs G. herself had her scalp torn off, her chest broken in, arm and leg broken and much else besides. In hospital, after the first fortnight of operations, the sister in charge of her said, 'I reckon I've pulled you through.'

'Why have you done it?'

And she went on to curse the sister, the hospital, everybody, for having brought her back to a life she hated. My friend was not, however, for all the curses, the sort of person who would lie down and die, and the situation proved it. She would go on living the next day, and the next, and the day after that. Whatever her conscious mind thought about it, she would get better. Today she looks younger than before the accident.

We seem to come back to a basic quirk or attitude which decides the reaction of the person to the situation. Another woman, perhaps a cheerful soul in everyday life, might have died in Mrs G.'s situation, even without the added shock of her son's death. She might have lacked the 'life-wish' which Mrs G. possessed (against her conscious desires) as surely as some primitive tribes possess, because they believe in, the 'death-wish' or death-urge. In Sir James Frazer's *The Golden Bough* the story is told of how, since the shadow of the mother-in-law passing over the body in sleep was considered fatal, a tribesman slept in the shade of a tree; but as he slept the sun moved round, and, when he woke, there was the fatal shadow cast upon him. Not immediately, but slowly he pined and died. By such compulsions 'civilised' man too is affected, though less obviously. Nothing but the situation will show who has the life-urge, who the death-urge. Given the situation, nothing will stop one person from dying, another from living in spite of all.

To some extent, as we shall see, and in certain situations, a certain type of body is useful: the big, burly, muscular person is less apt to survive than the lithe, wiry one. But it is as dangerous to generalise about this as it has proved to be about the ideal shape for an Everest climber. It is also true that a person can to some extent be trained to survival, just as he can be trained to hold his breath for long periods under water. I have before me the case of an airman who crash-landed recently in the Malayan jungle and who survived because of the equipment devised by the R.A.F. experts: ejection seat to throw him properly clear, a parachute which could be used for shelter and its thread for fishing, a Very pistol, food, compasses, knife, water ration, purifying tablets, mosquito net, hooks and floats for fishing, snares; in addition, a booklet called *What to Do*, giving all the answers. This man came out little the worse after three days and nights in the jungle. Without the equipment and training he might well have died because he expected to die.

What the preparation gave him, more important than any mosquito net or fishing hook, was the belief that if he reacted rightly, did the right things, he would not die. It was not *necessary* for a man who had crash-landed in jungle to die. Of this preparedness we shall see examples later, and it brings us back again to basic attitude, which training can improve but cannot implant. This rock bottom may, in one sense, be the psychologist's province; at the same time psychologists agree that they cannot give the answers. Bruno Bettelheim, for instance, a penetrating exponent of mass psychology, found his knowledge inadequate to explain behaviour in the concentration camps. He himself had spent a year at Dachau and Buchenwald, and I shall quote his opinions in a later chapter. What concerns us here is his stress on the importance of environment (which equals situation in the survival context) as against psychological premisses. In the camps there came to him 'the realisation that those persons who, according to psychoanalytic theory as I understood it then, should have stood up best under the rigour of camp experience, were often very poor examples of human behaviour under extreme stress. Others who, according to the same body of theory and the expectations based on it, should have done poorly, presented shining examples of human dignity and courage.'[1] Thus environment plays a far larger part in the bringing out of character than is generally supposed by those who look first to heredity, childhood disturbances or sexual impulse. In the camps, 'one and the same environment could bring about radical changes both for better and for worse.'

This idea of the importance of environment, or situation, fitted well with the idea which I, being no psychologist, already had in mind: to present a series of situations and see what came of them, rather than to attempt depth psychology (for which I am not competent) of the individuals concerned. In Bettelheim's view a bad or difficult environment, such as a concentration camp, which might be expected to turn

1. *The Informed Heart*, whence come also the other quotations.

4

out bad types, might equally 'evoke new meritorious qualitites in some who never evinced them before.' Thus psychoanalysis, which starts with the individual, and in the pre-war Freudian days tended to accept that the good society should and could be built through creating the good individual, was here of no help. 'Psychoanalysis, which I had come to view as the best key to all human problems, offered no suggestion or help towards the solution of how to survive and survive halfway decently in the camps.' Here Bettelheim had to fall back on qualities previously thought to be of little importance, while many which he had learned to stress were of no use at all.

Again, Bettelheim found that it was simply no solution, if some unlikely person did some outstandingly courageous act, to explain this away in terms of the death-instinct, aggression turned inward, megalomaniac denial of danger or exhibitionist narcissism. Such explanations seemed quite beside the point. It was not that psychoanalysis could not be applied, but that in viewing courageous or cowardly behaviour it fell 'shockingly short of the mark.' 'The way a person acted in a show-down could not be deduced from his inner, hidden motives, which, likely as not, were conflicting. Neither his heroic nor his cowardly dreams, his free associations or conscious fantasies, permitted correct prediction as to whether, in the next moment, he would risk his life to protect the life of others, or out of panic betray many in a vain effort to gain some advantage for himself.'

Psychoanalysis cannot explain why these men and women did what they did, any more than Freud's study of Leonardo da Vinci explains Leonardo's creative genius; the same childhood emotions and experiences might, in another person, have produced nothing but empty scribblings. We come back to the environment or situation. The situation would seem to draw out in the person some quality which he or she did not know was there, which psychoanalysis could not have told him was there, or, indeed, which may not have been there at all until the spark arrived to strike fire from the tinder. Moreover, situations will draw out different qualities even in individuals equally suited to meet them, while of both situations and individuals there is an infinite variety.

We lack terminology to describe the holistic state of the person *in* the environment. Normal phraseology puts environment and organism in opposition, yet they must be treated almost as a unit (art-and-artist, man-and-concentration camp, sailor-and-sea) if they are to be understood. Speaking personally, I recognise the new unit in myself, on a mountain. The man-on-mountain or rock-and-climber can accomplish things over which Noyce-on-the-plains would fumble incompetently. In deciding, therefore, to approach the person through the situation and to be implicit rather than explicit in my conclusions, I might have taken a whole kaleidoscope of cases, each shading into the next, to demonstrate the many ways in which it is possible to adjust to the new situation. It has seemed simpler to take a few outstanding cases from six or seven very broad types. Nobody would maintain that any type of survival is clear-cut and classifiable. Each situation is different; the reactions of each of us shade imperceptibly into those of our neighbour. But with this reservation it may be helpful to start with an example of 'basic' survival, in which nothing is called for but the endurance to sit it out, and to move on, through illness and accident, to situations in which a more and more co-operative, then positively active, part is required, until we reach a case in which a man volunteers for a long-term survival situation. I emphasise that there is no 'rising scale' in this progression. Finally, as example of the conditions in which moral as well as physical and mental endurance is called for, we shall consider the victim of a concentration camp.

Whether there is any link, any basic resemblance, between the cases, or any lesson for ourselves, we shall ask at the end.

2

Sitting it Out: The Collier and the Hermit

IT WAS AT THE TIME OF THE AGADIR EARTHQUAKE, IN the spring of 1960, that this book was born. The telephone rang. It was a leading London newspaper.

'We wondered whether you'd like to write an article about Agadir and survival,' the voice said.

'But I don't know anything about either.'

'You know that people are still being dug out alive, about ten days after the earthquake?'

'I didn't, actually.'

'There might be some connection between people who get buried like that and mountaineers.'

'But mountaineers don't survive that sort of thing, not unless they have to.'

'That's what I mean. Some sort of lesson people could learn from the ones who are trapped and *have* to do it.'

'Well, I'll think about it. It's very interesting. Only I don't know anything about it. . . . I'll let you know.'

'Let's see. We'd like it sent off tomorrow, or you could phone it to the office the day after. About fifteen hundred words?'

For once my slow-moving mind had to bestir itself. The Agadir earthquake had appalled me, as it appals everyone who thinks about it, as Lisbon appalled Voltaire: so great a calamity in so short a moment, bearer of such indiscriminate pain. But now, when I reflected, I had to admit that an objective curiosity about the survivors, buried for days on end under masonry or in cellars, did mingle with natural pity. By all accounts they were very ordinary people, the butcher, the baker, the candlestick-maker and their wives; that impression has been confirmed by conversation with Moroccans in Morocco. They survived, without food and water, conditions which would have killed many. And the very fact that there was nothing special about them was a good starting point for reflections about physical survival in other circumstances. These were the survivors who did nothing but wait (if that can be termed nothing), and, if they were Muslims, resign themselves to the hand of Allah. Had they some link with, or lesson for, other men and women who found or put themselves in survival situations?

When I came to the wider context, having no opportunity to visit Agadir, I looked for an example nearer home. Many have had this type of experience, and they offered it generously and to my profit: the skier trapped in a crevasse with broken leg, the holiday-maker stranded by the tide, the pot-holer caught underground, the airman upside-down in his wrecked plane. The case I am going to relate comes from the familiar scene of a British coal-mine. A little removed in time, the collier is John Brown, native of Midlothian and parishioner of Dailly in Ayrshire, during the year 1835.

The parish of Dailly extends along the banks of the Girvan, not far from the Ayrshire coast. On both sides of this valley rise hills of moderate height, while beside the winding river lie fields and woods quietly beautiful in a way common to the county of Burns. In those days Dailly village, which housed less than half of the parish's population of some 2,000, was pleasanter than most mining villages: built solidly from a grey stone quarried locally. None of the miners' cottages of 1835 now remains, but the church stands, and in the churchyard the gravestone of a quarryman killed while quarrying. Perhaps it is the humour of the place that this should be fashioned from the very stone that killed him.

Coal had been found near Dailly as early as 1415, and there is a record of the monks of a neighbouring monastery mining it in the sixteenth century. In 1835 Kilgrammie mine was a flourishing little mine worked by a 'lessee', or mineral tenant, who employed miners from the village and sold his coal at between 4s. 8d. and 5s. per ton of 24 cwts. The mine closed down at about the turn of the present century, but in the vigorous 1830s rich seams tempted the lessees to ever more daring excavations. The insecurity of these, together with ignorance of safety precautions, was the reason for the fall of October 8.

John Brown himself was a man of sixty-six, a bachelor. We have no picture of him. Though slightly deaf, he was otherwise hale and worked in the mine as hard as the rest. He had a reputation as a humorist of the phlegmatic sort. Sometimes, the story goes, his fellow miners would take his pick and finish off a stretch for him, so that he could sit and tell stories. In other respects he seems a typical Scottish miner of the period.

On the 6th, Brown, working alone in a hole at the end of the rail, was startled by a rumble above. Troubled, he climbed out to see what was happening. A truck, which had been standing empty on the rail, had rolled along and stopped a foot or so from the edge. Nobody was about, but it looked like a practical joke. That evening, however, his friends denied the joke, and on the evidence Brown had to acquit them. Another foot or two, and the heavy iron truck would have crushed him. Obviously, then, it was the Devil's work. Superstition lingered in these parts, and the Devil in person was no unfamiliar figure to the miners. He, Brown noted, 'seemed much more ready to push along empty hutches and endanger men's lives than to give any miner help in pushing them when full.'[1]

During the next day the pit creaked and groaned, the levels of the rails changed ominously, but the warning was ignored. The thick seam of coal had left, as it was extracted, a space, and this space was maintained by massive pillars, sixteen or seventeen feet broad and forty feet long. In order to remove more and more coal, the management

1. From 'The Colliers' by Sir Archibald Geikie, which later appeared in his book *Geological Sketches* (1882). This is the most detailed account of the accident, taken from miners who remembered it. The best contemporary account is that of Dr A. Hill, and appears as a note after his article on the Parish of Dailly in the *Statistical Account of Scotland*, vol. V (1845).

had reduced the size of these pillars until they became too weak to bear the enormous weight above. The creaks and grindings, as well as the trucks that ran on their own, showed an alteration of levels which meant that something was going to collapse somewhere soon. It was already clear, though the men worked on, that at least part of the pit would have to be abandoned.

The 'crush', however, came more swiftly than had been expected. At about five a.m. on the morning of the 8th the great rock mass above the galleries settled ponderously down with a rumble which most who heard it above ground thought must signify an earthquake. Rents appeared in the earth surface for several acres around, a pond-dam burst, the pit-ponies at the shaft-head went careering off, masterless, towards the village.

It is hard to believe now that the colliers below ground continued their work almost to the last moment. But the risks which they ran were nothing new to them; nor, for that matter, was the lessee's eagerness for coal. They worked on until the cry went up that the whole roof was settling down. Then they made a dash for it, first to the bottom of the main shaft, in the hope that the engine would haul them up. But this shaft had been caught by the roof's fall, so they made for a second shaft, only to find that this too was closed. The ground all about them creaked and groaned hideously, as they put it later, and they retreated to a part where the pillars still seemed to be firm. Then one of them remembered a tunnel or 'day-level' that led for over half-a-mile from the pit to a wood called Brunston Holm. As they started towards it, they realised that Brown was not with them.

Two younger men returned and found him. One of these, some thirty years later, described the scene to Sir Archibald Geikie when he visited the place collecting material for his article 'The Colliers'. When they came upon him Brown was still at work, 'as unconcernedly as if he were digging potatoes in his own garden'. Even when roused, and despite the creaks and crashes around, he was unwilling to come with them. Why, we cannot know. Had he suffered from too many false alarms before? Was he just plain obstinate? Being a little deaf, he had heard little of the din that terrified his friends.

The whole world seemed to be tumbling about their ears as they went stumbling, straining towards the others. Then, suddenly, John Brown remembered his jacket. He had left it behind. He refused to go on, for all their dragging.

'The jacket is a new one,' he said. 'And as for the pit, I have been at a crush before now, and will be through it this time too.'

Off he hurried, disappearing into the darkness of the mine to search for a coat. He had hardly gone when the roof finally collapsed. Brown must be either crushed or buried alive.

The day-level of a coal-pit resembles a drain or leat running horizontally through the hillside. It is built to carry off the underground water with which, along with mud, it is filled almost to the roof. The remaining miners had now to walk stooping through water which rose often to their shoulders. It was a clammily cold, eerie business, the roof and walls dark with slime in the lantern light, the mud sucking at their feet as they stepped forward. They were intensely relieved to be out, chilled and dripping wet, into the autumn fields and woods of Girvan valley.

They brought news of Brown's fate to the village, but there was no question of doing anything for him until the crush settled. The village now sensed that it stood above a man who was slowly dying. This point the minister, Dr A. Hill, did not fail to rub in to a receptive congregation the next Sunday. 'He made us feel deeply the horror of knowing that a human being was living beneath our feet, dying a most fearful death,' one of his congregation put it. That first Sunday everyone in the village felt that he was still alive, a terrible example to all. The next Sunday they felt that he must be dead. By the third Sunday they were just beginning to lose interest.

After some days the noises below ground had abated sufficiently for the work of rescue to begin. The miners dug willingly, and without pay, to cut a tunnel towards the place where they reckoned Brown to be. Their devotion was the more remarkable since they believed that he would by now be dead, and that either his ghost or the Devil, or both, would be occupying the spot where he lay. Several times men rushed out, pursued by strange gibberings borne upon the wind that whistled through the mine. Meanwhile the lessee employed miners from other parts to reopen the main colliery.

On the twenty-third day they cut through the last mass which separated them from the uncollapsed workings beyond. A rush of foul air put out their lights, threatening to suffocate them. They retreated. Finally, one of them went to fetch boards or corn-sieves with which to flail the air and create a current. Another advanced, waving his arms. In the darkness his hand struck a wagon standing in the roadway. The sound was followed by a human groan.

How John Brown had been feeling, what thinking, we are left to guess. Quite possibly, even if he had fully recovered afterwards, he would not have told us very much, though he himself thought otherwise. Lying in bed after his rescue, Brown turned to the miners sitting beside him and said with a puzzled expression, 'Ah, boys, when I'm through this I've a queer story to tell ye!' But that story he never told.

For over three weeks he had lain entombed in a chamber sixty yards long, twelve feet broad and six feet high. Gradually the air had become so foul, that when his rescuers arrived their lamps were extinguished sixty yards from where he lay. He had nothing with him but a quarter of an ounce of tobacco and an oil lamp. People wondered afterwards why he did not try to use the oil as food, and imagined that the thought had not crossed his head. But he had already, earlier in life, been trapped in an English pit, and had learned that to drink lamp-oil makes a man unpleasantly sick.

For two days he felt a fierce hunger. There is a story that he chewed his boot-laces.[1] Then, as happens when men are starving, hunger passed entirely. It was succeeded by unquenchable thirst. At first he was able to walk about, and drank the strongly impregnated water that flowed through the chamber; but after a fortnight he was too weak to do this.

He had always the feeling that he would be rescued. That, perhaps, does not need stating. Dr Hill, writing of the case in his memoir on

1. An old Dailly man, J. McCulloch, remembers being taught in school that Brown chewed the uppers of his boots. For much of my information about Dailly I am particularly indebted to John Duncan, of Ayr.

Dailly Parish, could not resist adding, 'That he was very sensible of the wonderful care which had been exercised over him, and of his very precarious state, may, it is hoped, be inferred from his asking to be commended to God in prayer;' while a contemporary newspaper goes so far as to attribute to him the words: 'In the darkness I was not alone; I had company the earth could not exclude, for God was with me.' It is at least probable, even if his words are unlikely to have been those ascribed to him, that he had that feeling, common to others in extreme ordeals, of the company of another person, and that, since he was a devout Presbyterian, that other person for him was God.

Apart from this, we know little. We know that at first only the sound of water came through, but that later he could faintly hear men working at the tunnel being dug in his direction, and that he was able, from the alternation of silence and sound, to form some impression of the passing of days. But we do not know whether he organised his time like Christopher Burney, who passed 526 days in solitary confinement at the hands of the Nazis,[1] by counting out the minutes, by the number of turns he took up and down, by the pauses between drinks. In total darkness, after the lamp went out, it would not have been simple to organise anything at all. Moreover, Brown's temperament was doubtless very unlike that of the sensitive, introspective Burney. To his reactions the survivors of the avalanche at Blons give a better key.

In January 1954 the small village of Blons, in Austria, was overwhelmed by avalanche.[2] The last survivor to be dug out, the shepherd Franz Bertel, had spent sixty-two hours under the snow, in conditions of extreme cold. Franz was 'a meek, blond, stoical fellow of twenty-nine, with a permanent happy smile on his face'. He was also a trifle simple. When he found himself buried in the stable, his first reaction was to remark, 'Something's happening in Blons.' Finding, after this monstrous understatement, that he was unable to get out, he became gradually bored and hungry and a trifle cold. He, too, felt certain that he would be rescued. Asked afterwards whether he prayed, he replied, 'A little. I reckoned the Lord was busy enough.'

1. *Solitary Confinement.*
2. *Avalanche!* by Joseph Wechsberg gives a graphic account of this catastrophe.

In fact he just sat it out and thought of nothing very much. From time to time he ate snow to stay his thirst, and he could see, through a little hole at the end of a long gallery, night changing to day and day to night. In something of the same mood Brown may have sat, and then lain, but for a much longer period. He did not have the advantage of seeing night change to day and day to night; moreover, every hour the air became fouler and the ground below colder, like a tomb. Perhaps the cold ground was a reason, along with haunting anxiety, why he slept little, 'being always on the rack from a consciousness of his dreadful situation'. Perhaps at first he beat his hands together, as he walked to and fro and to the water, then, choked with bad air and weak from lack of food, he lay and walked no longer. Anyone who has lain out on bare rock for a night will know that it is a very uncomfortable experience. To lie on rock for twenty-three days, with no blanket or sleeping bag, is an ordeal beyond the imagination of most.

Voices. A light through the pitchy blackness to which he has become accustomed. The light goes out, the muffled voices are gone too. Dear God, they've gone for ever! Silence again, and time passes. He knows that he cannot last long now, but hope deferred almost breaks resignation.

The voices are there again, but no light. Somebody is advancing, stumbling and talking, his arms hitting out. Something bangs against the pit wagon.

He tries to speak, but can only groan. He is heard. There is a cry, the man backs away and stumbles out. Time passes again. Now there are two of them talking together, and a voice shouts out, homely as the fields of Girvan, 'If that's your ain groan, John Brown, in the name o' God gi'e another!'

So they found him. At first they could not see him, not daring to light the lamps yet for fear of explosion. But they felt him, and his body was very cold, like a corpse. They called back to the others and started stripping off their jackets to cover him, and lay down with their naked backs against him, to warm his body. Then he spoke, or

In Memory of
JOHN BROWN Collier
who was enclosed in
Kilgrammie Coal Pit
By portion of it having fallen in
Oct.r 8th 1835,
And was taken out alive
and in full possession of his Mental faculties
But in a very exhausted state
Oct.r 31st,
Having been twenty three days
in utter seclusion from the world
And without a particle of food
He lived for three days after
Having quietly expired on the evening of
Nov.r 3d
aged 66 years.

hn Brown's gravestone (*W. Downie*)

Satopanth Glacier (*C. G. Wylie*)

whispered, 'Gi'e me a drink!' He was parched dry, for all the dripping walls around.

There were now a number of miners, and these conferred together. They were afraid to give him anything strong, in case, weak as he was, it should do him harm. One of them dipped a sleeve in a runnel of the pit wall and moistened Brown's lips with it. Brown asked them, or is reported to have asked them – and why not, for a sense of humour is strengthened rather than weakened by crisis? – 'not to make a fule o' me.' The water refreshed him and he spoke again: 'Eh, boys, but ye've been lang o' coming!'[1]

A remark that rang very true.

The time was three or four a.m. on 30 October, and there remained the problem of getting him above ground at this hour. One man returned to inform the lessee and summon help, while others continued to cover Brown with their coats and lie beside him. One rubbed butter from a piece of bread on to his lips. Brown said that he would like milk, and another man went off by the 'level' to raise a neighbour to milk her cow. By the time it was daylight a crowd had gathered at the pit-head.

Brown was laid on a board and pushed through the narrow tunnel hacked in the hard crushed roof, just wide enough for a man to crawl through on his elbows. In the cage in which he was to be hauled to the surface he was placed upon the knees of the lessee. 'Here it should be mentioned,' Sir Archibald Geikie writes, 'that upon the decayed timber props and old wooden boardings of a coal-pit an unseemly growth of white and yellow fungus takes root, hanging in tufts or bunches from the sides or roofs wherever the wood is decaying. As they rose into daylight, a sight which had only been faintly visible in the feeble lamp-light below presented itself, never seen before, and never to be forgotten. The coal-mine fungus had spread over the poor collier's body as it would have done over a rotting log. His beard had grown briskly during his confinement, and all through the hairs this white fungus had taken root.'

As they rose, hauled by the engine above, and as the daylight made

1. A woman of Dailly records that it was to John Scobie, her great-grandfather, that he said this.

15

the growth among his beard more visible, the lessee began pulling at the fungus, separating it from the hairs. Brown, so the lessee said later, pushed his hand away, murmuring, 'Na, noo, wad ye kittle [tickle] me?' He retained obstinacy and a wry humour to the end.

He was carried home to the village and put to bed. At nine a.m. the minister saw him, and thus described him: 'There was then an agreeable warmth on his skin, and, although he spoke slowly and little, yet he was perfectly collected. His appearance was very striking, from the length of his black and glossy beard, the hollowness of his eyes and their extreme brightness, as if they had been glazed. The odour of his breath was particularly offensive.'

Sir Archibald Geikie, after speaking with a miner who had been present, elaborates the picture: 'A more ghastly figure could hardly be pictured. His face had not the pallor of a fainting fit or of death, but wore a strange sallow hue like that of a mummy. His flesh seemed entirely gone, nothing left but the bones, under a thin covering of leather-like skin. This was specially marked about his face, where, in spite of the growth of hair, every bone looked as if it were coming through the skin, and his eyes, brightened into unnatural lustre, were sunk far into his skull.' Dr Sloan, who attended him, remembered that, when he put a hand over the pit of his stomach, he could feel distinctly the inner surface of the backbone.

One collier is known to have expressed the opinion, years later, that Brown came to the surface far too quickly, before he had been fed. Certainly in modern times, now that two world wars, earthquakes and avalanches and shipwrecks have given wide experience in treatment, his chances of complete recovery would have been that much greater. Nor was he helped by the crowds of sightseers who came to view this human miracle, to ask questions and to disturb his calm. He sank into a lethargy and died peacefully on the evening of 3 November, after it had seemed to the doctors that he was pulling through.

To those who thought of it at all, it must have seemed cruel that a man should survive the agony of twenty-three days underground and then die when by every expectation he was entitled to life. But it might be that the very qualities which pulled him through the ordeal were not those likely to help the more delicate operation of recovery. It might be that he was quite simply killed by kindness, or that the physical decay had set in so far that it won the upper hand so soon as the spirit which had held him together relaxed its watch. The causes of death were sufficiently obscure at the time for an examination of the body to be thought necessary.[1]

Any great feat of physical endurance breeds an almost reverential awe, and the Kilgrammie miners, it will be remembered, were superstitious. Why, they reasoned, should God bring him through the greater trial, to make him fall at the less? If God preserved him, why should it be for the useless end of dying later? And if not God, then who else . . .?

'Did ye fin' his feet?' they asked Dr Sloan.

Dr Sloan confessed that he had not looked at his feet immediately after he died, and to the end some miners believed that the Devil, cloven hoof and all, had come upon their friend in the dark and taken

1. The report of the examining doctors reads as follows:
Post mortem examination and Medical Report on John Brown. Dailly, 13 November 1835.

By virtue of a warrant from the Sheriff's Substitute of Ayr, dated 12 November 1835, we, the undersigned, have inspected the body of John Brown and report as follows.

Brain rather paler and firmer than usual; ventricles nearly empty; chloroid plexus pale.

Omentum nearly altogether absorbed, rests merely upon the colon; capable of being extended about two inches.

Heart small and flabby.

Stomach of medium size, empty at the cardial extremity; inflammation of the mucous coat extended about two inches in one direction, by one inch and a half in the other.

Mucous coat abraded in two places about one quarter of an inch.

Liver healthy; gall bladder very much distended; no mechanical obstruction.

Spleen very black – easily ruptured.

Intestines healthy; mucous coat dyed by a dark-coloured fluid.

Bladder, structure healthy – about half a pint of urine.

Kidneys healthy.

Lungs healthy; lobes loaded with black matter.

The body was extremely emaciated.

We have no reason to believe that improper medical treatment contributed to the man's death. This we state upon soul and conscience.

(Signed) John Wilson, M.D., C. F. Sloan, M.D., J. Blane, Surgeon, A. Vass, Surgeon.

possession of his body. Some would not even believe that he had in the proper sense died. His ghost haunted the tomb and was not exorcised until an inscription, written by the minister, had been carved upon a headstone. Then at last the ghost was laid, and the Devil departed from Dailly.

John Brown's survival may be termed 'basic' because he sat it out without active exertion, enduring and feeding upon fats stored through the years. There was nothing, indeed, that he could actively do; he could only conserve energy and practise a mental attitude which would buttress his hope of relief. These mental attitudes in modern Western man seem very personal, concerned with personal survival. In the case of the Agadir survivors the emphasis would be different, the emphasis of the Muslim faith, but they, too, were concerned to survive personally. However, it is possible to hibernate in a different direction, so to speak; to give the same performance, not through personal hope, but through forgetting personality.

Modern asceticism is generally associated with the East, and in thinking of ascetics a distinction needs to be drawn. Both Christendom and the East have had their great ascetics, between whom stretches a link that is often ignored. St Antony, 'the first of the Christian hermits', appeared between the Nile and the Red Sea during the reign of Diocletian. He, and his many followers after him, led lives of extreme rigour. 'Sleep and food and drink were reduced to the barest needs, and to less. A rivalry in repudiation ran about the desert, and the rumours of the gaunt and holy figures of its practitioners percolated through the bazaars of the great cities.'[1] But this asceticism had an object beyond the simple renunciation of the world, the flesh and the Devil. 'Alone, ascetic, emaciated, St Antony gave to the Church the same formula: "Your life and your death are with your neighbour".' The Way of Negation, in Charles Williams' phrase, complements the Way of Affirmation. Oversimplifying drastically, one could say that by renunciation, by prayer, a new relationship was to be set up with God, whose end was still to be the salvation of the 'neighbours', of all men.

It is instructive to take as parallel an Eastern ascetic, like the eleventh-century Tibetan saint, Milarepa. After the early years of 'notorious sin',

1. *The Descent of the Dove* by Charles Williams.

after the gruelling tutelage under Marpa the Translator, we find him saying a touching farewell to his beloved tutor and retiring to caves, some
of them not far from Everest, ultimately to attain Buddhahood. In
his charmingly personal autobiography, a book shot with poetry, he
records realistically that in the Dragkar-Taso Cave 'I had resolved on
the starvation diet of twenty measures of barley flour per year, and
now even that, after three years, had run out. I might have died without
being able to attain Buddhahood.'[1] He discovered a nettle-bed and
lived on nettle broth, using the empty flour sack to replace his disintegrating clothes. He describes his appearance: 'My body was
emaciated with privations and hardships; mine eyes were deeply
sunken into the sockets; my bones showed prominently; my colour
was of a bluish green; my muscles were all shrunken and shrivelled; a
growth of bluish-green hair covered my skeleton-like form; the hairs
of my head were stiff, and formed a formidable wig; and my limbs
appeared as if they were about to break.'

In one of his poems Milarepa 'justifies the life of ascetical seclusion
from the world. Unknown to the worldly multitude, who regard the
yogī as a useless member of society, he is, in fact, the most useful;
owing to his thought-force, broadcast like silent and invisible arrows
which fall among all nations, virtue and goodness are kept alive in the
world, and the Pathway leading to the Olympus of the Gods is guarded
and kept open.'[2]

And shot forth thus, the arrows fall midst all the Nations.
They strike the Faithful Ones,
And slay the Sprite of Selfishness.
Thus are the Enemies, all Evil Passions, overcome;
And protected are our Kindred.

Thus he, like St Antony, East as West, wills that the immense force of
his meditation shall not be consumed in himself alone, but spread abroad
to others. Nor is this aim incompatible with the quest for Buddhahood.

1. The translations are those given in *Tibet's Great Yogi Milarepa*, edited by
W. Y. Evans-Wentz. An excellent condensation of this work is *The Life of
Milarepa* by Lobsang Jivaka in John Murray's *Wisdom of the East* series.
2. W. Y. Evans-Wentz, op. cit.

We are not directly concerned with the ends of asceticism. All but a Voltaire will admit that important experience can be gained by some when the body is forgotten or indeed purposely neglected. The spiritual conclusions of the ascetics,[1] the true Way of Negation and the attainment of self-realisation (the avowed object of Milarepa) through solitude, are outside the scope of the present study. But it is not altogether outside it to contrast Brown's experience with that of a distinctly lower type of ascetic, whom one might call the professional hibernator.

Milarepa writes:

May I not lie steeped in Unconsciousness of Quietude;
But may the Blossom of the Superconsciousness bloom forth in me.

And Evans-Wentz comments: 'There are states of unconsciousness into which a *yogi* may fall, which do not lead to Enlightenment. A like state, which, however, is not necessarily a state of unconsciousness, is experienced in the *yogic* condition of suspended animation or *yogically* induced hibernation. Although a practised *yogi* may hibernate for very long periods – according to some *yogis* for centuries – and eventually revive in his physical form, it is not desirable that he should do so, if he be aiming – as Milarepa was – at deliverance from the Sangsāra.'

Thus the great ascetics were conscious that their powers could be prostituted. The Buddha himself, in the Eighth Episode of his life, practised miraculous fasting by living on a grain of rice a day over six years, until he collapsed and 'remained unconscious for many hours. When he came to himself he realised that this was not the path to true wisdom, and he went to a neighbouring village in search of nourishment.'[2] It is the same perhaps with other powers; for instance, levitation, which enabled Milarepa 'freely and without obstacle to explore the whole universe from the abyss of the infernal regions to the most

1. Including Western ascetics, whose experiences are examined by William James in *The Varieties of Religious Experience*, Chapter XIII.
2. F. Maraini, in *Secret Tibet*. Compare the Christian view: 'Ascetic practices, which in themselves strengthen the will, are only useful in so far as they enable the will to put its own house (the passions) in order. . . . They are necessary as a means; as an end they would be abominable'. *The Problem of Pain*, C. S. Lewis.

giddy heights', but which, among the Tibetan magicians described by Madame David-Neel, has become almost a trick. These stalwarts are also reputed able to dry ice-damp handkerchiefs with their naked bodies, so many in a night. Indeed, competitions are organised, to see who can dry the most. In this sense 'suspended animation' or '*yogically* induced hibernation' can become a trick too, and I take two examples which may have a bearing, by contrast, on John Brown. They happen to be particularly well authenticated, coming from the eye-witness account of Philip Mason, now Director of the Institute of Race Relations, at one time Deputy Commissioner for Garhwal.[1]

In May 1937 Philip Mason visited Kedarnath, an important shrine in the Himalayan district of Garhwal. To me, perhaps because I saw it first of the districts, it has always seemed the loveliest of all: in summer a land of huge peaks, dominated by Nanda Devi and Kamet, of mighty gorges on whose sides the pine and deodar climb dizzily, of terraced fields green and yellow with ripening barley, of high pastures beyond the upper tree-line. Kedarnath stands at 11,000 feet, a thousand feet higher than the more accessible Badrinath. Both these towns are places of pilgrimage, lying near to the source of the sacred Ganges. Their houses, roofed with wood or shingle, and their temples (Kedarnath's is particularly fine) are strongly built of stone, and they need to be, for in winter the scene is very different. Then the snows descend, storms rage for days and the villages are buried, cut off by huge drifts from the valleys around. Kedarnath lies in a small semi-circle of glaciers; peaks of some 23,000 feet glint frostily in the near distance, their rocks quite covered. At Badrinath there are hot springs; the town lies in an open valley and the snow is never so deep as at Kedarnath, where the houses are buried between October and April, and the inhabitants descend with their flocks to the plains.

The Garhwalis are a pastoral and agricultural people, moving up as the snow disappears to graze on the alps and plant their barley or potatoes in the higher valleys. They are round of face and sturdy, clad in homespun

1. From letters, conversation and the short story 'The Hermit' in his collection, *Whatever Dies.*

blankets for which you will often see them spinning the wool as they walk: a people not given to superstition, of which they see too much in some of the pilgrims flocking up during the summer months to wash away their sins. However, when Mason arrived he found tremors of excitement abroad. There were still, though it was May, twenty-foot drifts around, and they came to tell him that they had recently dug out a buried house in which they had found alive a *sadhu*, or saint, who had been there in the snow since the previous autumn. All he had had with him, they said, was a bag of *gur* (sugar molasses), which had disappeared.

Mason went to see him. The *sadhu* was a young man, looking thin and ill. He was very willing to talk, and told a long story of how he had indeed spent the winter there; of how 'great white spirits' – a race about twelve feet high and very white – had come to him from the snow outside. These sounded suspiciously like one version of the Abominable Snowman. They threatened him, telling him that this was their country during the time when the great snow fell. They took the *gur* and ate it, so that he had nothing.

'You did not go out to relieve yourself?'

'No. It was not necessary, because I was not eating anything.' For six months he had not been outside.

The man, when Mason saw him, was sitting wrapped in blankets in a patch of sunshine, like a convalescent after a serious illness. At first he could hardly walk, moving his limbs slowly and with difficulty. It was to take him a month to recover fully all his faculties. Meanwhile, he was enjoying the notice which his exploit brought him, the presents of food, the interested villagers who flocked to see him as Western crowds throng a champion boxer. To that extent he seemed something of a charlatan. Mason questioned him. What did his feat mean? Why had he done such a thing? He answered elusively, but, when pressed closely, said that he would come and explain it all to Mason in a dream. Either Mason slept too soundly, or no saint turned up that night.

About the feat itself, however, there seemed no doubt. Mason, then in the service of the Government of India, had travelled widely in his district and written with knowledge and sympathy of the Garhwalis.[1] The man had convinced everyone in the village of Kedarnath. The solid

1. See *The Wild Sweet Witch*, etc.

people of these places are used to impostors. They had certainly, they said, dug him out, and it would have been exceedingly difficult, had he crept away for a while, for him to have returned without tracks and popped back into the snow in time to be found. Could there have been a conspiracy? But there would have been no point, for Hindus are not interested in conversion by such means. The miracle is not a weapon of evangelism. And what object could there have been in faking an experience of this sort for a casual traveller?

Next year, in 1938, Mason saw the same man again, when he had repeated the performance. This time he was recovering more easily, as if he were used to it. But there were still no signs that he had undergone a great spiritual experience.

The second case is the more remarkable. In July 1939 Mason was visiting the larger pilgrim town of Badrinath, a holy place in which is found every manifestation in the gamut of religious experience, from frank imposture to deepest sincerity. Set in an open valley among hillsides thick with pine and deodar, it boasts a fine stone temple containing a sacred image of Vishnu, and hot springs in which the pilgrims, many of them arriving on foot from the plains of India, are accustomed to purge their sins. Many yogīs and *sadhus* are among the crowd, their bodies naked or covered with ashes. Some, like the Sannyasis or Gosainis (devotees of Siva), wear a red wig of coiled or matted hair over their shaven heads, giving them a grotesque appearance. In leopard- or deer-skin and with a gourd for offerings they go begging their way. One may also see the Kamphati yogīs, who split their ears so that the blood drawn may be offered to the gods. Not long since, human sacrifice was practised in Garhwal and Kumaon.

As at Rome or any other place of pilgrimage, the great mass of pilgrims are honest, hard-working people who have come to make the journey of their life before they die. The Rawal, or High Priest, and his attendants have somewhat the air of French *abbés*, practical and not easily taken in. Hearing that Mason was on his way up to the Satopanth Glacier, the Rawal said, 'Ah, then in that case you can tell us what has happened to the *sadhu* who went up last year.'

'And who is this *sadhu*?'

The man had gone up, he said, in the autumn, in September or early October, intending to sit the winter out on the glacier at a height of some 15,000 feet (about the height of Mont Blanc). The Rawal was positive that he had not come back, and it was now July. Next day, as he passed through the villages, Mason questioned the people that he met. Had they seen the hermit? Had he come down? These villages, up to Mana, the last before the Mana Pass, are inhabited during the summer months. In the autumn, as from Kedarnath, the inhabitants go down, driving their goats and sheep towards the plain, to bring back when they return commodities like sugar which they cannot otherwise obtain. The path is in constant use during the late autumn, until the snow comes and makes travel impossible. When not under snow, it is all bare rock and scree and short grass. It was hard to believe that anyone could have come down after the shepherds had gone, and that nobody had known about it.

The walk from Badrinath to the Satopanth takes two or three days. At Mana one turns left, up the stream of the Alaknanda, which is the infant Ganges. The valley becomes wilder, enclosed by lowering peaks, the stream a milky torrent. At last, beyond the point where the source of the Ganges issues from the combined snouts of the Satopanth and Bhagat Kharak Glaciers, one can climb by moraine on to the Satopanth. At the last camp site, stunted juniper provides the fuel; Mason camped here, on grass.

Next day he climbed on to the glacier. The going was hard, a bouldery scramble typical of many in the Himalaya, the boulders varying in size, so that one could not keep continuity of rhythm. Jump, skip, slither – and always the crusted grey ice below. At last the ice hummocks became less dirty, the pass at the glacier's head peeped out. It is a beautiful spot on a fine summer's day. The glacier, some six miles long, is hemmed by peaks that are the objective of mountaineering expeditions. Domi-nating the left (true right) bank stands Nilkanta (21,640 feet), among the most graceful mountains I have seen; but it is no place in which to spend a winter. After four hours of hard going Mason's party came to 'the tarn', as it is called, a small glacier pool in the ice. Beside it, sitting on a black buckskin, was the hermit.

They approached and questioned him. He looked an old man, withered and shrunken, completely naked but for a pair of spectacles of which one lens was broken. His hair was grey, a few straggling grey hairs grew over his chest. In his wizened face there was no beauty, no expression of the saint in ecstasy before the sublime vision. Only, as they questioned, Mason thought he detected in the other a certain pleasure at the thought that his feat surprised the foreigner. But perhaps that was unkind.

The hermit refused resolutely to talk either to Mason or to the Garhwali clerk accompanying him. Slowly he shook his head. Then, in the gravel heaped by the glacier's movement against a rock, he traced something with one skinny finger. It was the Sanskrit character for the sacred syllable *Om*, or *Aum*. This character stands for Brahma, who is 'the one without second or the inexpressible Absolute'. It has been said that *Om* is the ultimate word that can be uttered, after which there remains nothing but silence. Thus all prayer and worship are summed up by it; it is, as Marco Pallis says in *Peaks and Lamas*, 'the sound of all sounds, audible to the initiated ear, which is produced by the act of Manifestation, or, as we would say, of Creation. . . . It might be compared with Pythagoras's Music of the Spheres.'[1] In this context, it might have been taken to mean that it was the proper occupation of man to merge his consciousness in that music, into the great Nothingness that has neither beginning or end, rather than to answer frivolous questions. Certainly it was a sign of dismissal.

The cave in which the hermit had lived was formed, on the edge of the ice, by one stone tilted above another, leaving a space below into which it was possible for a man to crawl, and then to lie or kneel: about six feet long, three or four feet wide and two feet high. The floor was of grey, ice-ground gravel. The hermit was said to have gone up with two men, one of them carrying a sack of potatoes, the other half a maund (about 40lb) of flour. The potatoes he must have eaten raw. The flour he would have mixed with cold water, during the time when water flowed, and eaten raw also. Two ounces of flour a day, to keep out the cold of nine months.

1. It is, of course, also the first syllable of the Buddhist formula '*Om mani padme hum*', usually translated loosely 'sacred jewel of the lotus flower'.

Long periods of his stay the hermit must have passed in a 'state of *yogically* induced hibernation'. He was still in a sense entranced when Mason found him, hence the impossibility of conversation. Their minds were moving at different levels and speeds; they could find no common ground. How far he had gone beyond mere hibernation towards the real contemplative state, Mason could not guess. Perhaps the '*Om*' signified that he was far on the road to Enlightenment. If so, then none of Milarepa's 'arrows' fell upon his visitor, no reflection of the sublime experience. In silence Mason packed up, glanced back at the skinny figure squatted on the ice beside the little muddy lake, among the boulders. The shining peaks looked down, in a friendly way now, from a sky the blazing blue of Himalayan summer. But he could picture the scene in December. . . .

The hermit and John Brown (and with John Brown I think of all those trapped in avalanches, pits, mines, earthquakes like Agadir) both sat it out in impossible physical conditions for a length of time incredible by any 'normal' standard. One chose to do so for motives only half seen by us, the other had no choice. John Brown was a member of a community, always regarded himself as such and relied on the community to extract him and preserve that life which he himself could do nothing active to save. Whatever the strength he drew from religious faith, certainly he also drew great strength from his fellowship with the other miners. The hermit was alone because he chose to be alone. He differed widely from the Christian hermit, who seeks *life* in the sense used in St John's Gospel, through his seclusion, and who has, somewhere in his mind, the idea of a community being served or helped, it may be actively, it may be through prayer. The Satopanth hermit was not seeking life in that sense, or in any sense; rather he was losing it through a voluntary abstraction of the faculties generally associated with it. But, though one cannot say this with so much confidence of the second hermit as of the first, he differed also from the great sages of the Milarepa tradition in that his hibernation seemed to be an end in itself, having its own reward. If the way is a Way of Negation for its own sake, then it seems to lead nowhere.

We conclude that the reserves upon which the hermit drew cannot yet be expressed in chemical formulae or biological terms, though ideas even on that may be different in a hundred years' time. Already physiologists are at grips with the problem. Dr L. G. C. Pugh, for instance, records the case of a Nepalese pilgrim who sat out, without gloves, dressed in light cotton clothing, for four winter nights near the Base Camp of the Himalayan Scientific and Mountaineering Expedition (15,000 ft). Night temperatures recorded at the camp above during this period were – 13°C to – 15°C, and on the fourth night there was also a severe storm. On the fifth day scientists carried out two four-hour studies of body temperature and metabolism; on medical examination nothing abnormal was found, there was no sign of frostbite or cold injury, though he was a lean man. This was a puzzle. Just possibly there may be a link-up here with the processes used in artificial hypothermia, a technique now practised for heart surgery. Body temperature is lowered, metabolic processes slowed down, so that the blood supply to vital organs can be safely cut off for as long as twenty minutes.

Thus science can point out the ways in which the human body, when specially treated, survives temperatures which normally would kill it; but it cannot yet explain them. Nor does hibernation of animals serve as a parallel to that of the hermit. An American missionary, to whom Mason told his story, said, 'That's what bears do in winter,' and left it at that. But the bear lives on physical reserves of stored fat; the hermit had no fat at all, even when he started. On the other hand his reserves were not the mental reserves of John Brown, who loved and expected life and sat it out for that reason. The hermit's type stands apart from the main run of human, scientific, even of religious experience, and therefore I mention it now, partly as an obverse to Brown and partly to get it out of the way. It does not lead on, but remains static like a vast lake into whose dark depths, borne past them on the living stream, we dimly see. I shall not refer again, except incidentally, to the feats of 'mystics and magicians', but will note here and now that in simple terms of bodily survival these have never been equalled.

3

The Will to Live: Marceline and Others

DISEASE IS A JUNGLE IN WHICH THE LAYMAN QUICKLY LOSES himself. Gratefully he leaves the tracking of it to the professional guides. When he falls ill he can, if he likes, follow the Christian Scientists and deny that it exists. All honour to him if he follows that path success-fully. At the other extreme he can become a *malade imaginaire*, imagining himself about to die without the saving grace of doctors, or even with it. Or he can pursue the middle course of most of us, believing some afflictions to be mountains which no amount of faith will remove, while others can be overcome or at least moderated by an attitude which accepts but 'to submit declines'.

Everybody can think of cases in which attitude of mind has con-quered physical circumstances. Sometimes, like Mrs G. already quoted, the patient has lost a conscious wish to conquer, but the 'thing inside' ticks on and refuses to stop. Sometimes it is a need to live for wife or husband or children which brings him or her through, against the doctors' expectations; even if, being sensible people, the doctors did not commit themselves quite so far as the patient imagined. Sometimes it seems to be sheer determination to enjoy things enjoyed before. I am thinking of a skilled mountaineer, severely struck by poliomyelitis:

the iron lung, the danger list, tracheotomy and weeks of breathing 'from the machine', weeks of physiotherapy. Arms and body were hit, and legs too, one particularly. It was hinted, in those critical first two months, that he would never drive anything speedier than an invalid chair; a walking limit of one mile was mentioned. That was three years ago. He now drives a car, has climbed most of the peaks of Snowdonia – and has done rock climbs of Moderately Difficult standard.

In this case recovery seems largely a question of adaptability and co-operation: adaptability, when the virile man finds himself helpless and dominated by nurses and physiotherapists, and realises that a new pattern to life has set in; and co-operation in the slow process of regaining lost faculties. Co-operation is the new factor. The patient has not only the task of sitting it through, like the earthquake survivor, but of willing himself towards recovery and of assisting it through exercise, medicines, regularity in taking treatment – in fact what the doctor ordered and more besides. Whatever her first reactions to being saved, Mrs G. conscientiously did the exercises which restored the use of her limbs. It is a commonplace that any doctor needs the help of his patient in the job of getting him well, and any sensible patient helps.

That is true of recuperation from the great majority of diseases and accidents. But what of an apparently insuperable disease like cancer? Can an attitude of mind be adopted which will surmount that? Any enquiry is bound to be highly speculative, particularly for a non-medical man, and the choice of cancer is somewhat arbitrary. Moreover, drastic simplification tends to distortion. Let me say now, however, that the help I have been given, both by the profession and others, has been wonderfully generous. What little I have learned, I have learned from experts; and these have vigorously scrutinised the chapter which follows.

Even doctors are confronted, in an enquiry like this, by major difficulties at the outset. Many patients do not know they have cancer, and hospitals vary in how much they tell. It is possible to be cured without ever knowing the truth. Many who know, or suspect, push their knowledge to the back of their minds and prefer to forget. Further, cancer is arbitrary in its comings and goings. No two cases are alike;

a cancer which seems similar to a previous fatal case may equally well stop short and spare its victim. Surgery, drugs and radiotherapy help increasingly, but in the long run it can be the cancer which takes the decision. Thus a survival which seemed miraculous and partly due to supreme fortitude may be simply the result of a sudden, merciful cessation or 'spontaneous regression' which has a natural, if at present inexplicable, cause. With these and many other reservations in mind, let us look more closely.

Cancer is a 'malignant tumour', its main attributes starkly simple, even to the uninitiated. That is partly why I have chosen it. Cancer cells form alongside the ordinary cells of the body and then spread through multiplication, destroying the surrounding cells by pressure atrophy. They do not need oxygen. At first the cancer is local, usually reaching a free surface where there may have been a slight injury, and where micro-organisms of putrefaction can operate and produce an ulcer with thickened edges. The real menace of the disease lies in the 'secondaries' or 'metastases', born long before the ulcers visibly appear, from cells carried along the lymphatics to the lymphatic glands, and so to further groups, or else along the blood-stream to other parts of the body, particularly to liver and lungs. These cells Georges Beau,[1] in a comparison between the human body and society, compares to colonists who survive when the parent state has long since succumbed.

For even if the original cancer has been cut out or otherwise removed, the harm may have been done. To make things more difficult, these cells have an insidious way of taking over from some harmless tumour or some irritation of a well-defined type, such as that produced by clay-pipe-smoking (the classic case) or chronic mastitis, in a way to deceive doctor and patient alike. By the time diagnosis is sure, the cells have been carried to other parts of the body and the game begins again.

Cancer is likewise arbitrary in its duration and in its choice of site. Some, like Georges Beau, give evidence suggesting that cells may have

1. *Le Cancer.*

a life of their own quite independently of the total consciousness of the being of which they form part. They may react, assimilate, decide, remember, foresee, in a way to set new problems to the philosopher of the future. Certainly medical science does not yet know why in this country the great majority of cancers in men choose to site themselves along the alimentary tract, in women at the neck of the uterus or in the breast; nor why, though they spare no age, they prefer the adult and elderly to the very young. Treatment, whether by surgery, cytotoxic agents[1] (of which there are many) or radiotherapy, has advanced a long way, and research, as everyone knows, is pushed vigorously ahead by special centres, by hospitals and medical research councils. One day control will come, as it has almost come in the case of tuberculosis. We shall know what makes the spread of the cells sometimes stop quite suddenly at a certain point and sometimes go on; why, even in the generally fatal Hodgkin's disease – a form that presents exceptional intractability to treatment by radiation – the growth has nonetheless been known to give over, as if tired, and allow the victim to live against all expectation.

Such, simplified, is the textbook background. The question that no textbook can answer with certainty is: given that the patient knows of his or her condition, how far can a 'right attitude of mind' go towards overcoming it? At least it can be said at once that it is possible for mental attitude to affect the outcome negatively; that is to say, there are cases of sufferers from mild cancer, which there was every chance of curing, who have died although they had children, a happy marriage, a home to live for. Autopsy revealed no physical reason why they should have succumbed. They died because they were told that they had cancer, and, like the tribesman who feared the shadow of his mother-in-law, they believed that this fact would kill, as surely as the bone which the witch doctor points in the direction of his victim.

Is the opposite true, and can people live because they believe that they will live?

.   .   .   .   .

1. Chemical preparations injected into the body in an attempt to poison and kill cancer cells.

Let us take the case of Marceline, as I shall call her.[1] The foreground is a small cottage in one of those picturesque thatched villages of the Thames Valley. It is occupied by a woman, young to look at, slim, well built, with short hair over a brown complexion, but with a pronounced limp which clearly gives discomfort. With her are two girls, one aged sixteen and one thirteen. Not a typical village family, you would say after a second glance. It is not irrelevant to go back over earlier times, for a disease of this gravity needs to be thought of in the context of the whole life of the patient. Resistance to other adversity can be switched to the facing of disease, and vice versa. A climate of endurance is created.

If one can ever pinpoint the beginning of trouble, Marceline's started, as did those of many, in the war years. As girl and woman she had led a life which had swung between freedom and constriction, health and suffering, pleasure and pain. She was not a stranger to the operating theatre: tonsils at seven, TB glands at eight and again, more seriously, next year, when the infection lay close to the jugular vein and the first surgeon would not take the risk. She had run wild through a paradise of West Country woodland, then wrestled with the confinement of a hard boarding school. Here, earlier than most, she had gone through a period of 'intellectual excitement and spiritual crisis' which left her an agnostic. When she left school the headmistress told her that she had many good qualities and was a 'seeker after truth', but lacked endurance.

By the beginning of the Second World War she had passed through Oxford, studied shorthand and typing in London, worked for an Anglo-American family in Italy, then in Paris, where she stayed on after Munich giving English lessons. 'Life was passionately interesting' – and seemed to be forming a pattern, giving her a many-sidedness of experience which a sequestered office job would have denied. Above all, during those years, she had come to terms with herself in facing up to fear.

As illness had receded from her horizon, fear had taken its place as the enemy. Irrational terror would invade her at the likelihood of a

1. For this story I am indebted to the letters and conversation of 'Marceline' and to her doctors.

lift breaking, a train flying over an embankment, a cinema catching fire. She could tell these fears to nobody; by that much the more they added a nightmare proportion to the rest of life. Psychoanalysis might have removed them by tracing a source; as it was, she suffered silently.

Goethe records in *Dichtung und Wahrheit* that at Strasbourg he used to climb every evening on to a small slab, scarcely a yard square, at the very top of the cathedral tower. There he would stand for an hour, looking out over nothing but the distant fields and woods. 'This painfully frightening experience I repeated until it became quite indifferent to me.' He had faced and overcome his fear of heights. Marceline's fear was mastered in the same way with the help of a book, *Adventure* by Jack Seely (the late Lord Mottistone), which had appeared in the house one day. Here was a character she admired: handsome, courageous, a leader with all the qualities of the 'hero', who nevertheless confessed that he was often frightened and only overcame fears by facing them squarely and with a purpose, not slinking round the corner. Through Seely she came to admire courage above all things and to do as he would have done. She took every opportunity to ride in lifts, to travel in trains. It was a slow process, taking many years, indeed never truly complete, but it was successful.

Can the same process be applied to illness – 'First, a little, thence to more, He sampled all her killing store' – until at last an attitude of mind and fibre of body form themselves which can overcome even cancer?

In London, after a spell with the Land Army in 1939, Marceline joined an ambulance unit of the A.R.P. For the first time she fell deeply and happily in love. As to many more, the Blitz brought a bitter-sweet satisfaction among the misery. Sirens, bombers, crash of masonry and shrieks of the trapped, a smell of charred wood and smoke, long hours at first-aid in the black-out; all this interwoven with the comradeship of Londoners, the sense of being in it together, created an upside-down joy which many still remember with nostalgia, and which for her blended with the short-lived joy of her own love.

They Survived

All times I have enjoyed
Greatly, have suffered greatly, both with those
That loved me, and alone.

The Blitz ended. The war dragged on. In the W.R.N.S. she met a young French commando stationed at the same base. Again, like many others, both felt insecure on their own, as if only union would give that stability which life otherwise denied. He was due to take part in the invasion of France, and the bombs were coming over. The idea that the world might go on hardly seemed worth a thought; yet she longed for the sense of fulfilment that children give.

They were married in the spring of 1944. Before her first daughter was a year old, peace had come. She was 'repatriated', with husband and baby, to Brittany.

Inland Brittany is a strange home of tradition, where many still do not understand French. After the war food was short, the black market reigned. Marceline and the baby lived in one room, without sanitation or water, her husband having now been posted to Algeria. At last she had permission to rejoin him. At first she enjoyed the warm Mediterranean, the easier living, her beautiful small girl, but her husband began behaving strangely when she became pregnant a second time. The heat drove her to Scotland, where her parents lived, to have the baby, and she returned to scenes of violence and refusals to give money. She bore hunger more lightly than suspicion and mistrust, which bewildered her.

They returned to Brittany; then her husband went off to serve two years in Indo-China. When he returned, mistrust had deepened. He was now drinking heavily, frightening the children and often threatening to kill her. Her health began to give way; to general nervous exhaustion were added attacks of a painful gall bladder trouble, cholecystitis, and unaccountable spasms of pain in the chest. The doctor had no explanation. By now she knew she would have to leave her husband, but she could not think how, or when, or where to go. When he was sent to Madagascar the younger girl, after illness, was advised a change of air. Quite at a venture, they left for the Savoy Alps.

Next in the kaleidoscope of change contentment followed, for fifteen months. It seemed the old life of freedom, they felt themselves part of the country, accepted by the villagers and working with them. Health improved for them all, but she was not rid of the inexplicable pains in the chest, and one day noticed a small lump below the collar-bone. A cyst, most likely, said the village doctor. They were so intent on living, on the sledging and skiing of winter, the seed-time of spring and the haymaking and harvesting of summer, that they had no time to worry. In the mountains, on spring skiing expeditions, she found unsuspected reserves of physical strength, and drew moral comfort from reading the French philosopher Alain.

She had asked for separation. Her husband insisted on seeing her, but by now they were strangers. He went off to his parents in Brittany. Heavy-hearted, she packed bags for England.

Marceline's parents had opposed the marriage; they were even more rudely jolted by the separation. The jobs open to a woman with two small children in this country are strictly limited. She served as matron at a preparatory school, then on the domestic side of an adult education college: long hours each day, and three in one small room. But the fact of having a job, coupled with completion of the divorce and the grant of custody of the children, restored a measure of self-confidence. The past was past.

After a year of this work, however, she was physically exhausted again. A home of their own would help, nothing else. She had a little money in France and took a short holiday there, then joined the girls at her parents' home, now in Devon. One day she was taking one of them to the doctor, and decided to consult her about the lump on her own chest, which had swollen and was causing pain. The doctor sent her to see a surgeon. Two weeks later, in the sunny April of 1957, she was in hospital and knew that she had cancer.

·   ·   ·   ·   ·

It is impossible to picture, if one has had no similar experience, the deep shock of learning that malignancy is present in the breast and that it will have to be surgically removed. Add to this the worry of two young children and the need to be breadwinner of the family. The mastectomy (surgical removal) was performed on 25 April, while the children were put into a foster home by the local council. She left hospital in mid-May, but it remained to start a three weeks' course of radiotherapy.

It has been said that one has to be tough to stand up to modern medicine, and radiotherapy, or deep X-ray treatment, is as good an instance of this as any. This is, of course, one of the ways of attacking cancer cells, by directly 'burning them out', and does the job more effectively in general than cytotoxic agents. The danger lies in the possibility that normal tissue will suffer as well, and in the effect of treatment on the blood glands. The effect on morale is lowering. Here, to illustrate it, is a vignette.

'One waits in Outpatients. Mostly the others are rather old, and very tired and grey. They shuffle and peer about and hope there will be a nice cup of tea afterwards. An enormous woman dressed in thin artificial silk, flesh hung in folds about her, eyes tiny and buttonlike, expressionless, waddles from the treatment room. Everyone is very quiet except the old mad lady. She alone dares to protest against being kept waiting.

' "It makes my head ache! . . . Oh my eyes, my eyes!"

'Then she starts to hum, loud and tuneless.

'At last it is my turn. The area to be treated has been outlined by the doctor with a dye, the dose prescribed. Stripped, I lie on the table as the machine is adjusted over me, the nozzle pressed hard against my collar-bone. The radiotherapist goes out and switches on. I close my eyes and the darkness swings back and forth, back and forth. I open them and the room slides to a stop, but the movement continues sickeningly in my head, while the great machine buzzes and clicks above me. Through the glass window in the corner I see the shadow of the radiotherapist as she watches her switchboard. The buzzing stops – I must have had the full fifteen minutes – she comes in and stands beside me, to my dizzy sense like a great full-blown flower, very pink with a halo of fluffy curls and blue eyes, blue and meaningless as would be, just now, a chink of summer sky. I am sick and dizzy as I climb off the table; then overwhelmed, as if by a great weight. I want nothing but to crawl into a bed, to forget.

'I come again, as I am told, for another dose. And again. And again. "Radiation sickness" starts in earnest: nausea with vomiting, diarrhœa, dizziness, headaches; eyes ache and become inflamed, appetite goes. A burn appears on my skin, but I am not allowed to wash it, nor shall I be for several weeks after treatment has stopped, when it will be itching fiercely. Some of these ill-effects can be controlled by drugs, but not that sense of indefinite but real misery, as if life and all that it stood for were not worth the labour of living.'[1]

At the beginning of September the family, now reunited, left Devon for the village where they were to stay with friends and look for a house. But the effects of radiotherapy were slow in disappearing, and the doctor would not sign Marceline off. As she grew stronger, it became obvious that cottages were not so easy to come by. In September 1958, when they had still found nothing, another lump was discovered. This meant more radiotherapy. At that point their friends needed room for another baby, and the family had to move out. They were offered use of a fourteen- by six-foot caravan in the village, and accepted.

During that winter she was receiving radiotherapy while they lived in the little caravan, come rain, come frost, come snow. At nights they slept badly because of the cold, and all suffered from colds and sore throats. When it rained the leaks appeared faster than they could be patched up. When it did not rain, condensation streamed down the walls. Yet they tried to enjoy what they could and thereby to win half the battle; because if one enjoys, not only one's own but others' pleasures, one looks forward and out, not back and in. 'It had a certain crazy charm and we had some happy times there. In the evening the tiny doll's stove would burn merrily, we would draw the curtains

1. It should be added that by no means all who receive radiotherapy suffer radiation sickness in this way, though some who receive less than these very large doses suffer more. Individuals vary widely.

and the children snuggled down in their bunks while I read *Wuthering Heights* or *Oliver Twist* to them.'

In February 1959 they were offered a very small cottage in the village, in which an old lady had recently died. This was in so decrepit a state that at first it seemed impossible that they could live there. However, they started work. During that month she was receiving hormone injections, but in April discovered another lump, in the neck, which meant yet more radiotherapy. However, the cottage had still to be cleaned and prepared. First, she spent days removing layers of crumbling wallpaper, pulled out a myriad rusty nails, scraped and scrubbed. At week-ends children and friends joined in. Next, the garden needed digging in time for spring sowing. Then on 1 May, when one bedroom and the scullery were ready, they moved in and went on working, begging furniture from friends and relatives, visiting auctions and jumble sales: exhausting work, but satisfying, since they had never, even in France, had their own house. In this cottage, homely as they made it, they could take pride.

In July more lumps appeared on the chest – technically chest-wall recurrences and metastases, or secondary deposits, in the lymph nodes – and in September another operation was proposed. While she waited to go into hospital, the lumps spread until they looked like measles.

The operation to be attempted was adrenalectomy or removal of the adrenal glands. Not to go into details, which can be found in books like *Health and Hormones* by Stuart Mason, the vital importance of glands and their secretions, or hormones, has only recently been fully recognised. In the medulla of the adrenals, lying one on top of each kidney, is secreted adrenalin, the hormone responsible for our physical reactions of thumping heart, prickling scalp, pale skin, in face of danger. From a woman's adrenals and ovaries come, among other hormones, the female sex hormones. The removal of these glands, and of the ovaries, is something of a 'desperation measure', taken if other means have failed to stop the spread, in the hope that the cancer is hormone-dependent or activated by hormones, particularly the sex hormones. Marceline's doctor commented later that in his own mind he gave her a few months.

If the adrenals are simply cut out, death follows inevitably. The saviour from death is hydrocortisone, a hormone secreted in the cortex of the adrenal. The action of this is vital to the body, particularly in combating stress, and a form of it can nowadays be injected. 'The patient without adrenals is quickly fatigued and apathetic, even when the salt balance is adjusted. General misery is not just self-pity.'[1] It is hydrocortisone or cortisone which corrects the balance here, and allows a normal life.

During operation it was discovered that one adrenal gland contained secondary deposits of cancer cells. This had not been suspected. The three operations removing adrenals and ovaries took place within ten days of each other and were successful from the surgeon's point of view. The recurrences disappeared dramatically. Marceline herself noted that she had no doubt at all that she would come through, despite the obvious risks. Though left strengthless, she was cheered by the children, who came often, the support of friends, and letters and presents, sometimes from quite unknown villagers. When she returned in November she was still receiving cortisone, but it became clear that the chemical balance of blood and glands had been thrown out in other ways. She was suffering from dehydration and lack of salt (one of the adrenal hormones, aldosterone, affects salt balance), and during the next months she began to lose weight and to suffer frequent near black-outs. In June 1960 she returned to hospital for tests and began an eight-week course of Durabolin,[2] or male sex hormone, injections. In October she began to suffer sharp pain in one hip and leg, along with bouts of feverishness. This was a real puzzle, to doctors and patient alike.

In February 1961 she was treated with radiotherapy to the hip and concluded, rightly, that malignancy was suspected. At this point the traditional discretion of the medical profession seemed to be being carried too far and she demanded straight answers. She was in great pain and limped heavily. In the morass of pain mixed with uncertainty, morale sank very low. For three years she had believed that she would recover sufficiently to be able to take a job once more. Now she began

1. Stuart Mason, op. cit.
2. Described by the manufacturers as 'the most potent *anabolic* (building up) preparation actually available'. Male sex hormone is introduced without undesirable male side-effects.

to think that nothing remained but to hang on. This might mean National Assistance for life, the £8 a month contributed by her husband being used to make up the grants allowed. In addition to these the doctors succeeded in securing for her an extra 15s. a week to help buy nourishing foods. For clothes and amenities she would have to rely mainly on Christmas and birthday presents, and the cast-offs of friends.

The Welfare State does much for many people, but it cannot claim to be at its most generous in helping the breadwinners of families who are unable to win bread because of illness; the allowances for children are extremely small. We are not concerned with financial problems except in so far as they add a further dimension to the problem of survival. If one is a private patient, if one does not have to queue for buses and change twice in order to reach hospital, if one does not return to cooking, washing, ironing, mending, unstopping drains and repairing chairs, but to an environment of comfort, then one's chances of recovery are *a priori* greater. But it does not always work that way. In some people illness sets up a reaction tending towards recovery, and adversity intensifies that reaction, so that they derive more benefit thereby than the purely physical benefit which easier circumstances would have allowed.

In this case both struggles continued; the family found itself in financial straits. Whenever things hit rock bottom, help arrived, often from a quite unexpected source. Meanwhile, in June 1961, it was suggested that decalcification of the bone (due conceivably to the action of the parathyroid gland in the absence of adrenal hormone – another upsetting of the delicate balance) had caused the trouble in the hip. More Durabolin injections were ordered. These improved the hip generally, but by August the leg was worse and osteo-arthritis, possibly caused by decalcification, began to be suspected. In September Marceline started a course of physiotherapy designed to strengthen the muscles joining pelvis and thigh-bone. The exercises for this she enjoyed, because they seemed to be leading somewhere; she even constructed an apparatus so that they could be continued at home. By November, X-rays of the hip were satisfactory, but what had been taken for a calcified gland in the neck had started to multiply, and yet more radiotherapy was ordered. The whole game seemed to have begun again... [1]

Suffering breeds reflection, and in no minds more than in those which subscribe to no formal creed. If you are not – and we shall meet later some who are – moved by crisis from a position of religious unbelief, then the convictions that you hold already are likely to be strengthened and rationalised. The position of the agnostic who has been through it all and finds no cause to change his tenets is strong, because it is buttressed by great courage.

Here, if I may be allowed the first person, is what Marceline might say; much of it she has said, and I do no more than link her thoughts together.

'I know nothing of a beyond, nor have I, since I was sixteen, felt an impulse to believe in one. But I have a strong sense that we are, in Donne's phrase, not islands but linked each to each by chains no less real for being generally imperceptible, so that what each does has effect on the lives of others, diminishing but manifold. Thus, particularly for those nearest to me, it was important that I survive. If I gave up, something would be lost, and the loss would be theirs as well as mine, and through them the loss of others beyond.

'To face illness it helps to have ideals, even heroes. I admire courage, partly perhaps because I have been full of fears since I was a girl. I cry easily, and have to force myself to do things. But if you are afraid and can think how some admired person would behave, and expect you to behave, you will conquer fear. Courage is a quality not highly enough prized, perhaps: the only quality, Stendhal says, which cannot be imitated by hypocrisy. To have ideals to live up to, and to cultivate the courage with which to live up to them, is one path to survival.

'Hope is another. There have been many things to enjoy; we enjoyed even the caravan at times. There are many more that I want to experience. I love life, and do not want to leave the feast halfway through. Like André Chénier's young captive,

Qu'un stoique aux yeux secs vole embrasser la mort,
Moi, je pleure et j'espère; au noir souffle du nord

1. In spring of 1962 the pituitary glands were removed. Marceline died on 13 June, 1962.

Je plie et relève ma tête.
S'il est des jours amers, il en est de si doux!
Hélas! quel miel n'a laissé de dégoûts?
Quelle mer n'a point de tempête?

'At the same time it puzzles me that Christian sufferers should cling so tenaciously to life, when they believe that something better awaits them after it is over.

'Even if medical science said that nothing I could do or think would prolong my life, I would still believe that, if no vital organ were affected, I had it in me to last beyond expectation. When it comes to the everyday business of living, courage must be allied with patience in the slow grind uphill. If you survive a sharp, severe illness you can do it in a burst, like a sprinter. In a long illness it is a matter of putting one foot slowly in front of the other, as one would in a long climb over difficult ground; of harbouring strength and picking oneself up and going on again after every fall. Obstinacy comes in too, that *'obstination héroique'* of which Alain speaks, and which is undeterred by the thought of giving in. It is no use complaining; one accepts the obstacles and tackles them one by one.[1]

'Next, one must co-operate, and that applies even to cancer. This hardly needs saying, perhaps, but particularly in treatments like physiotherapy the doctor is helpless without the patient's lively co-operation and willing obedience to orders. In my view the doctor, too, should trust the patient, since they are working together, and help him to face a bad situation. All this could lead to too great a self-interest on the part of the patient, but as important as co-operation is the art of forgetting oneself and one's own trouble in the concerns of other people, the affection of family and friends, even the companionship of the great who have suffered and out of their suffering have made poems, paintings and music. By the same token it is good to keep one's outside interests going and to help those even less fortunate than oneself.

1. Alain in *Minerve, ou De la Sagesse*: '*Il ne s'étonnera point des obstacles, et il redoublera de courage, sachant bien que son courage dépend de lui seul*' etc.
Scientology too: 'One of the components of courage is duration of effort.' *The Science of Survival* by L. Ron Hubbard.

It is my regret that I am chained and cannot do this as I would wish, cannot help in a youth club and try to give some of the understanding which I needed and did not get when I was young. Last year, at least, we took in a six-year-old boy whose parents were looking for work. Illness has made me more tolerant of the problems and needs of others, of the old for example, and hence a believer that love, not sexual or specific but universal, is the main force propelling me over every obstacle.

'Lastly, a sense of humour. Perhaps that helped to bring John Brown above ground after twenty-three days. Humour involves detachment – the "second self" if you like, since we are all of us two people at least – the ability to stand outside a humiliating or horrifying situation and see something funny, because incongruous, in it. That is why hospital wards have their own brand of humour, often mildly obscene. It is a defence mechanism, one form of escape from suffering through surveying it, as if from above, in its comic aspect.

'In all this I believe that biological or biochemical factors are more fundamental even than psychological ones. Might not the blood-sugar level, or the oxygen content of the lungs, influence the way one reacts at a particular moment more than the presence or absence of this or that neurosis? Even the beneficial effects of prayer may have a physical explanation. I know that prayer helps some people in time of crisis, often people who have never prayed before. That may be because, by stopping and for a time otherwise occupying that part of their mind which was almost defeated, they were able automatically and instinctively to take the necessary action, or, in the case of disease, to turn towards health as if by a new and refreshing path.

'This may put me among the materialists, but the past four years have not changed my ideas. If they seem inadequate to others, for me they have stood the test of time and have satisfied me, so far as any ideas can, during a series of ordeals which often seemed insuperable. I have not felt a need to go beyond them and I have never experienced an urge to go back on them or to pray. I do not believe that either the answer to prayer or the working out of a subtle psychological complex is the key to survival.'

.   .   .   .   .

To some the concept of a life governed by hormones is a gloomy one. To think of Macbeth's 'I am settled, and bend up Each corporal agent to this terrible feat' as no more than an extra squirt of adrenalin pumped through the veins by his creator is to take the gilt from poetry. Besides, if one attitude can be produced artificially by adrenalin injections, may it not be so with others too? During the Battle of Britain it was rumoured that Luftwaffe pilots were being injected with some extract of the adrenal cortex to improve their performance. As a result, extensive research in the United States produced cortisone. This has the same action as hydrocortisone, the natural hormone which, as we have seen, combats stress. It turned out that healthy pilots have no need of extra cortisone. The original exercise was thus a failure, but cortisone remained, a signal advance in clinical medicine.[1] It may, however, still prove possible temporarily to induce qualities in human beings by the administration of drugs. Even the endurance necessary for extreme survival may one day be artificially induced.

What the biological outlook, as it might be called in Marceline's case, gives of special value is the willingness to face facts squarely and by trying to understand them not to fall into the trap of those who at the breath of a word – 'cancer' nowadays, as it was 'tuberculosis' sixty years ago – pack up and die. Obviously, if the accumulation of diseased cells is too great, or if a vital organ is affected, then you are doomed; but so is the man on a raft if a wave catches him, the mountaineer if an avalanche sweeps him from his steps, the marooned desert traveller if the water is two hundred miles away and not fifty. For all there is a point of no return, beyond which no effort, physical or mental, can serve to retain life. But this side of that point, by understanding, by co-operation and adaptability, a whole range of possibilities in survival can be found without going outside the human organism.

The willingness to face facts can, however, be combined with quite other beliefs. Those dissatisfied with the humanist standpoint will prefer to think that something outside and above ourselves takes a hand in the matter, either denying that disease exists except as a fantasy to be exorcised by proper belief in God, or accepting it as part of a divine pattern, asking God's help and consecrating illness as it were upon an

1. This story is told in *Health and Hormones* by Stuart Mason.

altar. Some there are who move to this last position from one closer to that suggested in the last pages.

At the pole farthest from the biological come the Christian Scientists, for instance, who believe mind, not matter, to be the reality in the universe. 'In the latter part of 1866' wrote Mrs Baker Eddy, prophetess of Christian Science, 'I gained the scientific certainty that all causation was Mind and every effect a mental phenomenon.' Cancer, therefore, is a mental phenomenon; like dyspepsia it 'does not come from God, is no thought in the Divine intelligence but a false belief of mortal mind, the child of fear'.[1] If somebody dies of cancer, it is not the cancer which kills, but the false widespread belief that cancer is lethal.

The way to survival, therefore, will be through mind-healing or conviction of the patient that he will get better because his illness does not exist. There is no space here to do justice to the real truths contained in Christian Science. 'The doctrine of mind cure . . . has always, and in every generation, entered as an element into the wisdom of the wise.'[2] Indeed, it is already one of the apparent themes of this book that attitude of mind plays the chief part in the survival of any ordeal. The Church of England admits mind-cure: at the 1962 Canterbury Convocation a resolution was passed asking the Archbishop to encourage the training of priest-psychotherapists. In this context the startling recent advances of psychotherapy used *in conjunction* with drugs should be studied. But the battle there is joined when the disease is recognised, evaluated for what it is and faced with every possible weapon, not relegated among the chimeras. Saluting in passing those who manage to survive by denying its very existence, we move to those whose main difference of opinion with Marceline is not that she did not survive an ordeal with courage, but that she gave no credit to a supernatural power; and whose quarrel with Mrs Eddy would be that she gave all the credit to that power and none to the more humdrum qualities of co-operation and adaptation shown by the sick person.

Let us start with someone in whom the disease itself produced a change of belief, and comment by the way that in these of our cases which touch illness we seem more directly concerned with spiritual

1. *Our New Religion*, H. A. L. Fisher.
2. Ibid.

experience than in the others. This may be partly because the patient has time on his hands in which to reflect upon his state, as most who find themselves in critical situations do not; partly because some illnesses are known to affect the chemical constitution of the brain and may, therefore, be responsible, in ways only now being defined,[1] for changing the process of thinking and hence the results of that process. Of these epilepsy is an extreme example. Taking leave for the time being of cancer, we turn to a disease which indeed attacks the brain. The story has been given to me by a friend.

Two years ago my friend succumbed suddenly to a severe attack of virus encephalitis. For the best part of two days she was afflicted with a strange headache and other sinister sensations. However, these symptoms receded; instinctively she knew that the worst danger was past. Because of the rarity of this disease and its subtle approaches, it still remained undetected at this stage. She herself knew that something was seriously amiss, but she was too feeble and distraught to combat the medical view that she was suffering from a bad attack of 'flu on top of overwork. Her relations living in the flats below were advised that, far from needing to be alarmed, they should give her the minimum necessary help for fear of 'spoiling' her – perfectly sensible advice had the basic premiss been correct. Thus she was left largely to take care of herself, and, despite extreme exhaustion and a variety of strange discomforts, she managed to do this so far as basic needs went. With the help of the telephone she even managed not to default entirely on her social and occupational responsibilities.

We are concerned here with the spiritual process which accompanied this crisis, and which became manifest on the third day. About this she has written:

'What happened was really very simple. Medical difficulties had mercifully kept me out of hospital and the most alarming symptoms had receded, but I was extremely weak, physically exhausted and in

1. *Battle for the Mind* by William Sargant describes lucidly and cogently the interplay of spiritual and physiological. See also the classic case of mescalin recorded in Aldous Huxley's *The Doors of Perception*.

Marceline in 1942 (*John Vickers*)

Ensio Tiira being carried down the gangway of the *Alendi Hill* (*Straits Times*)

Below left: Tiira's first meal in Singapore General Hospital (*Straits Times*)

After two weeks: ulcers healed (*Straits Times*)

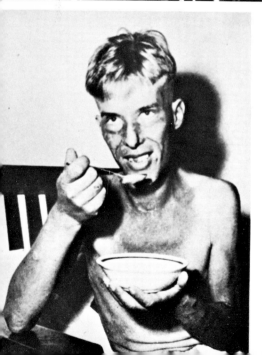

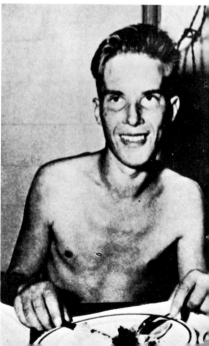

the grip of the mental attacks common to this condition. That is to say, I was excitable and extremely emotional, switching from tears to laughter on the slightest provocation. Reasoning processes were unimpaired, so that I was fully aware of my state; but distortion of powers of judgment spared me any deep anxiety or thought for the future. My mind was alert and buzzing with thoughts, with which I was quite content to occupy myself. I did not mind having to be much alone.

'One morning I telephoned a Catholic family with which I had long been on close terms. I spoke to Julie, who had just started her first term at secondary school. She was overflowing with happy excitement and her first words were: "It's such a lovely school. I'm learning French, I can say the Hail Mary in French." She was startled when I said that I did not know the prayer in any language, and delighted to fulfil my request to repeat it in English, French and Latin.

'Perhaps I should here explain that I only knew one other Catholic well, and that I had never discussed religion deeply with any of these people. I took myself for granted as a rational humanist, with a great respect for the faith of others, but I never felt that I too could be religious. I had picked up enough knowledge to be perfectly clear that, were I a Christian, I should be a Catholic; but it seemed to me impossible to overcome doubt by intellectual effort, and I could conceive of no other way. In any case the question had not troubled me.

'However, on this grey wet autumn Saturday morning my young friend's introduction to the Hail Mary left its mark. In my confused and rather hectic state of mind I felt that it would be deeply desirable to pray. But how? I really had no idea. The hours passed in not unhappy rumination, during which it was gradually borne in upon me that it was necessary for me to do something for myself; and at last I realised that what I must do was to find a priest. Why this was necessary I could not have said; I no longer feared that I might die, and I still had no conscious wish to become a Catholic. I simple had an overwhelming sense of need for something which I could not define.

'Knowing the priesthood to be human like any other profession, I felt that I should be selective. Some two years earlier my friend had told me of a certain priest with whom he had been at school, and whom he greatly trusted and admired. On my sickbed it seemed to me that here was my answer: I must find Father X.

'By now it was Saturday afternoon, and wetter than ever. I studied the possible approaches presented by the telephone directory, and for some reason selected the Catholic Education Council. Father Y answered. He cheerfully grasped my purpose without apparently thinking me insane, and he had personal knowledge of Father X, for whom he promised to search. A few more telephone exchanges, and there was Father X dripping and smiling on the doorstep, at 9.30 that same evening.

'When he was suitably installed I announced that I had not asked him to come because I wanted to be a Catholic, and I added that indeed I had no idea why I had pressed for him to come so speedily. I think I must have sounded very foolish, but I did not feel foolish, and he seemed to accept the situation cheerfully and without question. I cannot remember much about that talk, except that he told me some lovely stories and some interesting things about the Church, and that he left me after an hour or so with the promise of returning in a few days, and with encouragement to get on to my knees to pray as soon as I could. It was the greatest comfort and help that he was entirely unperturbed about my illness, and, indeed, that he took the whole event in his stride. His visit left me feeling refreshed and untroubled, and curiously relieved of that driving sense of indefinable responsibility which had goaded me to seek him out.

'His next visit was equally easy and cheerful. By this time my interest in the Church as such was stirred, and I had questions to ask. He explained to me towards the end the possibility and nature of a regular course of instruction, without commitment of entering the Church. He himself was going away for some months, but he left me with the name of another priest who would help me if I so wished.

'I was not moved to make any quick decision: I waited a little while, turning the matter over in my mind with a continued sense of deepest relief and comfort. Then the day came when, without another thought, I felt stirred to telephone Father Z, whom Father X had recommended. Three months of happy weekly visits to my sickroom for religious instruction followed, until I was well enough to be taken to see Father Z at his presbytery. By the early summer I was ready and eager formally to become a Catholic, so this was quietly arranged. Since then I have not had a single moment of regret. On the contrary, my sense of gratitude increases with the passage of time.

'One extraordinary feature of this change, which still surprises me, is that at no point since the arrival on the scene of Father X have I had the slightest intellectual doubt or hesitation. Despite the words with which in all honesty I greeted him, I had – and I remember this vividly – a perfect inner certitude that I was going to be a Catholic; and this knowledge never faded. During the months of instruction – and, indeed, it has been so ever since – I was hungry for as much knowledge and intellectual understanding of Christianity and the Church as I could cram in, so that it cannot be said that I was merely satisfying some passing emotional need. I often wondered at my lack of doubt, and indeed, I thought that, by the intellectual standards of my upbringing, I ought to feel ashamed of my inner submissiveness, but I never actually felt ashamed. And even this wondering ceased when I learned a little about the gift of Faith.

'A second point that interested me greatly is: how differently might I have responded had Father X proved either grudging, indifferent, pompous or diffident, as could so easily have happened? In the hyper-sensitive state I was in, I believe that I could not have borne any such disappointment, and that there would, therefore, have been no future in religion for me at that time. But the fact remains that this did not happen. Yet neither can it be said that I was carried away by Father X's personality, since I was perfectly content to be passed on to Father Z. Seldom among human beings – including those in the Church – do unexpected events move so smoothly and happily; yet they did just that when it happened to be crucially necessary for me. It was, therefore, impossible for me, both then and always, not to see the finger of God Himself intervening on my small behalf.

'Finally, it could well be asked: was not I very ill indeed at the time, in mind as well as body, and, therefore, might not this rapid conversion be the outcome of mental derangement? In one sense this is true: I *had* to be considerably deranged both to be aware of that driving sense of inner need and also to react to my need in such a highly un-conventional way. Like an infant that can only become aware of the reality of cold if stripped of its clothes, I could only feel my spiritual isolation and darkness (as I now know it was) when stripped of the overlying layers of normal intellectual and emotional functioning. But it does not follow that the religious experience as such was invalid. Its validity has, in fact, been tested and found certain by the only real test possible, namely by the passage of time, with all the vicissitudes that go with active living. The mental aspect of my illness now belongs to the distant past, while I have already made it plain that the religious seed sown at the time has never ceased to grow sturdily.

'Many months, even years, of storm and stress lay ahead, stemming largely from the consequences of my illness upon my particular, highly organised way of life. Knowing myself all too well, I find it impossible to believe that my morale would have remained unshattered, had I not throughout felt the strength, comfort and hope which flowed unfailingly from this experience.'

In this book conversion appears only as one of those things that can help a person to survive illness or other crises with morale actually raised. The deeper implications are studied, through many cases, by William James in a chapter of *The Varieties of Religious Experience*, and can be pursued thence through every shade of belief and unbelief. Of importance are the physiological processes involved, as described in Sargant's *Battle for the Mind*. These do not, of course, affect the validity of the conversion itself, but they do forbid us to think of the spiritual process apart from the physical.[1] What is certain is that con-version in stress of illness happens, is usually preceded by strong emotion and can entirely alter behaviour-patterns. But it happens to very few. The next story we shall consider might be that of many. We return to cancer of the gravest sort, to a cancer suffered by a person in whose case mental attitude proved vital, but whose religious faith

1. For a synthesis of spiritual and scientific values, written from an entirely different angle, Father Teilhard de Chardin's *The Phenomenon of Man* should be read.

remained solid, not vividly picked out like that of the convert, but a soberly cheering backcloth.

John Squire (that name will do as well as another) is a man of fifty-nine living, with his wife and son, in a comfortable house off one of the main roads south of London.[1] By profession he is a wholesale vegetable and fruit merchant. Each morning an arduous day begins at three a.m. With his son, who partners him in the business, he drives to London Bridge to sell the produce consigned thither. It is a long business. By three p.m. he is back after a twelve-hour day, by nine p.m. he is in bed. An exacting job, you would say, which most of us would shirk as we approached sixty. Not the sort of job for a man who has poor health.

It was in 1922 that trouble started, with appendicitis. Then four operations for duodenal ulcer followed one another. After that he felt no fear of operations, but was relieved to think that at last he was clear. So he was, for thirty years. In 1949 he began to suffer sharp pains in the abdomen. These subsided for a time but came on again in November 1951: fierce, gnawing pains, the eagle of Prometheus tearing at the vitals. In January 1952 he was admitted to hospital suffering from 'retro-peritoneal neoplasm'; a cancer in the abdomen.

In March an exploratory operation was performed and the growth was indeed found in the intestine, but in such a position as to be inoperable. Even a biopsy (removal of tissue for laboratory examination) was technically impossible. All that could be done was to straighten the colon, which lay awry, and to sew him up again.

Like many patients, Squire succeeded in surreptitiously reading his case sheet. He knew what was up. But the straightening of the colon had relieved the discomfort, and he thought at first that the operation had been successful and the growth removed. His wife, however, knew better.

Mrs Squire is a solid, cheerful, practical woman. She believes squarely that in order to survive any serious illness what the patient needs is a sense of cheerful affection around, of optimism, even if it

1. For this story also I am indebted to its subject, and to the hospital for his case history.

has to be laid on, of humour. A sick man, however apparently stable, becomes a small boy again; his wishes should be pampered, his insecurity bolstered by the old assurance that everything will be all right, his self-respect propped up by the loving interest of others. In short, he wants to be mothered and his recovery is, therefore, a combined operation. Putting theory into practice, she was one day joking openly when the ward sister called her across.

'How can you behave like that when your husband is so seriously ill?'

Mrs Squire was outraged. 'Do you think I don't know? Do you think I am not putting this on just for his sake, to cheer him up? Do you think I really feel cheerful?'

The sister, seeing how it was, apologised. What she really had to say was that Mrs Squire could take her husband home. This in effect was a death sentence. The hospital could do no more.

Faith, whether in the medical profession or in something above that directs even the knife and needle, is a first step to survival. In this case the faith was Mrs Squire's, since her husband at this stage thought that he was on the road to recovery. She refused to believe that it was intended that their family unit, they two and their son of seventeen, whom the perversity of this illness had matured sharply, should be broken up. The doctor and surgeon in charge, consulted, agreed that a course of radiotherapy at a leading London hospital should be tried.

Squire was seen by the Radiotherapy Department in April. His general condition was still reported good, but discomfort interfered with sleep, he confessed to pains, and his liver was enlarged. Six weeks after the operation, to allow time for the effects to wear off, radiotherapy started: the same routine, the area of skin defined with dye, the nozzle of the huge machine which whirred and clicked above, the absence of pain, but afterwards the utter draining of strength, the longing to lie down and give up. He had never felt so beaten.

After nearly six weeks, with one break for rest, the treatment stopped. He still felt some tenderness and discomfort round the navel and under the right ribs, but the cancer, as if by miracle, seemed to have gone. He had survived – for the time at any rate, for no one could tell whether it would recur, in the same place or by metastasis elsewhere.

That was nine years ago. By October 1952 he was starting light work, by December he felt really pleased with himself and had put on two stone in weight. In this agreeable progress family and job combined to add strength. The next year, however, he had a recurrence of pain, though not, it was thought, of cancer. In September he was opened up for the removal of a chronic peptic ulcer. With the permission of Squire and his wife the surgeon, while operating, examined the place where the cancer growth had been. It had vanished.

It seems likely that the deep X-ray had 'burnt it out'. Since then he has not looked back, except to be thankful. He has continued an arduous job, rising early and on the go for twelve hours a day. During the strike of late 1956 he and his son were forced to drive down to Kent each day, rising earlier than ever, to fetch the produce that was not being delivered at London Bridge, and to do the the manual work of unloading and sorting themselves. The way seemed, and still seems, clear.

Have an outside interest, a job, which takes you from your body and which needs you, to which you want to return: that seems to John Squire the first line to recovery. Next, trust your doctors, co-operate and feel sure that they will bring you through. Theirs is the power and, if they can't, then nobody can. Thirdly, surround yourself with affection, and this is where luck comes in. Some, we know, are not lucky. They are the orphans, the aliens, those who belong to nobody, and their struggle is ten times grimmer. The presence of a wife, her humouring, even when forced, gives confidence that she expects you to live, therefore live you must, in order not to disappoint.

Finally, religious faith can help. The Squires describe themselves as 'Church but not churchy'. Christian religion they regard as a solid assurance, a comfort and support in trouble, not an easy way out or even a means of salvation from suffering. Hospital chaplains are tempted, they think, to hunt souls,[1] those under stress being the most ready to turn towards outside aid. Also, since suffering, in one Christian view, is a necessary misfortune intended to wipe out our illusion of self-

1. A friend, an Anglican priest, writes: 'Never have I met a hospital chaplain taking advantage of his position to "hunt souls". He would soon be out of a job if he did so misuse his cloth.'

sufficiency, and according to some Anglican writers 'the redemptive effect of suffering lies chiefly in its tendency to reduce the rebel will' (C. S. Lewis), it follows that the unfortunates lying sick are those whose rebel will and sense of self-sufficiency are so uppish that they most need reducing. And at that game some of them are just not going to play. This thought at the back of the mind accounts for some of the resistance to the best intentioned and least proselytising of hospital visitors. 'There's enough emotion about already in a hospital,' John Squire put it, 'without their adding to it.' Let each keep his faith, as he knows it, and if it is the same faith, undisturbed, at the end of the ordeal, then that is as far as we can safely go, and at least ground for quiet satisfaction.

In some people the attitude to disease goes further than acceptance. They believe it to be part of God's plan that they should suffer, so that they may by example 'light a candle'.

Obviously, this belief is a great incentive towards the effort of survival, and that it may do much good is admitted even by those who doubt the premisses. I am thinking of people like the Reverend Brian Hession, who died recently of cancer, having in 1955 launched Cancer Anonymous. For my account I have no authority to go beyond what he wrote himself in his books.

He had for thirteen years, from the age of twenty-seven, been Vicar of Holy Trinity Church at Aylesbury. During that time he interested himself increasingly in pioneering religious films, for which he founded Dawn Trust. Then he began to suffer severe pains, attributed by doctors to hæmorrhoids and duodenal ulcer, and decided to surrender his living and devote himself to the making of religious films, to travelling in this connection and to preaching.

In 1954 he was in the United States on a tour which combined preaching, films and holiday, when on the way to Los Angeles the pain became unbearable. The doctors he consulted were amazed that he had been examined in England before he left and told that the swellings almost blocking the rectum were hæmorrhoids. Whether the American doctors could have been so rash as to give him three or four days to live, I do not know, but their prediction is recorded by Hession.

He and his wife hunted down a fine surgeon, John Howard Payne. The operation which he performed, colectomy, is not uncommon now, though highly disagreeable. It means removing the colon, and in this case everything within sight which might also be affected, and bringing the digestive tract to the surface much higher up, below the waistline.

Hession faced the ordeal with very great courage. He was helped in this by prayer, with his wife and then alone. He was also supported by hope: he managed to cable London, even at this moment, that Greystoke, a large house overlooking Poole Harbour, was to be bought for Dawn Trust as he was determined to survive. When it came, the operation was long and intricate. Incisions were made down back and front and the surgeon removed a large part of both lymphatics (the channels along which cancer cells pass), the rectum, Sigmoid colon and part of the pelvic walls. Metastasis had begun, and the operation seemed, therefore, to have been just in time.

After blood transfusions he was wheeled out. The coming round and slow recovery from the trauma of operation were intensely uncomfortable. He felt himself helped incalculably by his wife, who had prayed with two other women throughout the operation, by the messages of friends in America and by the thought of return to the work at Greystoke.

He showed courage and determination also in the difficult art of living with a colostomy. It takes time and patience to learn to control the muscles, to adjust the tube as the new dynamics of the body demand. Before long he was skiing at St Moritz. He records that he insisted on skiing down fast runs when it was snowing, to prove to himself that he was really alive.

Besides the work at Greystoke and his preaching, he wrote *Determined to Live*, with which we are concerned. He published three other books, and finally, in 1961, *Bridge to God*, but the first confronts in clearest form the problem of cancer. Doctrinally, it contains nothing that startles and a great deal that is standard Church of England pulpit exhortation. Suffering is sent from God, because the world has been disrupted by man. Its importance in our lives is underlined by Calvary. It is no use kicking against the pricks but advisable to 'give with the pain', not to blame God, but to yield to Him and be determined to turn suffering to good. The love of wife, family, friends – indeed, of all men – is vitally important in this process.

So far, standard belief which needs no amplifying from me. But there are those – and St Paul, himself an outstanding 'survivor', was one of them – who believe that they can, through their own sufferings, be a light to their fellows. 'My life must be a beacon to others', Hession writes, and goes on to the saying of Christ that no man lights a candle and hides it under a bushel, but puts it for all to see. He prays that God may grant him time in life so that he may help his fellows on the way. In this task he is, or may be, a chosen vessel of the Lord.

Now such a view may seem to some to put certain things out of focus, but it conduces to getting things done and will appeal to many 'ordinary' people who are sufferers from disease. Brian Hession is quoted as saying of the 1954 operation that he 'made a little bargain with God, that if I recovered I would devote a great deal of my time to helping other people, and especially cancer sufferers'. To many, the idea of bargaining with an Almighty, of treating suffering, death and life as counters in the deal, is repugnant. Others can accept it and point to the fruits achieved, the founding of Cancer Anonymous, which has eased the irrational fears of many. The point in our context is that this attitude of mind is, in extreme form, yet one other way of facing disease and living as long as the mechanics of the body allow. Possibly, if he had sat and taken it easy as the doctors ordered, Hession would have lived the same length of time; the metastases work out their own pattern in the body and the end comes inevitably. But up to that limit he survived, and tried to do something that made sense to him meanwhile.

The operation of 1954 was the most dramatic, but three others, at intervals, were performed in order to deal with metastases. In each case he was back at work very soon afterwards. He also received large doses of radiotherapy. The last operation, in July of 1961, seemed to have been successful, but in September he suffered a relapse, returned to hospital and died there in October.

Brian Hession was a man with a message. He believed it his job to illumine the dim corners of fear in which most people live through ignorance. To think that they should be illumined is, as we saw in the earlier part of this chapter, not a prerogative of the Christian. Like Marceline, but starting from different premises, Hession was convinced that if more people were educated to the facts of cancer, which in one form or another attacks one out of every four of us, fewer would be intimidated by it. Thus the edifice which he proposed to build in Cancer Anonymous rested on the twin pillars of medical science and faith. First, he interested himself in cancer research, delved for facts and figures, proclaimed that the answer would one day be found by science, in the chemistry of the human body and in cell metabolism. The patient can assist science by co-operating with the doctor. So far all would agree. Secondly, he believed that mental worry could cause cancer or at least create the conditions favourable to it through an imbalance of inter-cellular fluids. If that was so, peace of mind stemming from faith in God could prevent the disease as readily as abstention from cancer-inducive habits such as smoking. Medical opinion does not at the moment seem to support the view that attitude of mind makes a difference in the *occurrence* of cancer; but, as we have seen, attitude does, up to the point of no return, make a great difference to the bearing of it. The question is: exactly what attitude?

Hession believed that the attitude must be one of faith, that faith could work miracles when standard medical treatment had failed. Therefore, he believed in faith-healing and 'united sessions of prayer, thanksgiving and healing'. He also believed in the crisis of conversion, an example of which we have seen. And he believed that the action of faith on the metabolism might be responsible for what is now thought of as wholly spontaneous regression, the inexplicable stopping of cancer growth. Faith-healing had been practised by Christ, and, if you believed that, you must believe that Christ born in each person could likewise heal the apparently incurable disease.

Cancer Anonymous was launched in order to shed light. Its basic principle is that people who have had cancer should make their case known, under cover of anonymity to start with. Afterwards, those who have recovered, or who have learned to live with it, are encouraged to pass through the barrier, and by speaking or writing to share the 'victory', so that others who are afraid of having the disease, or who believe they have it, may not lie down and die but go forward in knowledge and faith. The motto is: 'Cancer can be cured or endured.'

Faith, as exemplified by the Church of England, is of course the keystone, and obviously the appeal is to Christians who need strength and to non-Christians who may be converted. This is not the place to refer either to the many letters received from those who have derived comfort by this means, or to those who feel that to be brought to God by illness, when one was not so brought in health, is like enjoying being bludgeoned to one's knees. Our point is still (at this stage) that Hession's view represents a firm and widely held belief, firstly that Christian faith can cure or mitigate disease; secondly, that faith professed is best professed in common, through the forms of prayer and worship; and, thirdly, that some people, like Hession himself, may be called to help light the faith of others by their suffering and by their acts.

We have considered briefly four very different people who had in common the fact that at one stage or another they were very near the limit, the end, death. How near, nobody can accurately say. 'Anyone who makes definite predictions about cancer is a fool,' an expert in radiotherapy said to me, and this goes for other diseases too. We can say that they were near enough to the edge for a tipping of the scale one way or the other to have sent them over, and that they endured beyond all expectation.

The four had more in common than at first sight one would suspect: a belief that attitude of mind made recovery possible within limits, and a belief in the value of sheer courage of the slow, painful sort, and of the co-operative effort of other people. These things are a common human denominator, and Christians who write off unbelievers as living 'dull, self-centred, colourless lives, chained to the prison of materialism' (Hession) must allow as much. The injunctions to look ahead and outside, not to give up hope, to regard courage as a long process, even to have faith, ring like echoes through the whole of this chapter. May their reverberations breed tolerance of the overbeliefs of others.

4

The Unsuspected Skill: Ensio Tiira

THE SURVIVORS OF ILLNESS FOUND AN UNSUSPECTED
capacity in themselves. Their part in the business was still sedentary, a
co-operation with their helpers and a talent for going beyond what their
helpers thought likely. But the unsuspected talent may come to the
fore in a different way, when human beings are flung violently into
circumstances for which they are unprepared and in which they stand
largely alone. Like Brown, they are often denied the companionship
that wins half the battle, but, unlike him, though waiting may be a
part of the ordeal, they have an active role to play as well. They discover
in themselves an ability which they never thought to possess; and
very often the apparently strong do not come off best in the end.

In desert and jungle, on mountains and sea, men are being flung
daily into survival situations for which they have no training at all.
Take the extreme case of Ensio Tiira and his companion, Fred Ericsson,
two young members of the French Foreign Legion.

Ensio Tiira, a Finn, had led an unsatisfying life, by his own account,[1]
plodding from failure to failure. In 1939 he had been evacuated from
Viipuri in Finland with his family, when the Russians attacked. At

1. *Raft of Despair*, written shortly after the experience described.

sixteen, in 1944, he had volunteered for the Army and served as an anti-aircraft gunner, but, feeling himself unsuccessful, was discharged and worked at a flour mill. He was of slight build, not strong, and unable to handle the heavy sacks. After a time in forestry he was called up (having lost the papers registering him as a war-time volunteer) and found himself in the Navy. But he suffered from anæmia and could only do light duties. He worked after that in the shipbuilding yards, joined a Finnish trader as deckhand and in 1951 married a girl of nineteen. They were intensely unhappy and separated, Tiira going to sea again. On one of his voyages he jumped ship at Rouen in a pique over shore leave. He had no money or food, and with four other Finns joined the Legion as a last hope.

About Fred Ericsson's background little is known. He was another rolling stone, a Swede, and a year younger, at twenty-three, than Tiira on the fateful day in 1953 when they decided to escape together. He had been a sailor and had travelled widely before joining the Legion, from which he had already tried to escape once. Thus he was a marked man. He was big and very strong, red-haired and rather loud-mouthed and aggressive. He seemed to know what he wanted.

These two found themselves aboard a Legion troopship, the *Skaubryn*, crossing the Indian Ocean and bound for the war in Indo-China. The idea of jumping ship and escaping had already been mooted in the Suez Canal, but the guards had been too watchful. In the Legion a curious but rigid code prevailed, as Tiira had discovered during his eight months' service. From mild beginnings the discipline had become frightening, a kill-or-cure routine: thirty-mile route marches under the Algerian sun with no water and terrible punishments for the defaulters; companions from every country who hated the Legion but hated each other more; an unwilling *esprit de corps* built on the basis of mere communal toughness (whose force in crisis he recognised one day when, surrounded by threatening Arabs, he was rescued by legionaries who appeared from nowhere, fist flailing, and then refused to be thanked). This code it was which encouraged men to escape in peace-time but branded them as deserting traitors if they did so once battle was joined.

The *Skaubryn* was not calling at Singapore. Thus, unless they escaped before Saigon, they would never escape, for they would be fighting. And they had signed on for five years. It was Ericsson who proposed the fairly simple plan whereby they would jump ship in the Straits of Malacca, using one of the small emergency rafts kept on deck. This would be enough to take them to the shores of Sumatra, where they imagined that nobody would question them. Tiira hesitated a long time, frightened of possible consequences, but at last agreed.

It remained to persuade members of the crew to help them by dropping a raft. Legionaries might inform upon them, but the crew was Scandinavian and would not. Three promised to help. They would need civilian clothes, food and drink. They would take no papers. The jump would be timed for the moment when the *Skaubryn* turned south-east into the Straits. After that, in the more crowded waters, guards would be doubled and escape impossible.

They collected or bought their equipment. By 22 February they had stowed under a lifeboat two life-jackets, two boxes of matches, two bandages, a rubber-encased flashlight. Both had knives and combs, Tiira had a mirror. On that day both became restless and uneasy. Sumatra had not appeared, their friends of the crew were not to be found. After lunch, however, Ericsson, who had waited by the companionway, came up.

'Off Sumatra at three a.m. We turn in north of We Island and head for Singapore.'

This was the jumping-off point recommended by the crew. Tiira would have liked to wait till next night, when they would be well and truly in the Straits with land on either side, but Ericsson, impatient, pointed out that if they jumped that night they would not be more than six miles from land: they could paddle that distance. Once they were in the Straits those extra guards would come on. Tiira again agreed.

The behaviour of the two that evening was very different. Tiira felt a great weight off him now that the decision had been made. Ericsson looked more worried than ever and wanted more cigarettes. Tiira proposed dinner and Ericsson said that he was a fool.

'You've got to swim tonight. If you eat you'll drown.'

Nevertheless, Tiira enjoyed a good dinner of roast beef and salad, potatoes and half a bottle of red wine. Afterwards, while Ericsson walked up and down deck, he joined a group of Germans in the lounge and went on with a Finnish lesson. Finally, he and Ericsson had a beer together with the last of the money. At 9.30 he went to bed, while Ericsson stayed on deck to prowl around, returning every so often to the cache of food and clothing under the lifeboat. To him Tiira seemed much too calm.

Tiira was called at 2.45a.m. on the 23rd and made his way up to the deck. Ericsson had called him early and was half-smoking cigarettes and throwing them over the side. Tiira enjoyed his cigarette while they waited for the crew. They changed into the civilian clothes left for them and went aft. In the sultry night they stood and argued about who should jump first. Suppose the other did not follow? They were still arguing as they descended to a lower deck, to make the jump easier.

'Tie yourselves together. That way you'll both have to go,' one of crew said with some justice, and threw down a long rope attached to one corner of the raft.

They were both tied at last, each grasping a post and waiting for the signal. Ericsson held the wine-bottle under his shirt, Tiira the food, bandages, cigarettes and matches in a plastic bag. Now it was Ericsson who looked eager, like a swimmer poised for the moment of the dive. Tiira felt only a terror that they were too near the propellers. The crew members cast-off the raft, Ericsson dived out in front, into the night. The rope tautened and Tiira, too, was in the water.

The raft was close by and they struggled towards it, then climbed in. Ericsson was complaining that the bottle had hurt his hip. Once inside they found it very much smaller than it had seemed, indeed 'nothing more than a bottomless four-foot square of metal tubing'. The flooring, now inches under the sea, was a network of canvas strips, each about five inches wide, with gaps between. Around the metal rim were draped a number of rope grips, to which drowning men could cling. The paddles were clearly intended for emergency, not for normal propulsion. They hoped they would not have to spend very long here.

Everything in raft technique had to be learned. First, Ericsson let go of the wine-bottle, which floated away. It took ten minutes to recover it with the one paddle they had been able to find. They tried to make a flooring out of life-jackets, to rest feet on rope stretched from one corner of the raft to the other. A breeze sprang up, and Ericsson complained that he was chilled right through. After some time lights appeared.

'It's Sumatra!' Tiira shouted. But it was the *Skaubryn*, returning to look for them.

The ship swung past them three times, its searchlight sweeping the water. Each time they prepared to throw over the stolen food, certain that they would be spotted, and cowered in fear below the rim; but a raft lying low in the water, if there is no motion, cannot easily be seen. By the time the *Skaubryn* came round for the last probe the sun was up. It seemed inevitable that they would be seen. When the ship was finally gone it left them incredulous in relief. Ericsson proposed a celebration and took a long pull at the bottle. Tiira took a shorter drink and advised him to put the bottle away. They were not on shore yet.

Ericsson agreed and started to sing. He had lost his white cap overboard and knotted a handkerchief for his head. They agreed to set their course towards the east, by the sun and by the direction which the *Skaubryn* had taken. Ericsson, who had had the responsibility of the night, went to sleep while Tiira paddled. They reckoned that Sumatra must be just over the horizon.

When Ericsson woke they quarrelled because he thought they were going in the wrong direction, since they could see neither land nor any other boat. The glare from the sea hurt them badly, especially Ericsson, who had no hat. Having by now the second paddle, they paddled towards Sumatra (as they thought) and looked at the fish below them. Soon, however, as they were watching a big pilot fish under the raft, they were dismayed to see three sharks, one of them a ten-footer, massing for attack. As the ten-footer swept in, Ericsson struck it with his paddle and shouted that he had hurt it. It rolled over, showing its white belly and rows of teeth, but came back in a moment, striking the raft and sending it smacking across the water.

63

The attack lasted for some ten minutes, and by the end the fish under the raft had scattered. Dr H. Lindemann of Bad Oldesloe, an authority on survival at sea, observes that the slower the boat, the more fish accompany it. The raft gave welcome shelter to many fish, and hence drew the sharks. Both men were tired, and Ericsson wanted more wine. Tiira suggested a smoke instead. When they sighted a ship they agreed to have lunch, to celebrate their continued good luck. The food in the plastic bag, originally some sardines, half a loaf, six small pieces of cheese and a small lump of garlic sausage, had run together. They divided a part of this mess and Ericsson, now very hungry, took one piece of cheese and suggested that Tiira should have the piece that was his due later, since he did not want it now.

The sun struck them hard in the afternoon. Ericsson, a reddish-haired man, found his face going red-raw. Tiira, almost a white blond, fared much better, and he had a small sailor's cap which gave some protection. They tried to paddle, but without success. They saw land, or thought they saw it, but it disappeared. Ericsson sang. They decided what they would do on landing, for they were still happy and confident. By throwing a rope they could tell the direction of the current and decided they must have drifted out of course.

'I think we'd better row now,' Tiira said.

But Ericsson was too tired. He took the discomfort badly, his eyes seemed to have sunk into his head and his cheeks to have drawn together, shrunken like a withered apple. A little rain in the afternoon cooled them, but they could not collect enough for a drink. Before sunset they ate some more of the crumbled mess, and Ericsson suggested that Tiira should now have his piece of cheese. Then Tiira tried to make the raft more comfortable, passing a length of rope back and forth to form some sort of platform. As the sun went down on their first day at sea, a strong breeze blew up from the south.

They had intended to paddle through the cooler night, and kept it up for some two hours. By the stars they confirmed their eastward course but could not know how far the current had dragged them west, into the Indian Ocean. At about ten o'clock Ericsson could do no more, and tried to sleep on the ropes; but unable to sleep, he sat wakeful while Tiira stretched out on the two life-jackets. Both dozed off, waking for a time when ships passed. Frantically Ericsson tried to signal S.O.S. with the torch, but the ships were too far away and passed by. At last, very cold, they settled on the life-jackets and slept fitfully, their backs together for warmth.

In the morning they could not at first move for stiffness, but the rising sun warmed them, and they took a cigarette each. They could see no land; Tiira reckoned they must have drifted twenty or thirty miles from Sumatra.

'If we don't see land soon or a ship we'll die,' he said.

'Not for a day or two. We ought to be able to live like this for at least three days.' They little knew what an understatement this was.

Neither of them thought that they could last long after the food and wine had gone. They decided to abstain during the day and only touch the food at evening, but at noon they felt impelled to have something: a little bread and two pieces of cheese. Ericsson was suffering badly from sun-glare and complained of sore eyes. Tiira felt much better, apart from a blistering face. More rain fell, but neither cupped hands nor cap would catch it. They rowed, refreshed by the rain, but soon tired and fell to cursing the Legion, their escape, even their own relief at not having been spotted by the returning *Skaubryn*. They were fools ever to have believed in the idyll of Sumatra.

In the afternoon it was too hot to paddle, and they sat talking of their chances. In Tiira's mind nagging presentiment had burst through to conscious thought: they were not going to reach Sumatra at all, but were drifting far out into the Indian Ocean, bound for Ceylon. In that case they were doomed, unless there was some miraculous, un-marked island between. They talked of catching rain-water in the wine-bottle, a converted hot-water-bottle with a rubber neck, and of eating the small fish that from time to time jumped into their laps.

'They wouldn't be good raw without salt,' Tiira said.

'When you're dying of hunger you eat anything. You don't worry about things like that.'

One of the reasons why I chose Tiira's case out of many open to me is that he had none of the advantages of training or knowledge.

He was ignorant of elementary survival techniques, and the right principles which he applied (personal hygiene, not drinking sea-water), he applied through some sixth sense, or just common sense, and not because a survival manual told him to. That is to say, the unexpected situation brought out the quality in the person. It is worth referring again to Dr Lindemann, who has in the last six years made three solo crossings of the Atlantic: in an African single-boom, a standard collapsible boat (this took seventy-two days) and an ocean-going yacht. His object was by scientific appraisal of the problems to help shipwrecked sailors, and he has described how, six months before his trip, he began conditioning himself for it by autogenic training. Thus, when he suffered the expected hallucinations and on one occasion saw a negro before him, he asked the negro which way he should be going. 'To the west,' said the negro. 'The post-hypnotic command breaks through even in hallucination.'[1]

Tiira and Ericsson had had none of the psychological preparation advocated by Dr Lindemann; indeed, the pre-jump tension and later fear of capture were probably a greater strain on morale than shipwreck would have been, and they expected to die soon after finishing their food. Their raft, intended for short emergencies only, had not even a cover, which in Dr Lindemann's view is a great morale-booster. As for raw fish, they knew nothing except that they were repelled by the idea of eating it. Dr Lindemann is of opinion that raw fish eaten with the organs is a protection against scurvy, but fish should not normally be eaten without fresh water. Dr Alain Bombard,[2] to prove that man could live from the sea, made his famous crossing of the Atlantic on a raft and used a *pressoir* to extract water from the fish, but he had conditioned himself beforehand by eating raw fish in moderation and drinking sea-water, and opinion seems to have swung against many of his findings.

Ericsson and Tiira would have cared for none of these things, even had they known about them. They saw a piece of driftwood covered with crabs, and hope revived. Ericsson felt too weak to paddle and

1. In a paper read to the Conference of the Shipping Medical Section of the German Association for Transport Medicine, 11 March 1960.
2. *The Bombard Story*. The journey was made in 1952.

tied his handkerchief over his eyes. He now sat, dejected and forlorn, saying nothing. At evening they looked at the food again. They had meant to keep some, but so little remained that they ate it all, sausage and cheese and bread fragments, some two mouthfuls each. They sipped the wine. It was the evening of the second day, and now they had nothing left to eat.

Again they determined to paddle, while the food still gave them strength. But Ericsson put it off till the dark and then, after half-an-hour, gave up. Tiira still felt convinced that land lay somewhere just over the horizon, but he could not manage the raft alone. He gave up too and huddled close to Ericsson for warmth. Around midnight he suggested that they paddle again, but Ericsson said that he was too cold.

'But if you paddle you'll feel better. We'll never make land if we drift this way, getting nowhere.' He could not understand Ericsson's apathy. The life had gone out of the strong man. He lay there, in a miserable cold heap', refusing even a cigarette. Tiira smoked one and made it last. He felt none too bad, but desperately cold.

In the morning he tried to curse Ericsson into rowing, but each time he gave up after a few strokes. Drifting bamboo caught them up, but it was rotten and soggy, as if it had been floating for months. Among some corks floated a turnip, but this was rotten too. As the sun grew hot they drank the last of the wine, spinning it out, rolling it round and round their mouths. When it was gone, they passed the bottle round from time to time, reckoning that the smell helped them. They discussed what one should do if the other died, and even where they wanted to be buried. Both wanted a land burial, and each promised to give this to the other.

'Lunch' was a cigarette and a sniff at the wine-bottle. Then a wind sprang up and Ericsson, who had brightened a little, suggested that they use his top shirt as a sail. So far as reaching Sumatra went this was madness, since the easterly wind was now blowing them farther into the Indian Ocean, but for Ericsson, indeed for them both, the very fact of movement stimulated. They thrust the paddles through the sleeves and held them erect. In this way they moved with astonishing speed, but in the wrong direction.

They could not hold the shirt-sail for long, and during one of the rests Ericsson had the idea of bathing, to relieve cramp and soreness. Though a risky operation, this seemed to do him good. Soon afterwards a storm hit them. For the first half-hour it was delicious; they held up their faces and let the rain pour upon them. But the rain turned very cold, the wind whipped them as they tried to shield their sore cheeks, and they were relieved, after an hour, when the sun shone again. They had caught nothing in the water-bottle.

After the storm Ericsson brightened once more, as it was his nature to do when there had been some action. They knew now, too, that the raft would stand bad weather. They hoisted the shirt and sped forward. A gin box stamped 'London', a great submerged tree, a covey of gulls at evening – all these gave hope that land might after all be near. The smallest sign was cause for hope, on which they lived. Both of them believed quite simply that they would not last long now that they had finished the food. But nowhere, perhaps, can the change from death to life, from torment to comfort, be more sudden and more appetising than at sea. At any moment their dream boat might steam over the horizon. Any one of their weary glances might pick up that magical island which within an hour or so would transform their state for ever. So they hoped on, and did not die.

The wind freshened as the sun went down, and Tiira feared that they would be washed overboard if both slept. He offered to take the watch and Ericsson did not refuse. Though it tasted bad and made them more thirsty, a cigarette stayed their hunger. Then the wind drove them on to more debris, bamboos full of grubs; they tried eating the white fungus that grew out of it, but they could not chew it into pieces small enough to swallow. Ericsson lay with one handkerchief over his eyes, another over his ears, stirring unhappily as the waves washed across. Tiira kept watch, bracing himself each time they descended into the pit. Each time that he moved to ease the numbness of his legs fresh pains shot through them. Dreams of land faded in an agony of regret at the decision that had brought him here. He thought with pain of home, of his mother who would be praying for him, as he knew. Then he played the counting game, like a child. Count to a hundred and see what happens. Another hundred . . . but still no ship.

He lay down beside Ericsson but did not sleep. The waves breaking against the raft told him, by their direction, whether it was going up or down. Tonight it was not cold, and at about midnight the bad weather cleared. Then they both slept. In the early morning of the fourth day, while it was still dark, he woke Ericsson and they had a cigarette, their breakfast. Still able to trot out the old joke, Ericsson remarked that this was their morning coffee and rolls, and added that he didn't like coffee much, anyway.

'It'll be a long time before we get morning coffee again," Tiira said.

'Not long. I'm good for another three or four days yet.'

'For me two days, no more.'

Ericsson was forcing the cheerfulness. His eyes were blank, he could see nothing. Tiira tried to cheer him, telling him that this would pass. He wanted to arrange the ropes to make a better bed, but Ericsson, now down again in despair because of his blindness, would not move. They hoisted the sail. They were not hungry now, and wanted nothing but water. The day was cloudless and again agonisingly hot. But at midday, as they smoked a cigarette that tasted of wood, Ericsson could still rise to calling it their lunch, 'soup and steak and vegetable'. He tried to practise some Finnish; then, resorting to the tactics of all who seek to survive, they broke into daydreams of the boat that would be coming soon. Tiira favoured a Panama vessel, Ericsson wanted a Swedish ship.

'We'd get food and drink and they'd pay us to work on a Swedish ship,' he said. 'We'd go home then and I'd be seeing Anna Lisa.'

They fell silent, dozed and daydreamed of home through the afternoon.

Ericsson woke, pleased that they were moving, and commented that they would soon be in Singapore. Tiira could not understand how he still had that idea and shouted at him that it was not Singapore they would be hitting, since they were drifting west, not east, but Ceylon if they were lucky and Africa if they were not. If they had jumped an hour later, when they were properly in the Straits, they would have hit Sumatra all right. They quarrelled over whose fault this was, and who was captain of the raft.

'Shut your mouth,' Ericsson growled at last.

The quarrel made Tiira unhappy. When one is a plaything of sky and sea it seems important that the human element should stand solid. He sank once more into despair, reviewing his past life and the mistakes that had pushed him, one by one, into this plight. He seemed to have made a series of false escapes, from Finland, from marriage, from his job in order to join the Legion, from the Legion to die in the sea. One cannot finally escape from an escape.

He stretched out a hand to tell Ericsson he was sorry that they had quarrelled.

That evening they had what seemed a wonderful stroke of luck. On the horizon, about three miles off, Tiira saw the big red sail of an Indonesian *prau*. At the same time Ericsson, whose eyes were now better, saw what he thought was a lighthouse on the western horizon. This turned out to be a destroyer steaming almost directly towards them. Suddenly, as they were about to signal, Ericsson said, 'It's French. I'm sure it's French.'

Earlier, in the storm, they had prayed to be picked up by anything, even the *Skaubryn*. But now that the chance had come they could not stand the thought of being locked in a French destroyer and turned over to the Legion. They cowered down in the raft and waited. The destroyer did not see them but was very slow in steaming past, and while it was there they did not dare signal to the *prau*. By the time it had gone the *prau* was far away and evening was advancing. Tiira thrust a paddle into Ericsson's hands, sure that they could cover the two or three miles of water between them, but Ericsson would not co-operate.

'We'd never get there,' he said.

Tiira tried paddling alone, but this was useless. In a fury at Ericsson sitting smugly there watching him, he stood up and threw his paddle overboard. This roused Ericsson, who set about trying to paddle towards it. For about five minutes Tiira watched, then he took over. Another quarter of an hour's hard work and he had recovered the missing paddle.

Then they quarrelled again about the *prau*, but ended by taking out a cigarette each. Quarrels did not last long, for they need energy. Tiira's first match failed to strike. From the second a spark flew off into their one remaining matchbox, which burst into flames. They both lit cigarettes from it, then second cigarettes from the first. These would be their last. Though their taste had become foul, the cigarettes had been of help, something to do, and a relief from hunger. Now they would miss them badly. Later they tried sitting with an unlit cigarette in the mouth, and found the taste not disagreeable.

The moon had come up, and during that night Ericsson began to suffer from hallucinations, such as are common among the shipwrecked. First, he gesticulated strangely, going through the useless motions of striking matches. Then he held an imaginary cigarette to his lips and pulled on it. A few minutes later came a loud splash. He could hardly be bathing at this hour. When he climbed dripping on to the raft he angrily accused Tiira of having pushed him, and would take no denial. Again they quarrelled, but soon huddled together and could not sleep; then slept, miserably, and woke to see the stern lights of a ship which must have passed within a quarter of a mile of them. By this time it was too late, though Ericsson flashed desperately with the torch: S.O.S. . . . S.O.S. . . .

They slept again, and when they woke were hungry once more. They always tried not to speak of food, though Ericsson broke the agreement by listing the menus on Swedish ships. Tiira could not keep from thinking of the butchers' shops of Rauma, his home town. (In this respect they were worse off than another remarkable survivor, Kenneth Cooke, one of two who survived out of fourteen after forty-nine days on an open raft. Cooke's main raft – there were three – was twelve feet by eight, provisioned with enough food and water for a meal and drink of a sort each day. Deaths were due partly to exposure, partly to the drinking of too much sea-water, partly to weakened morale over a long period.)[1] Tiira even thought with longing of the thick soup which legionaries received after a long march. They had not drunk for forty-eight hours, their tongues were thick and dry, their breath smelt rank. Now, on the morning of the fifth day, Ericsson still gave himself three or four days to live. Tiira continued to be less hopeful.

1. *What Cares the Sea?* by Kenneth Cooke. For some reason Ericsson and Tiira were not tempted by sea-water, the dangers of which are discussed at length by Lt-Cmdr G. W. R. Nicholl in *Survival at Sea.*

'If we don't get water by tomorrow, I'm through.'

It was about noon on this fifth day when Ericsson, seeing a crab which had climbed through the floor, broke off one of its legs and scraped out a few shreds of flesh with his fingers. He said that they were good. They pulled off the shell, but found very little meat. This was their first food from the sea and they felt happy to have found it, even if they had no intention of becoming Bombards.

Now the sun shone fiercely, and the metal floats of the raft burned them. Though incipient beards protected their cheeks, their ears and noses were painfully sore. They wrapped their second shirts round their heads for protection. Once, raising his shirt, Tiira saw a rain-shower some miles off. They started to paddle towards it, but Ericsson gave up and they sat there watching it, water that they could not use.

Meanwhile, the fish under the raft had increased in numbers, so thick they could have reached over the side and grabbed them. They must have run into a shoal. Unfortunately, this shoal had again attracted sharks; the usual escort of one big shark and five or six smaller had been increased by five more monsters, which cruised round and round, some sixty yards away. Suddenly they moved in to the attack. Again they were not, of course, attacking the raft itself but the fish below it. The raft they hardly seemed to notice. The first attack struck it a blow which sent Tiira to the bottom while Ericsson clung to the ropes around the sides. The air was full of small fish thrown high out of the water. Four big sharks were after them, coming in very fast and turning over so that their rows of teeth and white bellies seemed to slide past in procession. Ericsson and Tiira lashed out with paddles, but they had no effect. Each time that a shark struck, the whole raft tilted dangerously.

There was a tearing below. A blunt head broke through the canvas, a foot or so from their legs. Another lunge would bring it right up and tip them into the water. Both men struck furiously, again and again, till at last it sank back. A second hole was made in a few minutes, big enough for a man to fall through. Now they were afraid to put their feet on the floor; and if they put them on the side, they might fall out. Though raft and men must have weighed 300lb together, the sharks flicked them here and there like a child's toy.

The attack lasted about an hour, during which there was no peace:

each time the sharks submerged, the two knew this to be a preparation for the next attack. During one lull Tiira caught six small fish and put them in a jacket to be eaten later, but it was Ericsson who hit upon the idea of driving away the small fish which were attracting the sharks. They set to with their paddles, shouting and cursing meanwhile. By paddling a few yards and beating the fish off, they managed slowly to come clear. At last they had peace.

The effort of fighting the sharks had exhausted them. They lay still, trying to recover strength, restore courage. Then Tiira cut the flesh of one small fish into strips and they tried to eat it, but without water they could only swallow very small pieces. When they threw the remains overboard the water heaved and bubbled; they were afraid the sharks would attack again.

They thought of rigging the spare ropes across to form a sort of hammock, but Ericsson felt too tired. When the sun went down and he felt well enough to try, it was Tiira's turn to postpone the operation. As he fell asleep, he was aware that his heart was beating fast and loud.

They were wakened by the rain beating down. It was now sixty hours since they had drunk, and the relief was unspeakable. Ericsson caught the water in the hollow side of the bottle and they drank in turns. The water tasted of rubber, but they did not care. They felt renewed, new men. The tight feeling in the throat disappeared, saliva returned, their stomachs felt full. But they were soon cold, for the rain lasted an hour, and then hungry. The taste of raw fish lingered in their mouths. They could not bear to eat fish again.[1]

When the sun came up they set about rearranging the ropes. The 'hammock' kept them above the floor and out of reach of sharks; it would be more comfortable than lying on paddles and life-jackets. Ericsson spent much time counting the days and hours they had been away from the *Skaubryn:* five days and nine hours that morning. Tiira remarked that those five days of freedom had hardly been worth it. They lived through a hot, windless day and then, that night, came nearer to rescue than they had ever been. Three boats were in sight,

1. They were unlucky to be put off fish in this way. Cooke's party, for instance, ate a number of flying fish, a young shark, a dolphin, blue fish, ray and barnacles. They derived strength from these. But they had fresh water, even if very little.

73

not more than two or three miles away. Surely at least one would see them!

Ericsson almost fell out of the raft in excitement, signalling S.O.S., S.O.S., with the torch. To their joy, the nearest ship, now only half-a-mile away, seemed to reply. Tiira shouted, 'Keep it up! Keep it up!' and Ericsson kept it up, but now no light answered them. To their dismay the lights passed, the boat steamed on its course without turning. It left them near to tears.

Ericsson was, strangely, the more optimistic. Tiira's eyes were now very sore, and it was Ericsson's turn to assure him that this would pass. His own were better now. Then he found that his knife had dropped from his pocket and disappeared, but since they had Tiira's this did not matter.

'When we get ashore we'll need a knife,' Ericsson said. 'If we strike an island with no one on it, we'll certainly need something to kill animals with.'

Tiira knew that there would be no island. Ericsson was optimistic to the point of delusion.

They were now living on nothing but the smell of wine. On the afternoon of the seventh day, maddened by heat, Tiira stripped and plunged overboard, as Ericsson had done earlier. He had looked carefully for sharks, but even so Ericsson, from the raft, begged him to come in. He came in for a few minutes, then slid back, luxuriating in the cool freedom of the water. As he pulled out over the side a big shark whipped across underneath.

'You must be mad,' Ericsson stormed. Looking at him closely, Tiira could see that he really thought this. Each suspected the other's sanity. But Tiira did not feel mad. He washed and dried his socks, looked at his stomach and was amazed at how small it was, compared himself with Ericsson, shrunken and unhealthy to look at, and decided for the first time that he might last the longer. He tried to look at himself in the mirror, but its back had come off. Ericsson could not keep his mind from the imagined push overboard.

'You might have done it for a joke,' he grumbled.

Tiira said that to push a friend overboard was not his idea of a joke. Ericsson seemed satisfied, the delusion finally dispelled.

The eighth day, they lay still and could do nothing. They were dying from heat and thirst, exposure and lack of food. Their beards had stopped growing. Their hearts beat, they could feel that, and if something had urgently to be done it was done. Otherwise they just lay. They no longer felt hunger but, like John Brown, an 'unquenchable thirst'.

They had not the strength to row towards a rain-cloud spotted on the horizon, but at last, two hours before sunset, rain fell. Tiira had been asleep, and either in sleep or waking the thought had come to him that they could use the plastic bag for the collection of water. They brought it out and sat with bag and bottle on their knees, catching the rain as it streamed down. As the side of the bottle filled up they transferred the contents to the bag, then to the inside of the bottle. The raft jogged about and each time they spilt a drop they became angry, with their luck and with each other. This was the first water in three days, and they could not bear to lose it.

They collected about a litre in the bottle, but this presented a new problem. How much and how often could they allow themselves to drink? When night came they both wanted a drink badly, but Tiira, who from now on took command, refused the bottle. At midnight Ericsson woke him, pleading for water, but again Tiira refused. They must drink slowly, must keep some of the water until it rained again. In the morning, stiff and sore, shifting position continually for a comfort they could never find, they each had a little. Neither wanted to be the first to drink. Ericsson drank. Tiira watched his Adam's apple rise slowly once, then drop back. He, therefore, also took one swallow and put the bottle away.

Clouds gathered, but it did not rain. At midday they could not resist the impulse to drink again. As the water rolled cooling down the channel of their throats, all their good resolutions melted with it. They could not take the bottle from their lips. By nightfall it was empty, and they were left with their thirst again.

It was on the eleventh morning that Tiira found that his knife, like Ericsson's, had slipped out in the night and disappeared. Ericsson was upset by the thought that they would not be able to kill, even if they found anything. And on the next day, the twelfth, they did in fact find food.

It was a turtle, which woke them with a sharp tap on the raft side, swam away but then returned to the raft for protection. Making a big effort, Tiira jerked it over the side and threw it on its back. This was food. However, Ericsson had relapsed into pessimism and maintained they could do nothing without knives. Tiira remembered the mirror. He broke it against the side, hoping for a long sharp splinter. The fragments were the wrong shape and size, but they were sharp enough. He wrapped his hand in a handkerchief and went to work on the turtle, Ericsson holding the front flippers, Tiira kneeling on the back flippers and hacking away at the throat. After ten minutes he found that he had done little more than scratch the surface of the horny skin. Then he tried to choke it, but his hands were too weak.

Ericsson gave up, but for an hour Tiira worked with the mirror. It was their last chance of food, he knew, since they could not stomach fish. When he got through the outer skin rows of sharp 'thorns' barred the veins, and the veins themselves, which he thought to cut, were tough as rubber. When at last his sore fingers broke open the jugular a jet of dark thick blood spouted up and hit him in the face. Instinctively, he put his head down and let the blood flow into his mouth.

'My turn,' Ericsson said, and he had his turn too. Beards and faces and clothes were all smeared with blood. They washed before returning to the turtle. When Tiira picked it up by its back flippers more blood came spilling out, but now they felt nauseated at the sight of it dribbling into the reddened water and could drink no more. Ericsson fell asleep while Tiira tried to hack meat out of the neck. This was not bad to taste, but their mouths were too sore to take much. Ericsson chewed a very little and threw his over the side.

By great good fortune a shower of rain followed that afternoon; they could wash away the taste of blood and loosen tongues again. Tiira felt strong now, but Ericsson had tired from exertion and was worse than before. Tiira went to sleep with his feet on the turtle and next morning scraped all the shell and offered pieces of the now hardened flesh to Ericsson, who refused to eat them. 'I don't like it,' he kept saying, and turned his face away, half-asleep.

Tiira took some more and even tried to paddle, he felt so strong. Ericsson had lapsed again into listlessness. At one point he threw a turtle leg, meaty at that, into the sea. Tiira was furious.

'I work hard to get the food and you throw it away. It's food and not so bad.'

'It tastes bad and it smells bad to me,' Ericsson said dully. 'Let the sharks have it if they want it.' And the sharks did want it.

On the fourteenth day they thought that rescue had indeed come. Two ships approached to within five hundred yards. On the funnel of one of them could be plainly seen the three crowns of Sweden, two above and one below. Tiira stood up and waved. Ericsson, too weak, sat waving the bottle, the first thing that came to hand. The ship passed by without noticing them. So did a second ship, which had seemed to be running them down, so small was the gap between. The height of their hopes, particularly Ericsson's, made despair all the deeper. If these could not see them nobody could; it was as if an invisible veil had been drawn around them. Hope was gone; each sank into a private misery. Tiira hacked at the turtle, but Ericsson still would not eat. Now that the ships had passed by, they hardly cared.

Or so they thought. Yet when, on the early morning of the fifteenth day, a small tanker steamed right up to them, Ericsson, who clung perversely to his torch, fumbled the dots and dashes, and Tiira shouted, or tried to shout, across the water. He was sure that a voice answered him, but when he shouted again, no voice came back and the tanker passed on its way. For a long time Tiira sat and cursed the ship, all ships and everything. Ericsson took it very quietly, as if he accepted what had happened and his own end. In his wandering mind were confused days when he had escaped before and had been caught.

'You know,' he said, 'if a ship finds us now they can't put us in the cells.' It would be hospital for them, he prophesied. He drifted into sleep, no longer joking about the coffee and rolls for breakfast, no longer willing to talk at all.

Tiira, however, was only too wakeful. On that fifteenth day they were becalmed on a hot, glassy sea. The remains of the turtle now smelt horribly, and in the afternoon Tiira heaped them into the shell and pitched it over the side. In a few moments a big shark had swallowed the lot, and there followed a terrifying scene. The turtle-shell must have stuck in the shark's throat, for it threshed about, convulsed, skimming the water like a speed-boat and shaken by great tremors that ran through its whole body. Tiira feared that its convulsions would bring it near, that a flip of its tail would overturn the raft or kill them outright. He hoped that it would die and that the other sharks would eat it and leave them in peace. At last the turtle-shell broke loose and floated to the top, and another shark rose and bit off the head. After this, one huge shark remained with them always.

Knowing that Ericsson was dying, Tiira tried to find out where he lived, who were his parents, but the other would not answer. His mind had withdrawn, the colour had faded from his grey eyes, which were now milky white and glassy. Nevertheless, he mumbled that he felt better. In the early daylight of the sixteenth morning he awoke with a cry that he had lost the water-bottle, which he kept inside his shirt as Tiira kept the plastic bag. For a moment, panic. The bottle was everything to them, since without it they could not hold rain-water from the intermittent showers. On all the calm surface around, no bottle-top. Desperately searching, Tiira suddenly saw it resting on one of the canvas strips at the bottom of the raft. He grabbed it and kept it after that in his own shirt.

Rain came again at noon on the seventeenth day, and by now Tiira was expert at catching it in the bag and transferring it to the bottle. Ericsson pleaded for water even before there was enough to drink. After the rain he felt better, he said, but made no effort to move and lay back on the ropes. He had been lying there too long. He was covered with sores, emaciated, like a skeleton, unrecognisable as the handsome, vigorous man of a fortnight ago. His forehead was very hot, breath came gasping, lips were swollen and cracked. He kept calling for water, and apologised for drinking so much when it came.

'I'm so tired, Tiira. I can't help myself.'

He slept through the next night on his back and called for no more water. On the morning of the eighteenth day they had a quarter of a

Jack Sillito in 1943

Charles Houston in Rawalpindi on the day of return, 1953

Tony Streath

bottle left. Now Ericsson could only beckon with his hand for the bottle. He was unable to hold it and had to be helped. Some of the water spilt down his shirt.

After the drink he lay back, smiling. He did not know where he was and kept asking to be sent to hospital. He could find no comfort until Tiira turned him over on to his stomach. He groaned softly all the time, but did not want to be moved.

'No, it's better now.'

Only good rain could save him. The rain came at noon. Tiira jumped up to shake his shoulder, to fill the hollow of the water-bottle and press it on him.

'Ericsson! Wake up! Wake up!'

Ironically, the rain had come too late.

Tiira sat a long time holding Ericsson's pulse, unable to believe that he was dead. Difficult, exasperating, unpredictable, Ericsson had been his friend. The bond of hardship shared is stronger than any bond. Moreover, apart from physical help, he had lost the incalculable moral support which the presence of another person means in danger. Even when critical and carping, Ericsson had been a presence from whom strength could be drawn, just as he drew strength from Tiira.

At last Tiira set to and collected the water. It was a long shower, and at the end he had three-quarters of a bottle full. He felt very lonely and feared that he might go mad by himself. He also experienced strongly the sensation already mentioned, known to those who find themselves near their physical limit.

> I didn't pray, and I'm not a religious man usually, but for the whole voyage I'd had the strange feeling that someone else was with me, watching over me and keeping me safe from harm. I sensed it in the storm, when we nearly overturned, and many other times. It was as if there were sometimes three people on the raft, not two. With Ericsson dead I felt it more strongly than ever.[1]

To Tiira it seemed that the other person might be his mother: perhaps her prayers for him were penetrating space and time. There

1. *Raft of Despair.*

had always been a strong bond between them, for he was the eldest and in the 1939 evacuations had taken a man's part.

During the afternoon he had to drink several times, and he put this down to the upset caused by Ericsson's death. He took the heavy blue shirt, the best they had, and washed it for himself. With a torn piece of the white shirt he covered the dead man's eyes. Meanwhile, towards evening, the eastern sky darkened with cloud, lightning squirmed and flashed into the sea as storm slowly advanced upon him. In the glassy calm before it broke he had time to make everything fast, to secure the paddles and fragments of mirror under the life-jackets, and the water-bottle and plastic bag.

It was a hard storm, sharp waves coming close together rather than the majestic rollers of the first deluge. Wind shrieked as if it were blowing through a ship's rigging. He was blinded with spray, drenched as he lay along the ropes. He could not believe Ericsson would not be washed over the side, but he had little leisure to think of that as he gripped the ropes tighter and clung on.

The storm lasted three or four hours, and at the end he lay breathless on the ropes along which Ericsson still lolled. It was midnight, and after rearranging the tackle he fell asleep, forgetting cold and wet. He awoke several times, finding the raft tilted under Ericsson's heavier weight, and himself couched against the cold body's side.

Before sunrise the skies were very beautiful. Cloudlets in the east caught and held the long beams that seemed to probe up from the ocean floor. But once the sun burst savagely upon the scene it burned out all thought of beauty. Tiira was richer in water than he had ever been, and counted on lasting at least the three weeks he had now set himself. During that nineteenth day he slept for two or three hours, but found himself each time slipping against Ericsson. In the evening he arranged both life-jackets so that he could have the most comfortable 'bed' he had yet had on the raft. Now that there was nobody to talk to he found himself watching the sunset with an intenser interest.

The sun went as it had come, illuminating, long after it had sunk below the sea, islands of cloud in a great dazzle of coloured light. His mind, for a short time, seemed to leave the raft and wander there outside, in the sky. But the practical business of going to sleep brought him back with a bump. He could not lie on his left side, now a mass of ulcers, and to make any readjustment took a painfully long time, so tenuous had become the link between mind and limb.

On the twentieth day he washed his body and wondered at it, almost as if it belonged to somebody else. The skin flaked, ulcers from crown to toe gave off pus. He exposed it to the sun for a while, but when he came to put on his clothes found that this had not helped. And now the body of Ericsson, after two days, was beginning to decompose. Crabs and small fish were attacking parts of it that trailed in the water, and he could not keep them off. He sat to windward when he could, and wondered how far their promise to bury each other on land need carry.[1] If he were rescued, would he be accused of killing his friend if the body had disappeared? His mind had weakened. All he could decide was to take things as easily as possible, conserving strength.

That evening he finished the water, unable to stop himself. But he was lucky. In the night rain fell again, at first heavily, then through a light mist which set his teeth chattering as he shivered over the slow filling of bag and bottle. By the twenty-first morning two more big sharks had joined the escort, and the smell from the body drove him to wrap his head in the blue shirt. He did not dare to look at what the crabs and small fish were doing to Ericsson, but lay in the ropes, looking down at the sharks, trying to think of other things. The usual thought-avenues of escape did not work, for each only led him back to the horror of the corpse at his side.

By noon the sharks had increased to thirteen, but some of these later dropped off. He now made the first serious attempt to be rid of Ericsson's body, which had swollen and blackened beyond recognition. Surely no promise was meant to cover this predicament? But he had not reckoned on his own weakness. Struggling, he could push it to the

1. Kenneth Cooke and his companions buried each person who died immediately, overboard. So did Lt-Cmdr F. West, twenty-three days in a lifeboat with Sikhs, Lascars and Goanese in 1941: 'We always buried the British as soon as possible after they died, and said prayers.' (*Lifeboat Number Seven.*) The Sikhs buried their own dead. This was the rational thing to do, and Tiira undoubtedly added to his own torture. If he had acted at once he would have had the strength to dispose of the body.

side of the raft, but no further. He heaved and strained at it, ears roaring, but could not make the necessary lift. He fell back, feeling very ill.

That night rain came again, but in his weakness he spilt much of the water and nearly lost the bottle.

Clouds on the twenty-third day gave a cool morning, and in the afternoon rain fell. Welcome as it was, it seemed very cold, colder as he became weaker. He put on shoes and socks, which would also protect his feet from fish. Most of the clothes, even the blue shirt, were disintegrating with the salt water. He pinned the worst tears with safety-pins from the bandages and put bag and bottle in a life-jacket, since he was now so thin that his shirt would not hold them.

Sleeping in the afternoon, he dreamed of a rough sea. When he awoke, he noticed that two of the sound ropes had frayed through. Suspiciously, the frays were directly above the breaks in the canvas flooring, beneath which sharks cruised. Another anxiety beset him next night, when he awoke to find that he could hardly swallow water, his throat was so painfully constricted.

To add to his despair he had not seen a ship for seven days and was convinced that he was off the sea-lane and would now never be rescued. His conscious mind, in resignation, accepted death as the end and even hoped for it; for all that he went on with the jobs, doing everything that might help him to stay alive. At noon on the twenty-fourth day he saw a freighter, but scarcely felt disappointed when it went below the horizon without turning. Again he tried to get rid of the body, pulling and heaving at the belt, but could not. Then he thought, 'Perhaps it will help me after all if I am picked up and the body is still there.' He let it be.

On the morning of the next day a thunderstorm brought rain, but the wind made it very hard to collect water. In the following calm Tiira lay on the life-jackets, head wrapped in the shirt. Once, when he came out to drink, he noticed that the sharks were now ten, three new arrivals being the biggest he had seen, three times as long as the raft. Their attack was preceded by a reconnaissance. Sitting on the life-jackets, bottle and bag stowed below, he braced himself for the blow. The first shark struck hard, as if to see how strong the defences were, then flashed off. The shock was harder than they had ever received in the earlier fights. Then another shark came in, fin cutting the water, and struck under the float with its head so that the whole raft tilted. A blurred vision of the square, horrible brown and white face and it was off, while another, striking a glancing blow, rose glistening two or three feet above the water.

Now the water was torn and threshed all around; he could only shut his eyes and count the blows, then lose count. One fin he could not help watching, as it circled nearer. It disappeared and then, suddenly, there it was, a brown head and brown eye almost against his body. He found strength this time to hit it, striking wildly at the eye, but it was like hitting at bone. He jabbed again and again with the paddle, but the head was caught now in the mesh of ropes and it was a long time before it sank angrily through the broken floor.

Once or twice a shark would leap out of the water and he thought, 'If one of those comes in, that's the end.' Sometimes there were two furious heads up in the raft at the same time, struggling to disentangle, jostling Ericsson's body and taking some of it before they went down.

By now Tiira was paralysed, unable to do more than watch. Only three strips of canvas remained to the floor, and half the ropes. But he now knew that it was Ericsson the sharks wanted. If he could get the body overboard, he had a chance. In the lull he managed to crawl across on the ropes, and heaved once again at the body. He could lift the waist by the belt, but not the head or feet. In desperation he gripped the hair of the head, but it came away in his hand. Meanwhile, the sharks were coming in again, jabbing up through the floor. If he could have thrust the body down they could have taken it, for the thing had become, in a grisly way, a combined operation. But, though they tore at the flesh, they could not pull it, and they did not take the feet, which hung out over the water.

He knew well that if a little more of the rope went there would be nothing left to hang on to. Kneeling on three good strands, he put his hands under and tried to roll the body. Just then the sharks struck again, tilting the whole raft and unwittingly helping him. A last heave, the body balanced on the edge and was in the sea.

Before Tiira's eyes the sharks, lashing and tearing, fighting among themselves, took his friend away. He could not move but sat on the side of the raft in horror. Words came to his mind, through a veil:

'Our Father, which art in heaven, Hallowed be thy name. . . .'

He remembered parts of other prayers, of many years ago:

'Dust thou art, and unto dust shalt thou return. . . . .'
'The Lord Jesus Christ raise thee up. . . . .'

The sea boiled and flashed, then slowly subsided, as he drifted away. Pieces of clothing that he recognised came floating past.

After some time he began to look again at the raft. Ericsson's end had curiously strengthened the will to live. Only one canvas strip of flooring remained, but there was plenty of coiled rope. Working very slowly through the afternoon, resting often, he first cleaned off the tatters of flesh and clothing that clung all over the raft, then arranged an abundance of rope diagonally across it, so that for the first time he could stretch out his whole length. Because he was so light his body remained well above the water, out of reach of sharks. That night, pushed along by a good wind, he could really sleep, the bottle pressed like a cushion against his ulcered side.

He drifted like this for two days, refreshed by occasional rain, but on the morning of the twenty-eighth day noticed, to his dismay, that the wind had changed and he was going east, back towards Sumatra once more. His few hopes had been pinned on hitting Ceylon. To raise morale he tried to comb his hair, as he and Ericsson had always done when they saw a ship, but now he had no comb. He cleaned his ulcers and rinsed his sore mouth with sea-water and felt better. At about this time the use of his right arm left him. The poison from ulcers in the armpit had spread downward. During the twenty-ninth day the ulcers became even worse, the inside of his mouth more painful. He had eaten nothing since sixteen days ago, when he had chewed the last fragments of turtle. In the blistering heat he could not find any position of comfort for his body, nor, with the return of one of the big sharks, did he dare to trail in the water.

He tried to rig an awning against the sun, but nothing would keep it off. Now he no longer sweated and his voice had gone. However, as the sun disappeared he realised that he could still live, if he wished, through the cool night, and he had a little water. The next day he passed either in a coma or delirious dreams, and on the next, the thirty-first (March 25), he awoke convinced that he would die before sundown. Yet the day started with rain, and he managed to catch a little of it despite his arm. He found himself wanting to say prayers, as he had said them for Ericsson, but could remember only the Lord's Prayer and fragments:

> 'The Lord bless thee and keep thee. The Lord make His face to shine upon thee ... and give thee peace. ...'

As the day wore on, however, the conviction that he would die became stronger, and with it the sense of another person keeping him company since Ericsson's death disappeared. Night came and, to his own surprise, he was not dead but even felt stronger before he drifted into delirious sleep. The thirty-second day dawned, blending imperceptibly in impression with the previous day, and on it a dim procession of ships persuaded him that he had come back on to the sea-lane. A curious determination took shape: to live just one more day. The ships passed; nothing that he could do would attract them, but that scarcely seemed to matter. As night came he noticed that the torch battery had given out. He had no more hope from the S.O.S. Nevertheless, he must stay awake this one night; by will-power he would resist sleep. Will-power was not enough, and he slept.

At midnight that night two officers of the British freighter *Alendi Hill* were changing watch when they heard a noise as of two pieces of metal being struck together. In the brilliant moonlight their eyes were attracted to the raft, where Tiira, wakened by the ship that was riding almost on top of him, was beating the paddle against the metal float. They called the captain. For three hours the big freighter manœuvred – three hours of heart-breaking suspense for Tiira, who thought each time they turned that they were going away – before it could come alongside the tiny raft and lower a rope. As they pulled him over the side, they could see dimly the sharks thrashing and bubbling round the raft, as if in fury that their chance had gone. The time was 3.20 a.m., almost exactly thirty-two days since Ericsson and Tiira had jumped the *Skaubryn*.

When he was taken aboard, a skeleton with parchment-like skin and suppurating ulcers, Tiira seemed as close to death as a man can be. In another day he would probably have died. He was about a third of his normal weight (five days later, after feeding, he weighed 56lbs out of a normal 132). Yet the human body, unless some positive illness is present, seems able to start the upward climb almost immediately. Prudently the officers of the *Alendi Hill* took him in very slow stages through milk, a little at a time, and fruit-juice, to solid food. After five days, when they arrived at Singapore, he was sitting up. After nine days, he had put on sixteen pounds in hospital. Apart from a worry that he would be turned over to the Legion, a worry slow to dispel, his mind was at rest. He started then and there to write of his journey. In May, on a Finnish ship, he set sail for home.

There have been many stories of endurance at sea and longer periods have, of course, been passed in the open. In 1942, Poon Lim, a Chinese steward on the *Ben Lomond*, spent 133 days at sea on a raft, feeding himself by catching fish with a bent nail prised from the wood.[1] But I have chosen this story, partly because of the extremity to which Tiira came without dying, partly because he had none of the aids or knowledge advocated in survival manuals,[2] partly because he and Ericsson contrast in exemplary fashion as the survivor and non-survivor, and partly because certain facets of Tiira's self-revelation cast light on certain of the qualities that make human beings tick in extreme situations and come through, even when they think that they are going under.

Neither of these men expected the situation with which they were

1. As told in *The Ben Line* by G. Blake. This feat, of which there are not many details, is almost inexplicable in any terms. A particular problem is how he got enough fresh water to keep alive. He caught rain-water and the raft had food for fifty days.
2. Compare the precepts contained in *Survival at Sea* by Lt-Cmdr G. W. R. Nicholl, in this connection.

faced, though as legionaries they were prepared for the sudden-death type of crisis. Both had worked on big ships, but Ericsson, the sailor of the party, did not survive. (Here Cooke and his friends, as also Lt-Cmdr West,[1] had an advantage, being nautically minded and having a good idea of where they were going.) Ericsson did not survive, partly because of his physical disposition. A big, red-haired man, he may have been the ideal companion for a tough, short-term situation in battle, but he was not suited to a long period of extreme temperature and discomfort. Like many big men he was nervous, swinging from cheerful optimism to despair, from friendly fellow-feeling to real hate. He could not adapt his personality to circumstance. He could not row when they needed to row, if he was not in the mood; he could not resist the water, when he knew it must be conserved; he preferred to lie in discomfort, when he knew that rearrangement of the ropes would make for a better night and hence longer life; he was possessive, not letting the torch out of his grasp even when he knew that Tiira would be staying awake.

In his experiments with dogs, Pavlov noted four basic types: the 'strong excitatory', the 'weak inhibitory', the 'lively' and the 'calm imperturbable'. He noted also that more severe and prolonged stresses could be applied to the last two types before they broke down than to the first two. If these categories can be applied to human beings, as psychotherapists seem to think that they can, then Ericsson was certainly of the 'strong excitatory' type and Tiira, who ate a good dinner and gave a Finnish lesson before the jump, was among the 'calm imperturbables'. A slight man, light blond in complexion, he had kept himself to himself among the legionaries. He had had to be talked into the escape by the eloquent Ericsson. Once they had jumped, however, something in him fixed itself stubbornly as a determination not to die. At first this something was conscious, and skills which he had not suspected came to the fore in the arrangement of ropes, methods of water-collecting and killing and cutting up the turtle. Ericsson's

1. Op. cit., footnote p. 81. It should be added that Dr Lindemann considers experience on a steamer to be of no help for survival in a small boat or raft. There is no contact with the sea. 'From the bridge or deck of an ocean-going steamer it is as good as lost.'

bright ideas came in flashes, like his suggestion that they scatter the fish when the sharks attacked. Later, when his conscious mind was convinced that he would die, the small something in Tiira crystallised as a subconscious refusal to accept that conviction. 'Die I will not', said the voice inside, when he had come so far.

Though they often quarrelled, the companionship with Ericsson was undoubtedly of supreme value to Tiira. What the issue would have been had Ericsson died earlier, no one can say. His presence meant less physical comfort, less water, more worry; and the communal paddling proved useless anyway. Tiira survived fifteen days without him. Yet he was a companion, with all that this means, and when he had gone the feeling that someone else was there grew stronger. After Ericsson's death Tiira prayed for the first time.

Somebody who, as a result of shelling, found himself in an open boat for six days, has told me of the atmosphere of prayerfulness which came over the least 'religious' castaways.[1] Some of the prayer was specifically for rescue, and when a Spanish ship finally appeared and picked them up there was a general sense that this intervention was directly due to prayer. It would not have been kind to remind them of the thousands of boats drifting over the Atlantic in which the same prayers must have been offered without the same result. What interests us here is that in Tiira's case prayer first came after the intense emotional shock of losing Ericsson's body in horrifying circumstances. It came again on the day when he was convinced that he was going to die. It was not, that is to say, a request but a reconciliation, both with his friend and with something beyond his friend. He did not, when he was picked up, feel that the extraordinary luck whereby he had been spotted on the very night after the torch battery had given out was due to appeal on his part, but rather that the words which he had

1. Cf. also Kenneth Cooke: 'On the night of the seventh day one of us heard Little John praying. He humbly asked the apprentice to pray for us all. . . . All joined in the request and the day was finished with a heartfelt prayer from all aboard the two rafts.'

Lt-Cmdr F. West wrote in *Lifeboat Number Seven:* 'We are all praying for rain or a ship' and: 'Praying seems to come easier when one is in trouble. . . . I found the hours of silent prayer and the complete solitude into which I was able to cast myself on these occasions, a source of strength, giving one renewed hope.'

tried to whisper had put him somehow at rights, both with Ericsson and with the universe of which they were a minute floating scrap, so that it did not matter any more whether he lived or died.

'The Lord make His face to shine upon thee . . . and give thee peace.'

5

The Disciplined Skill:
Two Deserts and Two Mountains

SOME HAVE THE ORDEAL THRUST UPON THEM IN SUCH A WAY that they can do nothing but sit and wait. Those who are well suited to this pastime, like the shepherd of Blons, come out of it comparatively intact. In the case of the hospital patient an effort of co-operative adaptation is required besides. Skill, albeit acquired by sheer force of necessity, saved Tiira when no amount of fortitude would have availed. But there are some who, although not voluntarily exposing themselves to survival situations, because of the nature of their sport or calling accept the risk of their occurrence. Anyone who pursues an adventure such as long-distance sailing, or greater mountaineering, or polar exploration, is mentally prepared for situations in which he will have to make strenuous efforts if he is to go on living. He is prepared in a sense in which John Brown, a 'natural' survivor, was not, when he descended to his daily work one October morning.

Nobody in his senses seeks to be avalanched or marooned waterless in the sands, yet anybody who climbs mountains or explores deserts is aware that one of these predicaments may conceivably be his. To meet it, a man can fortify himself with techniques and disciplines of the sort

which apply also to armed forces. Visiting the library of the Scott
Polar Research Institute at Cambridge recently, I was bewildered
by the number of books[1] and manuals, the latter particularly from
the U.S.A.F., which instruct a man in everything from signalling to
the striking of fire, from the best methods of cooking snakes to the
ways of finding home. Basically, the theme of all of them is the same:
given adaptability, the human being can cope with almost any situation.
It is the unadaptable, the Ericssons, who go under. To some extent a
man can learn to adapt, both through survival 'courses', which put
him in some of the situations that might be met, and through books
which illustrate the situations that cannot easily be demonstrated.

Disciplines of this sort, suggested from outside, can get one a long
way. Self-discipline, that elusive quality, does the rest. It is self-
discipline which enables one man, though he has none of the aids,
to come through the ordeal, while another, who has read all the
books, goes under. It is the aim of the manuals to instil that self-
awareness without which no book-learning is of any use at all.

It would be possible to tell many stories of disciplined skill which
has pulled through, for this is the best stocked of my somewhat
artificial categories. To illustrate the self-disciplinarian and soldier I
shall tell briefly of two cases, one well known and one not well
known, before dealing in more detail with a mountaineer whose
experience sums up that of many more.

Sven Hedin is famous as a Swedish scientist, explorer and linguist.
In 1894 he set out on the great journey whose object was 'to traverse
Asia from west to east, from the Caspian Sea to Peking, and in par-
ticular to explore the intermediate regions which are least known.'[2]
The first part of his journey went well. After passing through the
Pamirs he made his daring attempt on Muztagh Ata (24,388 ft),
reaching by yak a height which he thought to be over 20,000 ft.
After a winter spent at Kashgar he proposed to cross the Takla Makan
Desert of East Turkestan from west to east.

1. Among longer works might be mentioned *The Survival Book* by P. H.
Nesbitt, A. W. Pond and W. H. Allen. One or two others are given in the biblio-
graphy.
2. *Through Asia*, vol. I. The other quotations come from this important book.

The purpose of this journey was scientific and archæological. I emphasise that. Very little was known of this region beyond rumours of 'a thousand and one cities' buried in the desert sand. Sven Hedin started from Merket, on the western fringe, on 10 April 1895, with local men and a hundred gallons of water on eight camels. For the first thirteen days water was found for the camels through digging, and the party reached two small lakes. On the 23rd they entered the real desert. The sand of the Takla Makan, sifted by wind, is microscopically fine and blown into shifting crests sometimes 350 feet high, infinitely toilsome to pass. On the 24th a dust-storm obliterated the ground, while the sun still shone fiercely above. By the 26th they found themselves short of water. With desperate energy a well was dug; at a depth of three feet the ground became damp, but no more. Sven Hedin reckoned that there remained enough in the tanks for two cupfuls a day.

On the 29th two quarts of water remained, to be stolen by one of the guides. There was no sign of the Khotan Daria, the river towards which they were steering.

On 1 May, Sven Hedin and his four men pitched the 'Camp of Death'. Everyone – camels, too – seemed to feel that this was the end. A sheep was slaughtered, but they could not drink its thickened blood. Two men who had drunk camels' urine mixed with vinegar and sugar died later.[1] At sunset, with the other two men, Islam and Kasim, Sven Hedin pushed on. At first he rode a camel, then walked by lantern light. At midnight, after only two and a half miles, they had to leave Islam and the camels. Next day they rested, buried naked to the neck in the sand with clothes hung above on a spade for shelter. At night they crept on. On the morning of 3 May, Kasim spotted a tamarisk in the far distance. When they reached it, 'we thanked God for His mercy, and I have never before so forcibly realised that the

1. Many others, like D. R. G. Cameron, who made a remarkable survival in the Sahara, have observed that urine is likely to be poisonous. (*A Saharan Venture.*) But others again, like Jack Sillito, who is quoted later, have not been affected. A doctor writes that the acids in urine, if taken without fresh water, would be poisonous, but that in Sillito's case the amount taken, owing to de-hydration, was so small that it probably did not affect the issue one way or the other.

Mohammedans have the same God as the Christians'. They chewed the juicy needles of the tamarisk 'like animals'. In the evening they reached three poplars and tried to dig a well, but they were too weak.

They were not saved yet. On 4 May they were again in sand. During the heat they rested their dried-up bodies under a tamarisk, and at evening Kasim was not strong enough to continue. Sven Hedin continued alone until one a.m. and then 'sank down in utter fatigue under a tamarisk'. Here Kasim rejoined him and they staggered on together like dying men. On 5 May they saw a dark line on the horizon – the woods of the Khotan Daria. They reached these at last and rested under poplars. At seven p.m. Sven Hedin continued. 'Kasim remained where he was, lying on his back, motionless, with eyes wide open and mouth gaping, and he did not answer when I asked him to go with me.'

The wood ended and a white plain showed in the moonlight. This must be the dry bed of the river. In five hours he had come no more than two miles. Suddenly a duck flew up, water splashed. It was a pool, left in the deepest bed where the stream had last flowed. By an act of restraint which has become proverbial, Sven Hedin took his own pulse before drinking. It was forty-nine. Then he filled his boot with water and returned to Kasim. Much later they were rejoined by Islam, who had been rescued by merchants and who brought Sven Hedin's precious instruments.

This, in bare outline, is one episode from a life of disciplined exploration. Let us admit that luck was with Sven Hedin, as it refused to be with Burke and Wills on their great crossing of Australia from Melbourne to the Gulf of Carpentaria in 1860. Though they reached the mouth of the Flinders River, everything went wrong and they died. Only one member of the party, King, survived, befriended by a local tribe.[1] Yet, discounting luck, Sven Hedin had schooled himself from boyhood, by his studies and by early journeys, for the tasks which he coolly proposed. Therefore he was half-prepared for a situation which had killed others. It was characteristic of him to have made quite sure, next time he crossed the desert, that the journey was

1. For the accounts see *Australia Discovery* by E. Scott, vol. II.

'a series of triumphs'. On it he discovered the city of Takla Makan, lost for 1,500 years in the dunes.

Comparable with Sven Hedin's are experiences like those of Sir Douglas Mawson in the Antarctic, when he fought through alone after the death of Mertz. Transferring the idea of discipline to armed forces, one is confronted with two ideas rather than one. On the one side there is the discipline which many of us knew – 'bull', the cleaning of boots and buttons, the ability to turn to right or left correctly. This enables men to fight with ordered courage, as the Guards fought, rather than to adapt themselves to the totally unexpected. It was this tight discipline which almost broke down in the disastrous Arctic expedition of 1879, led by Lt A. Greely of the United States Navy. Greely spent two winters in Lady Franklin Bay, 250 miles from the North Pole, after which the relief ship *Proteus* was crushed by ice and he spent a third winter. The desperate struggle to return ended in a bivouac, no more, under an upturned boat at Cape Sabine. Food ran out, the party lived on little but shrimps. Most died of cold or starvation. Routine naval discipline was not enough when men stole food. One man was shot by Greely's order, and cannibalism, it was learned later, had been practised on others. It is abundantly clear from the accounts that those who came out best were the self-disciplined, like Sergeant Brainard.[1]

In contrast with routine discipline from the top is the training of the Chindits, for instance. Much of this took the form of direct experience, and much of that experience was a 'survival of the fittest'. There are now many special services, designed for operations behind enemy lines. Circumstances often demand qualities beyond and above, but supplementing, training. There come to mind many stories, some, like those of Jan Baalsrud[2] and F. Spencer Chapman,[3] too well known to be quoted here at length. Baalsrud, survivor of a Norwegian sabotage expedition in 1943, was trying to reach the

1. *The Long Rescue* by T. Powell.
2. *We Die Alone* by David Howarth.
3. *The Jungle is Neutral* by F. Spencer Chapman.

Swedish border. At one time he lay in a sleeping bag for twenty-seven consecutive days, out in the snow at 3,000 ft, and had to amputate his own toes.

Chapman, in Malaya, commented that some regular British units in the campaign gave up earlier than they need have done. Cut off by the Japanese in the jungle, they found themselves outside the routine discipline to which they were accustomed, and even the situations for which they had been trained. They were disorientated, rather than driven, towards their surrender. (This is not to belittle their courage or endurance. In captivity and escape, the fortitude of many was a matter for marvel.) Of six British soldiers who died in jungle conditions Chapman wrote that they died, 'not of any specific disease but because they lacked the right mental attitude'.

He himself is an exponent of the principle that, granted willingness of spirit, it is no use the flesh saying it is weak. It can do almost anything. He spent three and a half years behind Japanese lines as a guerilla: he was unconscious seventeen days during a dangerous illness; he suffered at various times from blackwater fever, pneumonia, tick-typhus and almost chronic malaria; he once took twelve days to cover ten miles through jungle, and on another occasion marched six days barefoot without food, yet he never seemed to lack the energy to blow up just one more Japanese train. What he had applied in Arctic Greenland he applied equally in Malaya. The 'military' ordeal, however, upon which I have chosen to enlarge is much shorter, though in its own way as demanding, and little known. Chapman once said that a man can work hard without food for eight days, provided he has water. But without water . . .?

In 1942 Jack Sillito was a parachutist in B Squadron, 1st Special Air Service. Rommel had advanced victorious across Africa to El Alamein, and it was the job of the S.A.S. operating in the Libyan desert to send out small jeep-parties on raids behind his lines. That November, Sillito found himself navigator to a party of four, in two jeeps, which left Kufra oasis to attack the coast railway line between Tobruk and Bardia.[1] They were to lay explosives and blow up track and passing trains. He

1. The story has been given and checked by Jack Sillito. A short account appears in *Born of the Desert* by Malcolm James.

navigated the party 300 miles to Hatiet Etla, a wadi in which a three-ton truck had been abandoned with a stock of food and water. From here they drove the further 140 miles to the line.

It was midnight when the four men, having left the jeeps, crept forward to reconnoitre. The line seemed deserted. Suddenly, however, music broke the silence beside them: they had stumbled on an Italian dug-out. The S.A.S. officer decided to attack, quickly, with their revolvers and one tommy-gun. But the tommy-gun jammed, hand grenades greeted them and from the desert a machine-gun opened fire. This fire pinned Sillito to earth; when he finally wormed his way clear, at three a.m., it was to find that his companions had given him up for dead. The jeeps were gone.

He had the choice of surrender, which he did not fancy, or a 300-mile walk along the Mediterranean coast to British lines, or the 140 miles back to Hatiet Etla, to food and water. He chose the last. He set off with a greatcoat, compass and revolver; nothing else.

He felt very fit and full of confidence. For the first two days he found a little brackish water in cans scattered where battles had been, but no food. On the third day he found an abandoned British tank and in it, to his delight, a tin of bully beef. But he had not realised how he had dried up. The saliva had gone; when he crammed the beef into his mouth he could not swallow a mouthful. He kept the tin and drank his own urine from it. This helped him, he thought.

The heat was at its worst between eleven a.m. and two p.m. He rested then, with greatcoat draped over head and knees for protection, but the coat became too heavy and he threw it away. The ground was now stonier and frighteningly bare: no bush, no trees. His shoes began to disintegrate and his feet to blister, so that each step seemed more painful than the last. He had to take frequent compass bearings. When he felt exhausted he lay down; when he awoke he staggered on. During the sixth day he caught sight of three moving objects – a mirage, he thought at first. He looked again. They were three S.A.S. jeeps! He tried to shout, but no sound came. He tried to run, and shambled across the sand towards them. He set fire to his shirt, but they went on, like Tiira's ships, and did not see him.

By his own account despair took him at this point. He picked up a large stone, but 'I found I hadn't even the strength to commit suicide. I couldn't even give myself a headache.' He tried burying himself in the sand, but by the time he was down the fit had passed and he was deciding to walk again. 'Like a robot' he walked on, or like a man in a trance, head sunk on chest. On the seventh day, not seen till he was on top of them, he found several sets of jeep-tracks. He followed those which led him along his compass course. At last, through a white heat, he saw the wadi.

When he reached it he could find no sign of the truck. Bitterly disappointed, he concluded that he had hit the wrong wadi and staggered back twenty miles. Then he saw, lying beside the track, a pack which he remembered had been dropped by the driver of his own jeep. This meant that the last wadi must have been the right wadi after all, but that he had not seen the truck. Almost unable to walk, he stumbled the last, worst twenty miles back towards it. But there was still no truck. As he swayed there, hopeless and undecided, a cloudburst of rain struck the wadi, filling it inches deep in a few minutes. He rolled into the water, luxuriating in it, and drank six mess-tins full. Then he climbed on to the bank and fainted.

He was awakened by voices. An S.A.S. jeep was passing, bound on the same mission which for him had ended so critically. He was saved.

He had spent eight days without food and almost without water, walking 180 miles in the Libyan desert. He had weighed thirteen stone and now weighed eight. In less than a month he was out of hospital and back in action, this being in his view the normal course to take.

There is discipline and discipline, therefore, and a too rigid acceptance of any code, civil or military, stultifies equally. Sillito's endurance was admirable, and indeed through the feats of soldiers it is easy to appreciate the dichotomy that worried Alfred de Vigny: however deeply I abominate war, however brutal and senseless the organisation of armies seems, it is impossible to withhold admiration from many of the qualities that make a good soldier. Here I need only remark that a soldier of the adventurous type, trained through experience in unusual conditions, may be supremely good at overcoming survival hazards which he has learned to accept as part of his calling.

Occasionally one finds a soldier (meaning a man with military, naval or air force training) who also submits himself to the other discipline, that of exploration, mountaineering, small-boat sailing, for its own sake. Mountaineers, like anyone else with a kink, are good, bad and indifferent. In so far as they are monomaniacs they may become less useful members of society, but they also become in a sense artists who express themselves in rock and ice and snow, in technique and endurance, as the painter expresses himself in paint and canvas. In a person who is both soldier and mountaineer one may find someone endowed to an extraordinary degree with the 'something' needed for survival, and I pass to an example which can be elaborated: the story of K2 and Haramosh.

Chapman had been a mountaineer and explorer, and became an 'irregular' soldier in time of war. Tony Streather joined the Indian Army in 1944 at the age of eighteen, partly inspired by a lecture at school. He gained his Army experience the direct way. At the time of Partition (1947) he was on the frontier with Pathan troops and saw something of the turmoil and bloodshed into which the sub-continent had been flung. Everybody took sides, and he became a staunch supporter of Pakistan. He stayed on, seconded to the Pakistan Army, and in 1949/50 found himself a captain in the Chitral Scouts, responsible for the movements of men in mountain districts remote from central control. In 1950 a Norwegian expedition had permission to attempt Tirich Mir (25,264 ft) in Chitral, and Streather was invited to be transport officer. He did not go as a climbing member of the party, but adapted himself so immediately to climbing conditions that he was found indispensable and went with them the whole way up the mountain to the top.

Most of us begin our climbing in this country, walking the hills and climbing rocks of an ever-increasing steepness and difficulty. Streather started with a twenty-five-thousander and only gradually came to enjoy the different delights of Welsh and Scottish hills. He never joined the ranks of rock experts happy to spend a whole day on specks of cliff a hundred feet high, at which one would not so much as glance in the Himalaya. A mountain for him remained a stretch of wide, high country, presenting problems of transport and supply and personnel, obstacles demanding a variety of techniques, dangers from storm and avalanche: problems, in fact, similar to those of a military situation.

In 1953 he was invited to join the Americans on K2, at 28,250 ft the second highest mountain in the world. He would again be transport officer. The story of that expedition is rousingly told by Charles Houston, the leader, and Robert Bates in *K2: The Savage Mountain*. Streather has provided me with further details. The days that concern us here are those after 2 August. At that time a party of eight, two more than had been originally intended, was camped 25,500 feet up, on the Abruzzi Spur. It was their eighth camp and hopes stood high for the summit. Then the weather, which had been worsening, turned really bad. On the morning of the 3rd they could only lie and wait, while a grey mist blanketed everything and sharp flakes tore at the lips of any who passed from tent to tent. Of the days spent here Houston wrote words which I have quoted in a different context:

Can such an ordeal be remotely conceived as 'pleasure' or 'sport'? Are we masochists to 'enjoy' such a battering, such cold, such wind, lack of food, lack of sleep, lack of water? Our stay at Camp VIII, ten days of hardship and anxiety, was terribly hard. It brought each of us down to fundamentals. The deepest springs of character were tapped for our survival. The lack of oxygen at great altitudes may dull the mind and weaken the body, but there is an inner strength of spirit, a bigger power which emerges undiminished, even magnified, to bring a man through such an experience. We faced nature's wildest forces with our pitifully feeble tents and clothing as our only weapons, plus our determination. Perhaps it is this conquest, conquest of one's self through survival of such an ordeal, that brings a man back to frontiers again and again. It may be a storm at sea, the arctic cold, or the desert heat. It may be a frontier of the spirit or of the mind. By testing himself beyond endurance man learns to know himself. He endures and grows.

In this atmosphere the stage was set for the struggle to survive, a struggle made more difficult by the dead weight of inertia upon the mind. It is so much easier, at 25,000 feet, to lie still and do nothing. Owing to lack of oxygen every effort, even for the simple jobs of doing up a boot or washing a pan, seems too great.

On 7 August, when the weather brightened a little, they prepared to go down. There was no alternative. 'Schoening, Streather and Gilkey seemed to be the strongest,' Houston wrote, 'but all of us were weaker than we had been a few days before.' Tents were torn; frostbite was creeping over their limbs. As they packed up, Art Gilkey, who had looked so strong, quite suddenly collapsed. Houston examined him and found thrombophlebitis of the left leg – blood clots which might be fatal even at a lower altitude. This was bad indeed. Desperately they wrapped him in his sleeping-bag and a torn tent, and started off down, pulling and pushing; but soon the whole slope threatened to avalanche under the weight of new snow, and with immense difficulty they climbed back to camp. They did not know what to do.

Craig and Schoening succeeded, through wind and cloud, in re-connoitring a line down the rock-ribs to the right (looking down) of the dangerous slope: steeper, snow-plastered and more difficult, but safe from avalanche. Next day, while the party waited on the weather, these two roped and climbed for 400 feet *upward* – a last gesture to the mountain. That evening Gilkey developed a pulmonary embolism as well, which made his chances of a safe descent very small indeed.

When a weak sun had filtered through, on that morning of the 8th, luck had seemed to be turning. Such tiny signs of better fortune are clutched at and magnified and made the vessels of hope. 'This looks to be a good day, maybe the beginning of the good weather,' Streather had said. But that evening, despite the move uphill, the main feeling must have been of despair. One tent had been torn away, and now two of the three remaining two-man tents had to house three each. Gilkey's cough and the wind, in full strength once more, forbade sleep. Frostbite and lack of food weakened them further. Yet the sense of solidarity among the Americans was stronger than ever; not only would they not abandon Gilkey, but they would do their damnedest to bring him safely down. Curiously, the very qualities which gave them greater fortitude and will to survive lessened their actual chances of survival, and in determining to get Gilkey down, at whatever cost, they were aware that they might effectively destroy themselves. This much Bates implicitly admits, when he writes:

> We all knew that some of us might never get down the mountain alive. Each had long recognised the near impossibility of evacuating an injured man from the upper ledges of K2. We had told one another that 'if somebody broke a leg, you could never get him down the mountain', but now that we were faced with Gilkey's helplessness, we realised that we *had* to get him down. We didn't know how, but we had to do it.

Earlier this same year, on Everest, we were discussing what would happen to a party of two, using closed-circuit oxygen, if one of the sets gave out. Would they both shuffle along, trying to work on the one set, in which case both of them would probably be doomed? We felt little doubt that something like that would be tried. There are times when the hundred-to-one chance of the whole group surviving seems preferable to the certain survival of any one member.

The wind pounded so hard that they had to shout, even in the tent. On the morning of the 10th somebody said, 'What? Move in this storm?' and Houston, the leader, who had been on K2 before and knew the risks, replied, 'We've got to. He'll soon be dead if we don't get him down.' He was equally likely to die on the way, but Houston's was not exactly a reasoned decision, because at times like this one does not make decisions of the reflective type made at sea-level. The brain is numb, can only deal with the next immediate problem: in this case, it was how to get Gilkey as far as the next camp below. Granted a party's solidarity, there could be no other problem; where a party is scattered, however, as happened to the Germans strung out at several points along the ridge of Nanga Parbat in 1937, a race for life can develop.

They packed light loads, two tents, chocolate and meat bars, and set off. The descent was even worse than they had expected. Molenaar and Schoening went ahead to reconnoitre the way. Gilkey, bundled in eiderdown, was pulled by Craig and Bell in front, while Houston, Bates and Streather controlled him from behind. They worked over to the rock-rib through a screaming wind, then down alongside, towards a snow-shute and ice gully. They would not have chosen this route for preference, but they had no choice, since they had to go where they could lower a helpless man. They realised also that they could not now go back.

The work was desperately slow. Fingers and toes had lost sensation. No one knew how, when they reached the steep pitch, somebody managed to tie two 120-ft lengths of nylon rope together so that they could lower 240 feet at a stretch. At last Craig disappeared with Gilkey, always uncomplaining. 'I'm fine, just fine,' he would murmur when anybody asked how he was getting along. Streather descended now to see what was happening to them. There was a cry: 'Hold on tight! They're being carried away by an avalanche!' The whole slope of granulated pellets had slid away, snow blotted everything. When it cleared, the two men were still there. Craig, clinging hard to the rope, was grey and chilled but safe. So was Gilkey, who would have suffered severely had they not drugged him with sleeping pills. The last two climbed slowly down.

They had reached the top of a small cliff. Craig, exhausted from the avalanche, was belayed (protected with the rope) down and across the ice until he could reach the ledge which, at 24,500 feet, had provided a temporary Camp 7 on the upward reconnaissance. Gilkey was then lowered down the cliff, Schoening remaining as sheet anchor and the others descending, roped in twos, until they were spread out on the ice slope of forty-five degrees below. (See diagram p. 105).

It was Bell who slipped, but it might have been anyone. When one is very tired a shift of wind or a pack that slips round the wrong way is enough to throw balance awry, and the wind was tearing, racing, biting. Bell went slithering then hurtling down the slope, dragging down Streather, and after him Houston and Bates, who were roped to each other below. Fortunately, Molenaar had just attached his rope to Gilkey, who was being held by Schoening above. This rope caught the four falling men, but pulled off Molenaar, and the weight of all six came on Schoening. By a most powerful piece of belaying, clinging for life to his ice-axe driven into the snow, Schoening held them all.

Bell had slid three hundred feet, the others varying distances. Ropes were badly tangled, but that scarcely mattered to men who had thought themselves dead. Already in a bad way physically, they were far worse by the time they had struggled to their feet. Bell's hands were white and stiff, and he had lost his glasses; Houston had fallen over rocks, was suffering from concussion and did not know where he was; Molenaar had cracked a rib and cut his thigh; Schoening above, his hands frozen, could not go on holding. Craig at last could come over to relieve him, and they anchored Gilkey, still recumbent on the slope, with two ice-axes. Somehow the others dragged themselves one by one to the platform, and put up the bivouac tents. As they hacked at the slope to make a platform they heard Gilkey calling twice, but the storm blurred his words. Some ten minutes after the second call Streather, Bates and Craig were ready to move back across the slope for him. Wind lashed the surface, obscuring it with snow. When for a moment it cleared, Gilkey was no longer there.

It was Streather who had started to move towards him, belayed by the others. But even the ice-axes had been torn away by the avalanche that had taken Gilkey. Streather experienced a deep sense of shock, but for the moment little more. Only one part of his mind was working, and that part had other worries pressing upon it. Soon they might all be dead, as Gilkey was now. Meanwhile, for them all, there remained the urgent problem of packing seven climbers into two tents, one designed for two men, the other for one. Also, Bell's hands and feet were frozen, and Houston still could not understand where they were. All through the night he kept wanting to cut a hole in the tent fabric to let in more air. Schoening was having trouble with his breathing. It was a ghastly night, long-drawn-out and nightmare-ridden, for them all.

During it they had leisure to reflect upon the loss of Gilkey, the brave companion who would have sacrificed himself, if he could, in the storm.[1] Nobody, perhaps, dared ask himself the question: how

1. It is possible that he did. They never knew the reason for his second call, whether it was the avalanche coming, the ice-axes slipping, or whether he could have pulled them out. In his drugged state this last was very unlikely, however.

would the night have been if Gilkey had been with them? How much further would they have been able to drag him?

In the morning 'Tony Streather, who with Craig and Schoening had been brewing tea for us all during the night, looked more himself than anyone did' (Bates). Storm gathering once more, the party packed up, squeezed Bell's frostbitten feet into boots and set off down the relentlessly steep 1,200 feet to Camp 6. Bell having lost his glasses, unable to see where to put his feet, and Houston still puzzling over where he was, they would be lucky to escape another fall. When Houston had gone only a few yards down the slope he stopped and sat down in a perplexed sort of way. Schoening, who was with him, shook out the rope after a few moments and called down, 'Come on, Charlie, let's go!' Houston got up and went on climbing down. Bates noted that throughout this descent a sense of fatalism had crept over their minds. The accident, the miraculous escape, the loss of Gilkey, the night spent in insecure tents which might well have rolled them down the mountainside – all these made them feel like puppets on a string. If the worst happened now, then that was that. They could do no more. They could only go on and hope that they would be protected, as they seemed to have been protected so far.

On an exposed col at the top of the steepest slope they had to stop and take off their crampons, or ice-claws, in order to descend rocks. Anyone who has performed this fairly simple operation in great cold knows how painful it is: gloves must be removed, straps are stiff with ice and will not go through the buckles, every minute or so numb fingers are thrust back into pockets to warm up. Add a searing wind, the whistle of snow pellets, the delay while they helped Bell – and this was the cold inferno in which Tibetans believe.

Luckily the fixed ropes could be used; but, below that, loose rock hampered men who were near to breaking point. Once Streather, 'the strongest man on our rope' (Bates), climbed twenty feet down the wrong place and had to climb back: an almost superhuman effort. But at last, none too soon, they were back at Camp 6 (23,330 ft). During their absence snow had drifted into the tents, but the first arrivals cleared this and then food and drink could be heated. They knew that

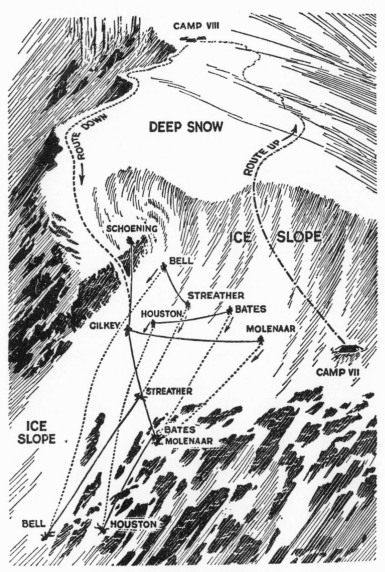

The accident on K2.

the worst part of the route was over. From now on they would be unlucky not to get down safely.

They had still ahead of them another crowded night, with Houston trying to climb out of the tent; a stormbound day during which Streather and Schoening descended to Camp 5; the job of digging a tent out of the snow; and the descent to Camp 4, ending with a difficult chimney, called House's Chimney because it was first climbed by Bill House in 1938. It is worth pausing a moment over Houston's experience in this 150-ft vertical fault, difficult enough at sea-level and a real obstacle at 22,000 feet. Everyone had worried over being caught in storm above it, and now the whole party was there, beset by storm, gathering darkness, exhaustion and injury. However, to spend another night above was unthinkable. The climbers descended slowly, one by one, held on the rope by Houston and Bates above. As leader, Houston insisted on coming down last. It was now pitch-dark; the wind roared, snow blew about.

Charles Houston has given me this account of his experience. It does not appear in his book:

Houston realised that he could not climb down. He was still suffering from his fall and could not move his head without pain; there was no practical way to secure himself from above. Worst of all, the three ropes hanging in the chimney were indistinguishable by feel in the dark, but two of them (left in 1938 and 1939) were rotten, and only their own would hold him. He dared not trust any of them but must climb down unaided. He was still not fully rational and should not have insisted on being last – another man would have had a better chance. Many thoughts went through his head constantly: the tragedy of their defeat, their failure, and, above all, their friend's death. Now the impossibility of his descent, another defeat, another death. He decided to jump, ending the hopeless struggle without the risk of falling down the chimney and perhaps sweeping away those below. But he must have had some inner strength left, for he hesitated, unable to do this to family and friends. Time passed, unintelligible shouts came faintly from below. He knelt in the snow and whispered the Lord's Prayer. Peace and certainty came to him.

Looking back over the years, Houston recalls those minutes with photographic detail, but he has no recollection whatever of the next half hour. How he climbed down is a blank – his next memory is of being helped across the steep snow at the bottom of the chimney and down to the snug security of Camp 4, where hot tea, food and friends were waiting. To him, as to them, this safe descent was yet another miracle in their tragic epic. To this day it is difficult for any of them to talk of the whole descent. The blood on the rocks, the impossible miracles, the cold and privation are locked in each man's memories.[1]

When they reached Camp 2, two days later, they were exhausted far beyond the point at which they would have thought a man must drop. But already at Camp 6 they had known in their hearts that they had come through.

'Ce qui fait tenir, c'est la pensée des camarades.'

So said a Belgian Resistance campaigner, the victim of a concentration camp, when asked what had made him hold out under torture. What pulled the Americans and Streather through was the thought that if one gave up, the whole party must be lost, and the corresponding sensation of strength from the support of friends. Each man drew his strength from a reservoir in which it seemed that the others also were drawing theirs. To some it seemed to come also from a source outside and above that reservoir.

To sum up, the Americans of the party had experienced that sense

1. It was in connection with the story of this prayer that Marceline made the observation on prayer quoted on page 143.

R. A. Hodgkin, in an article in *The Guardian*, Nov. 1961, wrote: 'The very act of letting go of fear and launching out on a dangerous but skilful act is akin to both art and prayer. "Not in my strength alone!" "Into Thy hands, O Lord!". . . . The Christian who utters a prayer in the face of danger is seeking no miraculous help; he is willing (asking) that whatever power is available in his small being may be free to flow, unimpeded, into his action.'

Cf. also the French philosopher, Alain, on prayer: *'Vous vous confiez; vous flottez un moment dans un grand univers, vous vous laissez porter.'*

We shall return to this theme in the last chapter.

of a larger whole which a well-balanced expedition can give. This sense we experienced, as I have indicated, very strongly on Everest in the same year. It was not two individuals, but the expedition which reached the summit, and that thought made nonsense of the political controversy as to whether Hillary or Tenzing was the first to place his foot there. Houston must have had some such conception in mind when he refused to send down over the radio, from Camp 8, the names of the intended summit pair. This sense of community, however strongly it may brace morale towards an end, goes deeper even than the instinct for survival, for self-preservation. As we have seen, had these men been concerned first with their own survival, they would logically have abandoned Gilkey at Camp 8. Given the unity of the expedition, that course was impossible, even if the alternative meant the death of all.

Streather kept an equanimity at which his friends wondered. He kept it not only because he felt himself to be a member of the party, but possibly also because, having accepted the conditions which his calling imposes, he was mentally prepared for the crises, through soldiering plus mountaineering, as the others were prepared through mountaineering alone.

Experience, if it does not deter, strengthens. In 1955 Tony Streather joined Charles Evans' party to Kangchenjunga (28,146 ft), that 'reconnaissance' expedition which brilliantly climbed the third highest mountain of the world. This time things went well, for the weather in the later stages favoured. Streather and Norman Hardie, using oxygen, reached the summit, or rather twenty feet below it, the day after George Band and Joe Brown. Only one crowded night, at the top camp, may have recalled the ordeal of Camp 7.

The survival situation chooses some of us as haphazardly as it passes others by. In 1957 nothing could have been further from Streather's thoughts than to repeat, in even grimmer form, a part of the experience of K2.[1] He was now married, with one child, and instructing at Sand-

1. In this section I am indebted to the book *The Last Blue Mountain* by Ralph Barker, but also to personal accounts and amplifications from Tony Streather and John Emery.

hurst. Although he had good reasons for not returning to the Kara-koram, when the invitation to lead an Oxford party to Haramosh came he found even stronger ones for going. He was lured by the country, since different landscapes lay hold on the imagination of different types of people, and he was following the logical sequence well known to mountaineers. Once one has accepted the initial illogic-ality of the urge to climb up a mountain and then come down, the rest follows unsolicited. One accepts the chance to go out to Alps or Andes or Himalaya, because it is 'fun' and one has always thought of it as fun, even knowing quite well that the fun will involve discomfort, hard food, harder exercise and a possibility of real torment. No one appreciated the possibility better than Tony Streather; both as moun-taineer and soldier he was prepared to accept these possibilities and to set about minimising them by safe planning.

Haramosh (24,270 ft) stands splendidly on its own in the Gilgit Agency of north-west Pakistan. As one flies from Rawalpindi north-ward up the Indus valley to Gilgit, one is struck first by the ugly great mass of Nanga Parbat (26,620 ft) towering up on the right. Smaller and more delicately chiselled, Haramosh rears icy walls towards the elegant rock cone of its summit. Further north still, the great jumble of peaks culminating in Rakaposhi (25,550 ft) dominates Gilgit, the starting point.

The party which formed itself from a nucleus of members of the Oxford University Mountaineering Club had in mind no more than a reconnaissance. There would not be time for more, unless the route proved straightforward. Bernard Jillott, secretary and prime mover of the expedition, was a man of great drive, impulsive, single-minded, living for mountains and hoping for a future as climber-writer; a man who did not, perhaps, see far on either side of his path into the people around it, but who got things done. John Emery was then a medical student at St Mary's, a man with a first-class brain, easy in manner and easy to get on with, a fine rock-climber like Jillott. Neither he nor Rae Culbert had difficulty with relationships. Culbert, a New Zealander, had been studying botany at Oxford after work in the field; he was a person direct in manner and speech as New Zealanders are, who somehow made touch with all the others at different levels.

It was impossible not to be his friend. Scott Hamilton, the American, was not to be directly involved in the crisis until much later.

The scene is the fourth camp along the north-east ridge of Haramosh, 20,000 feet up. With the help of Hunza porters in the lower part, and after a number of setbacks due to bad weather, the party had at last forced a way up this north-eastern flank of the mountain, but they realised that they were still, really, on Haramosh II, a subsidiary summit of 21,930 feet. The main summit could not be reached from Haramosh II without a descent for which they would not have time.

The chief obstacle had been the snow: for days on end it had snowed, burying tents until they were invisible. The Karakoram, unlike the main Himalaya to the south-east, do not receive a regular monsoon in May or early June. Throughout the summer, periods of fine weather alternate with periods of bad, snowfall being particularly heavy on peaks like Haramosh and Nanga Parbat, which jut southward from the main chain.

Temperamentally, therefore, a Karakoram mountaineer needs to be good at lying about. Isolated at Camp 4 by drifting snow, two climbers, Culbert and Emery, lay for four days doing nothing, talking and sleeping, melting snow and cooking, eating and sleeping again. One can get to know and like a man very thoroughly on these occasions, though conversation rarely strikes a deep note.

These two had been left here on 7 September, when the three others made their last trip up with loads. Snow had fallen heavily and communication between camps had been impossible. On the afternoon of the 11th, however, it cleared a little and they ploughed a thigh-deep furrow down towards Camp 3, in case the others should be coming up. Some way down lay a line of crevasse which they had crossed by a snow-bridge; wind-driven fresh snow had corniced the bridge and Emery, cautiously probing and keeping well on the safe side of the old tracks, as he thought, suddenly went through into black nothing.

The rope jerked him with suffocating force. He could not hang long like this. Kicking, he was able at last to find footing on a small snow-ledge and eventually to shout up to Culbert above for more rope.

John Emery in camp on Haramosh

Jillott and Emery set off towards the Cardinal's Hat. Avalanche slope to the right

Richard E. Byrd (*G. P. Putnam's Sons*)

This had to be fetched from Camp 4, and meant a cold wait. By working along inside the crevasse, protected from above, Emery was at last able to climb through and out at the far end. The whole operation had taken two and a half hours, and dusk was falling.

'Nice to see you, you old bugger,' Culbert grinned down.

'Thanks, you old bastard,' Emery answered.

They lay in the snow and laughed. But the incident was a prelude.

The true crest of Haramosh II's north-east ridge, which would give them the view of the mountain that they wanted before they must return home, was about 1,000 feet above Camp 4. On the 13th the two forced a route some way up towards this and on the 14th went farther, through deep snow and over crevassed ground. The weather was improving and at last, after seven days of isolation, they were joined by Streather and Jillott. Only Scott Hamilton remained below, at Camp 3.

The 15th was to be the last day of upward progress. Mist cleared to a fine morning and the party, after routine chores, set off at eleven a.m. The first part of the route was now well stamped, frozen and solid. At the highest point reached by Culbert and Emery they paused for lunch. Then they went on, crossing a crevasse, labouring up deep snow towards the corniced crest which must, surely, be the north-east ridge on the other side of which would be the view they had come to see. The cornice leaned over towards them, quite small at the point they had chosen. Streather flogged a hole through it with his axe and shouted down, 'Come on up! You can't imagine what you'll see!'

It was one of those moments that make the labour of months worth enduring. A superb view greeted them. Their own ridge led over a tangle of minor summits to Haramósh II. Thence it sagged as it swung round to the final 3,000 feet uprush of Haramosh I. From the glacier between the two peaks there cascaded the huge north face of the mountain, dropping 13,000 feet to the Mani Glacier and the tiny village among green pastures below it.

They chose a safe place to sit, and Jillott said, 'I can't see much chance along there.'

They felt a relief that there was no route after all, but perhaps they would get a better view from a little way farther along, from the top of a conspicuous hump nicknamed the Cardinal's Hat. Jillott, eager to push ahead till the last moment, thought so, and he wanted to photograph. Emery agreed to go too, so that the others could take a picture of the party as near to the top as it would arrive. They roped up. In their talk Streather had already commented on the great mass of ice bent to the left, hanging over space. He did not like it. 'Keep well back from the cornice,' he shouted as they moved away.

The cornice was enormous. Jillott and Emery therefore kept well down on the right, on the slope that was the beginning of the downrush into the north face. As they rose they were getting, Emery later remembered, an even better view of the mountain's upper reaches, and decided that the route would 'go' after all.[1] Forty feet short of the top he stopped and belayed the rope round his ice-axe thrust into the snow. As Jillott moved up to the crest he heard a muffled explosion, a crunching and grinding sound. The whole slope began to move – in the opposite direction from that which they had been fearing.

For a moment, to Streather and Culbert, it looked like a joke; then, like two puppets comically jerking arms and legs, the others disappeared. Through the snow-dust the two on the ridge could see the avalanche billowing out far below, smashing itself in a cloud-like powder.

In any sudden transition from carefree happiness to disaster the mind for a time is stunned. Streather and Culbert stayed immobile a long while before they pulled their thoughts together. Then they traversed out towards the hard ground which the avalanche had swept clear. The feel of the day, beautiful and bright with all the peaks sparkling around, had changed. The mountains, which a minute ago had smiled in a friendly way, were ominous and heavy with menace. But Streather was accustomed to concentrate on 'next problems', and that meant trying to see down over the concave slope, to the right of the crest, which hid the upper part of the north face. It was this slope which had avalanched. At last Streather, belayed by Culbert, was able to look

1. The mountain was climbed next year by an Austrian party, using substantially this route. Conditions seem to have been very different, with much less snow.

over into a snow-basin tucked into the great mountainside nearly a thousand feet below. Waves of powder snow were still settling, but he detected, far down on the white plain, one figure in a green windproof: Jillott. Then, after some time, another climbed out and both stood, shaking themselves. The two were saved.

It had been a miraculous salvation. A whole plate-like slab the size of a large room had slid off, bearing Emery and Jillott helpless upon it. Their minds, like their bodies cocooned in snow, lost touch with time and reality. They knew that they were slipping, faster and faster. They knew that at some point they were sailing through air, over cliffs it must be. They went on falling, then rolling down an easier slope, until at last they came to rest. Slowly they came round to their full senses, as if from an anæsthetic.

Emery's left hip hurt badly, his leg dragged as he struggled to kneel. The ball must have dislocated itself from the socket. As they looked up, they realised what they had come down, and also how fragile were their chances of climbing out. Three-hundred-foot ice-cliffs barred the whole slope above, only dwindling towards the right. Below these ran a line of bergschrund, or big crevasse. This might be crossed if they had ice-axes, but in the fall both had lost them. To do the climb without axes was almost unthinkable; but the only other way, down the north face, did not appeal.

Turning to look once more, Emery made a movement which must have jerked his hip, for suddenly ball and socket were back in place and he could stand.

Since there was obviously no point in going straight up to the cliffs over which they had fallen, they decided to bear right, towards the place where the cliffs petered out. Moving slowly, and feeling impotent without their axes, they climbed up and then along the schrund, until it became a fairly innocuous crevasse which could be crossed.

Once across it, however, they found themselves cut off and unable to work back along its upper lip. The alternative was to climb straight up, and this they tried to do. The slope steepened to bare ice, in which they tried, ineffectively, to kick steps. Soon they had slipped and were rolling back helplessly towards the crevasse. Jillott shot over it and continued down the slope below. Emery came to rest across the lower lip. There seemed no point in trying again.

They decided to return to the avalanche tracks, where they would be more easily spotted by the others when they descended, and to stamp out a platform for the night. It was now almost dark, the cold gripped them, but the weather remained fine. Emery unzipped his windproof trousers and held his hands in his crutch. Jillott did the same. Emery was also suffering from mild dysentery, and stamped around every few minutes. Both of them had spent the night out on a mountain before, but had never dreamed of doing it as high as this. They knew the dangers, and what had happened to the French on Annapurna.[1]

About halfway through the night they saw a light on the slopes above. They shouted upwards, then decided to climb towards it, at least to the bergschrund, but in the dark Emery fell over a twenty-foot ice-cliff which he had been unable to see, and they realised that it was no use. After stamping out another platform, they waited for the dawn, even sleeping fitfully; but Jillott felt the cold keenly and was unable to control his shivering. They shouted when they saw the light again. Dawn came slowly, and it was bitterly cold.

The light had certainly belonged to Streather and Culbert. After the intense relief of seeing the two below still alive had come the immense worry of how to get them out. Culbert remained cheerful, sure that they could do it, radiant with strength. Streather found himself nervous about the lateness of the hour, the dangers of a slope which had already avalanched. Obviously they must return to camp, rest a little and collect food and more warm clothing. But first they would try to send down a rucksack full of eiderdown clothing, spare scarves and gloves, sweets and chocolate. They packed the sack and Streather moved out towards the point where the avalanche had started. The sack slid off all right, but when it reappeared below the cliffs it was going

1. Annapurna (26,492 ft.) was climbed in 1950. Partly as a result of an enforced night out, Herzog and Lachenal, the summit pair, lost their toes and Herzog parts of his fingers. Rébuffat and Terray, the supporting party, recovered.

well wide of the others and finally disappeared down the north face. This was not their lucky day.

They hurried back to Camp 4, therefore, in failing light: four hours coming up, just over an hour going down. They cooked, ate well, found a spare shirt and a spare jersey, filled two thermos-flasks with soup and started up. At ten o'clock they had reached the ridge again; the moment had come for deciding what to do. Looking down, they could see very little, since the slope curved bulging out of sight, the sort of slope one would avoid. Streather decided to go down the full length of the three hundred feet of rope they had with them, secured by Culbert from the top. The moon was up, but it hid behind cloud and both men used torches. At first the snow was soft, then hardened, where the avalanche had peeled off, and also steepened. Streather faced inwards, kicking steps as he went, flashing his torch and shouting every so often down into the basin. At last he heard answering shouts from below.

The slope was now very steep, perhaps sixty degrees, and that feels very steep indeed when you are on it in the dark. He must have been at the end of the rope, but no sound came from above. There was nothing for it but to climb up again and rejoin Culbert, whose voice, he found, had been cut off by the bulge of the slope. Streather shortened the rope to one hundred feet and they started down, securing each other at each rope's length. The dawn began to lighten.

They could see Jillott and Emery now, waving and shouting to them. At first Streather could not think why; then he saw that he was nearing a drop below, the top of the ice-cliffs, in fact, over which the others had fallen. They were waving to him to move over to the right, towards the point where they had crossed the crevasse. He looked horizontally across the line he would have to traverse in order to do that, leaving the avalanche track. It still looked very steep.

It proved to be not only steep but icy. Two or three hours, they had thought, but it soon looked as if it would take all day. The ice was extremely hard, splintering under the axe instead of caving in to make good steps. The effort of bringing the inside leg through to the next step called for a prodigious twist of the body. At over 20,000 feet an immense thirst develops, due to dehydration caused by altitude, and physiological research has shown that the body needs six pints of liquid a day to combat it. They had been climbing all night without food or drink. Meanwhile, Jillott and Emery reached the point at which they would cross the crevasse and sat there in a stupor, waiting. The sun blazed down.

The traverse eased to an angle of some fifty-five degrees and lost a little height. But at the end of it, in the late afternoon, they would have to climb down at another very steep angle into the basin. Just before they left the traverse Culbert was leading. In one of the steps Streather noticed something dark: it was a crampon which must have come off. As Culbert turned to recover it, the rope flicked it out of the step and it slid off down the slope, into the bergschrund.

Mountaineers nowadays wear boots with moulded rubber soles. These are perfectly secure on ice, and more comfortable than nailed boots, provided one has strapped on to them the sets of metal spikes without which it would be folly so much as to look at a snow and ice mountain, for without crampons rubber-soled boots skid and slither on ice helplessly. Streather and Culbert, facing each other, caught each other's eye. Both realised that the loss of this crampon was very serious indeed.

Streather led over the remainder of the traverse, while Culbert took off the canvas overboot whose grip was even worse than that of a boot. They descended the steep slope at the end of the traverse as they had descended the slope above: facing inwards and kicking hard into the snow. This is a tiring and exasperating movement, particularly when the snow lies over ice and is rotten. But kicking was preferable to cutting. As the light began to fail they were down at the crevasse and sending a rope over to Jillott and Emery, who tied on and crossed. The party was again united.

One of the thermos-flasks of soup had broken, but the other was handed over: the first food or drink Jillott and Emery had taken for well over twenty-four hours. The weather remained fine and hopes rose. They roped up to climb out of the basin, never doubting that this was a better course than to sit it out a second night. In twilight they started off confidently, rediscovering in the fact of being roped together the sense of forming a party. Culbert led, then came Streather, Jillott and Emery.

They had climbed two hundred of the three hundred feet to the beginning of the traverse, and could just make out the platform that marked its start. Culbert had been having difficulty with his left foot in the holds. Suddenly it slipped out, he fell backwards, and in the fall knocked off Streather. The other two stood no chance and all four, entangled, rolled backward over the bergschrund, to the slope beyond. Nobody was hurt, but Streather had lost his ice-axe.

They tried again, this time with Streather leading and using Culbert's axe. At the end of each rope-length he belayed by securing the rope round the axe, and protected the others one by one as they climbed. This system promised to work well, provided nobody fell off while Streather was stepping up. Again they reached a point shortly below the platform. Then Jillott, going to sleep in his steps, fell and dragged the whole party down two hundred feet, back to where they had started. In the fall they lost the last ice-axe.

Though physically unhurt, they were now badly shocked, exhausted and dispirited. They realised that they had underestimated the problem of climbing out. They found a ledge in the crevasse and huddled there while loose snow blew over them. Streather suggested that Culbert should take the sock off his left foot, which felt frozen now that the overboot was off, and put it under Streather's shirt. This might save it. In the night they slept a little, but Jillott's mind wandered, he kept moving about, and Streather asked Emery to give him a morphia injection. Emery had lost his gloves in one fall, and a spare pair of somebody's socks in another. This was, therefore, his second night out without gloves in the snow at 20,000 feet. His fingers could not cut the top off the phial and he had to give it back to Streather. Streather filled the syringe, then Emery pushed back the shirt and gave the injection in the buttock. The vigorous protests stopped, and Jillott fell into a deep sleep.

When it grew light, Streather climbed stiffly out and went down to disentangle the rope. He could not see the ice-axes. Jillott, now feeling much better, thought that he saw an axe sticking out of the snow four hundred yards to the left, and went over with Culbert, who had had a hard time getting the boot on to his swollen left foot, to try a route that way. With or without axes, Streather believed that they must climb out today, if they were to remain alive. Streather and Emery crossed the schrund and started up the slope of last night, kicking and punching to remake the steps which their falls had obliterated. The other two also crossed the schrund farther left and found what they had been after; but it was only a broken, useless shaft and they went back to catch up the others. This they quickly did, for the step-kicking and punching was proving very slow, painful work. The party was un-roped now, for Streather reckoned that to rope would mean that all would be dragged down if one fell.

At first it had seemed a straightforward matter of climbing out. Only gradually it had become clear that they might not be able to climb out at all. As on K2, actions were becoming less a result of con-scious decision than a series of numbed responses to situations as each arose: the next job, and the next, and the next. Used to the unexpected and the snap decision, and acclimatised by the experience of K2, Streather was prepared for this ordeal as most men are not. Even when exhausted, he continued to react instinctively.

A hundred feet below the platform Emery spotted Culbert's axe, the axe that Streather had been holding at the time of the second fall. Using this to cut steps, Streather reached the platform and brought up Emery on the rope. Then Emery held the others while Streather started to clear the steps of the traverse, now covered over with drift snow. Time passed; it must have been well after noon, but they lost the sense of time. They seemed to be playing the game out in a white eternity, removed even from sensations. Yet thirst pressed on them continually, and occasionally they sucked snow, which does not quench thirst.

The steps were so well covered that Streather very soon lost the track and found himself too high. Very carefully he cut and kicked downward, until he regained the original line. Then he went on, without looking round. Coming down behind him through the now rotting snow Emery suddenly felt himself slip. He turned frantically, dug his crampons in and stopped himself before he had slid too far. Then he followed on.

The last stretch of the traverse descended slightly, for here they had gone up a little, on the first descent, to round the top of the ice-cliffs. A descending traverse on steep ice with only one crampon is all but impossible. Culbert had mastered his disadvantage so far with a quiet courage. He had asked for nothing. But here, before the last hundred feet or so to safety, he stopped. He edged his left foot forward and knew for certain that it would slide out of the step. He called out, 'Do you think you could give me a belay over this bit?'

Streather shouted back that he would finish the traverse and belay in the better snow beyond. He and Emery tied the two ropes together, then Streather climbed on up the good snow of the original avalanche track, wedged his axe in firmly and hitched the rope around it. He told Emery to go on up the more straightforward slope, and that they would be following. Culbert launched out on the last descending line of steps and almost immediately came off. As he pendulum-swung below, his whole weight came with sudden force on the rope. It jerked Streather from his step, even from the axe, and in an instant they were both falling back over the ice-cliffs which the others had passed two days earlier, over the bergschrund and down the slopes beyond.

The shock of this second passage was even greater than that of the first, because this time no cushioning mass of snow fell with them. They fell as it seemed into nothing, until the slope below welcomed them roughly and rolled them over and over beyond the bergschrund. Apart from the brutal roughness of it they knew little. They lay stunned a long time. From far above, through a blanket of unreality, Streather heard a voice shouting, 'We'll go back to camp and get some food. . . . We'll come and help you as soon as we can.'

It was now dark. At last they rose with immense and painful effort and dragged themselves up the slope. They found some level snow in the crevasse and there, huddled together, dropped at once into unconsciousness rather than sleep. 'Sleep didn't add up,' Streather said later. It was the evening of the 17th, two and a half days after the original accident.

The voice from above had been Jillott's. There was nothing else he could do. He crossed the last part of the traverse himself and climbed on, shouting up to Emery, who stopped, astonished to be joined by Jillott and not by the other two. The bitterness of the situation came home to them. Now the rescuers were below, the rescued free to climb out. And there was nothing that they could do except climb on and vow to return for the two below.

They struck the ridge, finally, in the dark, at the point of the avalanche. Emery led off towards the break in the cornice through which they had first climbed, but he could see nothing and almost immediately fell heavily through the cornice himself. This new fall of some thirty feet shook him badly and dislocated his hip again. Again he managed to turn so that the joint slipped back into position. He called up, 'Keep going along the ridge. I'll meet you at the cut in the cornice.'

Here, where Streather had flogged a way through on the 15th, they met and started searching for the rucksacks left behind. In one of them was a water-bottle, and each in turn had to tear at it before he could convince himself that the contents were frozen solid. In their haste and confusion they searched only one rucksack thoroughly and failed to find the glucose tablets.

They started down. Soon they were jumping the big crevasse fifty feet below the cornice. It was so dark that Jillott, jumping second, landed on top of Emery and knocked him over. Troubled again by dysentery, Emery was forced to relieve himself; then they went on. After a few steps Emery said that they should wait for the moon to come up, since they could see nothing, but Jillott had no thought but to push on down, and on occasions like this the man who makes the move has the whip hand. He went on, unroped, and Emery knew that he must keep with him. Jillott seemed to be finding the way very skilfully, but instead of detouring round the crevasse area, as they had done before, he started to go straight through it. Emery, following, shouted, but there was no answer. He remembered the crevasse at the bottom, where the angle of the slope changed, and hoped that he would catch Jillott up before they had to negotiate it. Going on, he came suddenly to bare ice, where Jillott must have kicked off the surface snow, and once again he was slipping, falling, down towards the crevasse.

His next memory is of a dream that he had fallen into a crevasse and could not get out. In his dream he seemed to be asleep in his tent at Base Camp, dreaming that he was in a crevasse, and that, if he made an effort, he would wake up. But however hard he tried he could not stop

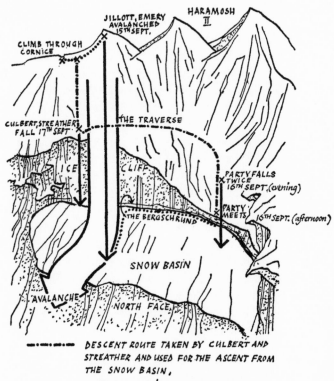

DESCENT ROUTE TAKEN BY CULBERT AND
STREATHER AND USED FOR THE ASCENT FROM
THE SNOW BASIN,

EMERY & JILLOTT'S CLIMB OUT OF SNOW BASIN

The Accident on Haramosh II

this dream.

At last he did wake up. It was daylight, but the light had a cool, filtered quality from the ice-walls around. He was jammed in the crevasse where its walls narrowed like an hour-glass, pinioned at the pelvis. One leg hung below, but he felt no emotion at the situation, as if he was detached from it, his mind 'agreeably insulated'. After some time he kicked out with the free leg but made contact with nothing. He drew the leg up, jammed it and levered himself until he could free the other leg. Then, with crampons against the wall opposite, he started to 'chimney' sideways in the crevasse.

Of his state of mind while he did this he has written:

These movements, though slow and deliberate, were logical; the curious thing was that I seemed to be rather separate from them.

121

I considered and performed them almost automatically, for only part of me seemed to be concerned with them; a large part of my consciousness was hardly interested in them at all. It was rather as if I had two minds or as if I was two people. One mind, or person, was occupied with the drudgery of movement; the other was completely detached, simply an observer. At times the observer was the only one in possession, and I would do nothing at all: at other moments the odd conflict would begin again, the impulse to action would assert itself, and I would move on a bit farther between the walls, while that other half of me just watched and watched.

At last he came to a place where the crevasse opened out into a depression. He climbed the short distance to the surface on frozen snow-patches, and fell asleep. When he awoke, the sun was shining from a blue sky. Jillott's footsteps were near him. 'My dichotomy of the mind had gone; I could think clearly, seeing the next steps ahead. I moved on again.'

Going on through the crevasse area, he came to a point where, on a steep slope, Jillott had slipped to the bottom, then got up and gone off to the right, in the direction of the old tracks. Emery cut straight across the slope to reach the tracks above the point where Jillott would have joined them. When he reached them, he turned left. When Jillott's tracks came in from the crevasse area he expected to see them turn left also, towards the tents, but they went straight on, to the ridge five or six feet beyond. On the other side the ground fell sheer into the great crevasse, which at this point bit into the ridge, then, six hundred feet on, down towards the Stak Valley in the distance. Jillott must have walked straight over.

He could not believe it and called down hopelessly. Then dazed, conscious only of the next thing he must do, he went on down to the tents. He needed drink more than anything: for three days, apart from a few mouthfuls of soup, he had taken nothing but snow melted in the mouth, and of this one cannot take much. He tried to open a tin of grapefruit juice, but his hands were numb, lifeless, and as he pressed he noticed, as if they belonged to somebody else, strips of skin peeling from the fingers, leaving a red jelly underneath. His hands did not hurt; they were not *his* hands. He took about half the tin and felt better.

He decided to get the primus going, but fell asleep and slept, fully clothed, until late afternoon. When he came round he started work on the primus, but his hands would not obey him, the matches were damp and it took over an hour to light it. He made a drink, then started water for soup. The tent was growing dark when he heard a voice outside. It was Streather, alone.

Streather and Culbert recovered consciousness when it grew light on the 18th. They moved very slowly across to the beginning of the climb-out, but the morning was cold and windy, and they sheltered again until the sun came up. Streather's eyes were playing tricks; he had lost his snow-goggles and was partially blind. He saw two dots above, to the right, which he thought must be Jillott and Emery. While he shouted, a small avalanche obliterated them, but they were still there after the avalanche, for they were only holes in the snow or jutting rocks.

They started to climb out again. Uncovering the old steps, Streather saw them red from the blood of his knuckles, where he punched them. On his left hand he still had a woollen glove and overmitt. With his teeth he pulled the sleeve of his jersey down over his right hand. Soon Culbert's left foot slipped, he came off again and slid back to the bottom.

'Are you all right, Rae?'

'Yes, I'm all right. I'll try again.'

This time Streather had almost reached the platform and Culbert was coming up well, when again there was a slither behind and again Culbert was sitting at the bottom. This time he was all in.

Streather balanced in the steps, his half-blind eyes searching for the others. Short of taking off his own crampons – and this Culbert would not allow, even if they fitted – there was nothing he could do. He was aware dimly that it was after midday; they had made no progress at all, had not even started the traverse. Somebody must go on up. He shouted down, 'Hang on where you are for a bit. I'll go on making the steps. The others are sure to be down soon, then we'll be able to help you.'

He went on. He knew little now, having passed beyond conscious thought, but that he must go on. As he worked, he kept looking vainly for the others.

He began to traverse. Loose snow had been blown over and obscured the steps, and he used his frozen overmitt as a tool with which to clear them. He dreaded the last, downward-slanting hundred feet, where Culbert had come off, because there, with his overmitt, he could reach only the beginning of each step; but miraculously he got across, and in the better snow beyond he found the ice-axe with which he had tried to belay Culbert the day before. He was, however, beyond feeling pleasure or relief.

He moved up painfully, slowly, using elbows to help clear the steps. As he climbed he gradually began to sense something, somebody above, helping to pull him out, as if from a black pit. This was a personality rather than a person, in the sense in which Tiira felt another to be with him. With this somebody or something he must co-operate by doing his own part. If he climbed, he would be helped.

Streather, like Tiira, describes himself as not having been a religious man in the conventional sense. Indeed, the hypocrisy of some who clasp their Bibles and then refuse to help down-and-outs used to revolt him. Yet the feeling that he had then of having for a time been 'over the other side' remains with him, a boulder of impression, in William James' phrase, wedged for ever in the spirit, unforgotten if unexplained, making for tolerance in everyday life, for kindness, for love.

Towards evening he reached the ridge and moved left towards the break in the cornice. He found the glucose packets but could not open them with his hands, and they spilled in the snow. He scooped them up and crunched them with snow, which tortured his cracked lips, and went on down. Where the new track bent leftward he followed it; like Emery he slipped and fell, above the crevasse, but managed to push himself clear and landed heavily on the other side. Then he followed Emery's track beyond. It was almost dark, on the evening of the 18th, when he reached Camp 4.

Once these two were together again, in the comparative comfort of a tent, surrounded by food and drink, there was a reasonable chance that, whatever the discomforts, even amputations,[1] they might have to

1. In Emery's case extensive, for he had stood about without gloves for a very

124

suffer, they would survive. But they still clung to the myth that they were going back for Culbert. Streather even returned unsteadily up the slope to shout down at the point where Jillott might have been, for the mind will not accept facts if it does not want to, and they could not allow, having been so close to them for so long, that the other two had died. At any moment, it seemed, Culbert's grin might appear in the doorway.

They set about organising themselves. First, they moved into the second tent, which was higher and easier to enter, and examined their feet: Emery's were a bluish colour, Streather's showed a blue line above the toes. They put on dry socks. Streather climbed out for the primus and they started to brew. They had a craving for liquid, but their faces and lips were so sore that they could not eat. They put Ovaltine, soup, Complan, everything they could find, in the brews, drank and dozed off, drank again, then lay in great pain from their frostbitten extremities, from their swollen and bleeding lips and the torture at the back of their eyes. (Snow-blindness gives a sensation as of sandpaper rubbing on the eyeballs.) At last Streather put out the primus, they took sleeping pills and slept deeply.

Their avowed intention was still to go back for Culbert next morning. Emery had been able to walk down, but, getting up in the morning, he at first could not stand, much less climb slopes of sixty degrees. To go down now was not so much a decision as an acceptance, like the gradual, instinctive acceptance of changing situations in the basin. But the going was no less painful for that: an agony of unaccepted loss. Sometimes, when men or women act collectively, they degrade themselves as the Nazis did. At higher levels the community instinct is one of fellowship, positing that type of love of which it was said, 'Greater love hath no man than this, that a man lay down his life for his friends.' This type of love had developed very strongly among the four of them, and particularly between each and Culbert, a man with a flair for finding common ground with others. But even had he been

---

long time. Hands were built with skin grafted from the chest, feet were amputated before the toes. It is a measure of his resilience and courage that he took his medical degree, practises as a research physiologist and climbs again. For cases parallel in some ways with his compare Masherbrum, 1938, and Makalu, 1961.

the greatest rogue on earth it would have been inconceivable to abandon a member of the party while strength remained to help him, for, as we have seen, the sense of community can run counter even to the instinct for self-survival. Both his own way of life and his experience with Gilkey had accustomed Streather to think in these terms. He had without hesitation passed Culbert the rope which caused the second major fall. When he left him in the basin, it was still in the expectation that the others would soon be back. After a certain point he had known, in himself if not in conscious thought, that he must go on up. Now there was no course but to go down.

The survival of these two from now on would depend on Streather. He packed the rucksacks, packed a tent in case it should be needed that night and left a sleeping bag and food, with a note, ready for Culbert. This was irrational, but even now they could not accept that he would not come down. Emery meanwhile practised walking and at last, with hands on ski-sticks, succeeded in hobbling along, gradually accustoming himself to the lack of sensation in the front part of his frostbitten feet.

The route down to Camp 3 included a steep slope, now almost ice. Streather found here that dragging the tent along was a dangerous as well as an irksome business. He let it slide, hoping that it would strike the glacier below in the right direction, but it veered over to the left and disappeared down a crevasse. This meant that they must at all costs reach Camp 3 that day. Down the slope he lowered Emery, who was fumbling with his feet, then cut steps to rejoin him, rope-length by rope-length. It was slow, deliberate work, but at last they were down, and in great tiredness dragged themselves towards the distant tent of Camp 3. There they found Scott Hamilton.

The sight of Hamilton broke the closed circle that had bound the four together and made Streather realise his loss in terms of the outside world. For the first and only time he broke down. To Hamilton, accustomed to immediate human contacts, as many Americans are, the British façade which hides a companionship no less real for not being obvious had seemed impenetrable. Now, perhaps, he understood that the very qualities which had seemed to make Streather unapproachable had pulled him through. By the time Emery, a little way behind, had arrived, Streather's fit had passed.

The struggle was not over. Apart from the pain in their extremities, the black scabs over their lips made even drinking painful. In sleep they were disturbed by nightmares. Streather still could not relax control. In the morning it was he who had to organise the descent, deciding to take one tent in case they were benighted. Emery could still only take a few steps at a time. Once, when as last man he was about to cross the ladder left over a crevasse, Streather called up, 'Come on, John, this is our last big hurdle.' And he came on.

Descending the icefall that was still the chief obstacle between Camps 3 and 2, they slid a hundred feet down a steep slope and lost both ice-axes. In mist they pitched the tent on the spot. Hamilton lay between them, to give them more room on the outside, but Emery and Streather, feeling a need to be together, changed places and lay side by side, dreaming bad dreams.

Next day the mist was still low, but Hamilton went ahead in a clearing and found Camp 2, where they rested for the remainder of the day. But they were still not down, and the last two days were to show how near the end they were. Hamilton, who seemed to have been stunned during the first day, had recovered sufficiently to take over the lead. They dug out aluminium stakes to replace the lost ice-axes and descended very cautiously, systematically, slopes that had been easy before, belaying continually. The snow surface here was treacherous, but Streather and Emery could not use their hands to climb the rocks alongside. Darkness came; they cleared a rock platform and lay out in their sleeping bags.

Next morning it was snowing, and they waited for it to clear before they continued. Just before they set off, Emery's rucksack slipped from the platform and disappeared. They started down, hoping they would not need it and wondering now whether the Hunzas had packed and gone, giving them up for lost. There seemed to be no sign of life in the valley. They went on, with desperate slowness, and not till after mid-day thought they saw figures on the scree a thousand feet below. It was the Hunza porters, climbing strongly to their rescue. They stopped and sat down. The struggle was over, even if a part of the pain would be always with them.

6

The Volunteer Survivor: Augustine Courtauld and Richard Byrd

SOME MEN, VERY FEW, VOLUNTEER FOR SURVIVAL SITUATIONS; not just for the tough, short struggle with danger but for months at a stretch. The two 'volunteer survivors' that I have in mind were different in age and temperament. Augustine Courtauld was a young man of twenty-six, a member of a comparatively small party to Greenland. Admiral Richard Byrd was forty-six years old, had flown over the North and South Poles and was leader of a large-scale American expedition to Antarctica. There were similarities too. Neither, when he left home, could have foreseen that he was going to man the fort – in this case a meteorological station – alone. Each, without knowing what he was in for, welcomed the test when it came, but then found that the experience was almost too strong for him.

Byrd wrote a revealing book, analysing his reactions. For that reason I shall use *Alone* mainly as a corroboration of or contrast with the less known story of Courtauld. Though widely acknowledged at the time and receiving extra unwelcome publicity from the fluster of the proposed rescue expedition, Courtauld's feat was never written of by itself. In his autobiography he passes with tantalising speed over

those months, to us the most absorbing of his life. I am indebted to
J. M. Scott's excellent *Portrait of an Ice Cap* and to Courtauld's personal
diaries (many entries are quoted in Scott's book), which I use by permission of his widow. From these I hope to present a vignette to parallel
Byrd's broader canvas.

For some time Byrd had wanted experience of solitude, and it is
not impossible that Courtauld's sojourn, two and a half years earlier,
fired him. 'Above everything else, and beyond the solid worth of
weather and auroral observations in the hitherto unoccupied interior
of Antarctica and my interest in these studies, I really wanted to go for
the experience's sake.' Originally it had been intended that three men
should man the advance base which was to be set up as a meteorological
station 400 miles from the Ross Sea throughout the winter of 1934,
but the expedition ran into difficulties even before reaching Little
America, the main base in the Bay of Whales on the Ross Sea. Blizzard,
cold, engine trouble with the tractors, the approaching disappearance
of the sun, all made it impossible for the party setting up advance base
to stock it for more than one man. Byrd jumped at the chance, despite
the twinges of conscience to which a married man is inevitably prey.
'This was an experience I hungered for, as soon as I grasped the possibilities.' On 22 March he flew in to the base, set in a snowy waste
123 miles from the sea instead of the hoped-for four hundred. On the
28th, after the last unloading and farewells, after many complications
caused by the intense cold of approaching winter, he found himself
alone.

Unlike the American set-up, the British Arctic Air Route Expedition 1930/31 was a small affair led by Gino Watkins, recently a
Cambridge undergraduate, and consisting of fourteen men having an
average age of twenty-five. Their avowed object was 'to explore the
possibilities of an air route to Canada by the great circle.' Apart from
mapping the east coast[1] and general exploration, they would set up
on the spine of the Ice Cap itself, a meteorological station which would
make winter observations. Little at that time was known of the Ice Cap,
a great mass of piled flour, in Scott's simile, frozen by its own weight,

---

1. In the view of L. P. Kirwan this was their most important contribution.
The White Road.

dropping out at the edges over the rim of surrounding mountains near the sea. It had been first crossed by Nansen in 1888; Peary, de Quervain, Koch and Rasmussen followed; segments were cut off by a criss-crosss of journeys; but still nobody knew it in winter. Two expeditions, one British and one German under Dr Wegener, set out to man stations on or near the middle line, at a height of 8,200 ft.

Watkin's ship, the *Quest* landed its party in the bay south of Angmagssalik on 26 July 1930, and he immediately organised a first journey to set up the central station. He has been called the most remarkable young man of his time; certainly he inspired others by example and personality as few men of that age have done. On this occasion he had been ill-informed by the weather experts, who predicted short storms only during the winter. It was hoped that the Ice Cap station could be relieved at regular intervals between October and May, parties of two at a time taking over the meteorological work.

The first party of five, Dr Bingham, Martin Lindsay, Quintin Riley, John Rymill and J. M. Scott, was to set up the station. The journey Scott described as a summer journey, 'scarcely more testing than an arduous holiday', but arduous it was to men who knew nothing about ice-cap travel, and only one of whom knew anything about sledging. The rest learned the hard way. To get on to the plateau it was necessary to climb the steepening glacier above base, one particularly nasty section, known politely in print as Bugbear Bank, taking two days and needing combined tactics. Once on the plateau they steered a straight course and flagged the route. On 28 August they reached the point, 8,200 feet high, at which the station was to be, and set about putting it up.[1] (See diagram, p. 153).

This station was very much simpler than Byrd's: an umbrella-shaped tent with a length of brass tubing at the top for ventilation, nine feet

[1]. It may simplify the story to give at this stage a bare outline of events leading up to Courtauld's sojourn.

August 28. Station established by Jamie Scott, 'Doc' Bingham, Quintin Riley, John Rymill and Martin Lindsay. Riley and Lindsay left there.

October 2. Station reached by Gino Watkins, Freddie Spencer Chapman, Jimmy D'Aeth, Scott, Rymill and Bingham. Bingham and D'Aeth left in place of Riley and Lindsay.

December 3. Station reached by Chapman, Lawrence Wager and Augustine Courtauld. Courtauld left in place of Bingham and D'Aeth.

in diameter and just over six feet high under the apex. Double canvas covered the eight wooden ribs. One entered by a twenty-foot tunnel which came up through the floor. Later, side-exits gave access to small snow-houses. Only the tent was put up by the whole party; the two first volunteers, Lindsay and Riley, did the rest when the others had gone. First they set up the instruments – nephoscope, Stevenson screen, anemometer or 'whirligig' as Lindsay called it – and dug an ice closet, a deep pit with sledge over it for seat. Then other amenities were added, such as the first snow-house in case the tent later proved too cold. They stayed longer than they had expected. By 19 September they were beginning a discussion on walking out, supposing that the relief party did not appear in the next fortnight. They had not enough food for the winter, and it was understood that, if the relief party did not arrive, the garrison was at liberty to quit without dishonour.

Life, however, slid quietly from day to day. They dug a second snow-house, of special design, and took the three-hourly observations. In the morning this was a cold business, but at evening, when the sun lingered on into twilight and filled the sky with dazzling contrasts of pink, pale blue, purple and orange and gold, they would stand outside, entranced. At night there was the beauty of the northern lights, 'a muster of dim lances, close serried, standing erect to the sky' (Lindsay). They read for hours from a library which grew with each arrival, played chess, tried their hand at cooking. The Central Station gave far more leisure than Byrd was to have, for besides a formidable battery of instruments, 'eight in continuous operation', which ruled his life, Byrd had radio schedules to keep, for which he would start to prepare two hours beforehand. Later, when he was compelled to crank the generator by hand, the strain of keeping the schedules far outweighed any comfort he derived from contact with the outside world.

Lindsay and Riley were relieved on 2 October by a cheerful party: Watkins, Chapman, Scott, Bingham, Rymill and D'Aeth. For a day or two the friendly, explosive companionship broke the silence of the Ice Cap. Then, when the support party had withdrawn, leaving Bingham and D'Aeth alone, a few steps in the flat whiteness outside the tent led back into an Ice Age, in which it seemed that man had never existed.

Bingham and D'Aeth expected the second relief early in November. 'Watkins's plan, based on absurdly optimistic meteorological forecasts, had been to relieve the central weather station on the ice sheet every month. But the blizzards, blandly prophesied as infrequent by the weather experts, blew weekly during October at over a hundred miles an hour.'[1] Relief did not arrive till 3 December. The two service men seem to have borne the delay with competent fortitude, working outside at clearing snow and building an eight-foot wall round the 'courtyard', making improvements inside, reading, smoking, talking, playing cards. In the reasons for this delay lies the explanation of Courtauld's subsequent five months alone.

Watkins and Scott had set off southward, intending to explore down the spine of the Ice Cap before turning east towards base. Storm and the behaviour of their dogs dramatically curtailed this programme; they could only make ninety miles out of the proposed three hundred before heading for the coast. On 10 November, back in the coastal zone, they saw black dots ahead against the white: Chapman's relief party returning, as Watkins imagined on first seeing them, from relieving the others and installing Hampton and Stephenson in their place. In fact, they were still on their way out. (See map p. 137.)

Only Chapman,[2] the leader of this contingent, had visited the station before. Besides Hampton and Stephenson and Lt Lemon, responsible for the wireless, he had Lawrence Wager, later to climb to 28,100 feet on Everest, and Augustine Courtauld. Courtauld had not at first been chosen for this spell at the Ice Cap station. Officially he was 'surveyor and in charge of boats'. He had been to Greenland twice before, with J. M. Wordie, and the second time, in a party with Wordie and Bunny (Sir Vivian) Fuchs, had climbed Petermann Peak. He had also travelled in the Sahara with the Tuaregs. After the Cambridge of the 1920s – hunting, the odd quirks, like starving for three days just to see what would happen, adventures with a home-made boat – he had found the traditional 'settling down' to a bowler-hatted London irksome. An indulgent father had made possible the first two trips to Greenland.

1. L. P. Kirwan, op. cit.
2. Of course the Chapman of *The Jungle is Neutral* and author of *Watkins' Last Expedition*. On that expedition he spent a month alone on the coast.

It was after the second that he had fallen in with Gino Watkins. On the expedition his job so far had been to map the coast to the north in the *Quest*, using aeroplane when possible. With the Ice Cap he was unfamiliar.

Courtauld was in many ways typical of this remarkable expedition under a remarkable leader. They were all still undergraduate in humour, yet deadly earnest in expedition matters; flippant in tone but serious in judgment and as ready to pass judgment on the world, the flesh and literature as in the twenties one normally is. 'A delightful book,' Quintin Riley wrote in all seriousness after reading *Wuthering Heights*, and the same Riley, arriving at the station, began by hanging his crucifix over his sleeping bag and on the first Sunday read from St Paul, St John and the *Imitation of Christ*. He noted how much he missed Communion.

There were, they found, only two seasons on the Ice Cap. No autumn intervened to divide summer from the bitter, driving winter. It was the storms which delayed them, the wind which had already delayed the start by reaching, even at base, 129 miles an hour and blowing away the wind-gauge. In fifteen days they did fifteen miles, fighting for every mile. On days when they were able to start at all it might take six hours to clear the snow, pack the sledges and be away. On some days there was nothing to do but lie up and listen to the blizzard.

The writing of a diary on an expedition is a personal solace. The wilderness of mountain or ice cap does not mean privacy. One is never truly alone; every function of the human body is performed within inches of one's fellows. In the diary, written half-inside the sleeping bag with numb fingers while the socks are drying, the supper cooking, each can give vent to private hopes, fears, reflections on the universe. On 3 November, Courtauld's diary gives the first hint of doubt: 'If this continues, it will be a long time before we can reach the Central Station and we shall be short of food.' On the 5th:

> The fornicator [usual name for the wind] blew all day. Snow drifted right up over the tent entrance, so causing the two walls to come together and make the tent very cold. Got out about 3 p.m.

to feed the dogs. Wind furious. Could only walk against it with face turned away. Most of the dogs were buried in the snow with only their noses out. Some of them did not seem to want their pemmican. Inside of tent covered with hoar frost, which drips on to us. We are now on half-rations, which, fortunately, are large enough to keep us going.

On 7 November came the first change of plan. There would not be enough food to keep all six sledges going. Lemon, Chapman and Stephenson would go on while the others returned. But then, on the 10th, they met Watkins and Scott, and a new plan formed itself.

About noon Freddie, who was in front, came running back. He had seen a sledge away to the left. It was Gino and Jimmy returning from the Southern Journey. We stopped our sledges and ran to meet them. They, like us, have had awful weather. . . . Gino was very perturbed that we had got no further in and seemed to think we should have a very difficult task to get there at all. He told us we must get the people there out at all costs, if necessary feed the dogs on each other. Freddie has decided to push on with three sledges, himself, Wager and self, while the other three will return to the base. If the three of us get there with enough food to keep the C.S. going till the spring, Wager and I will stay there.

'So revolves the kaleidoscope of chance,' Stephenson recorded in some disappointment the same day. The party divided on the 11th. Lemon, the wireless expert, returned, and nobody in the end knew for sure what became of the transmitter. The teams struggled on. It was that evening that Chapman wrote: 'Courtauld came into our tent this morning and suggested that he should stay alone at the Ice Cap station.' The reason he gave was the common worry that they had not enough supplies for two men. Further, the bad weather had started early and might continue into March, making it impossible to land an aeroplane or send relief. Chapman confessed himself moved by this argument.

The idea must have come suddenly. Courtauld cannot have ruminated long, as Byrd did, because before the 10th he did not expect to be going to the station at all. In exactly what spirit he made the offer, and then persisted in it, one is left to guess. Remember that the manning of the station was a routine job, not the public achievement that it became later, in part owing to the failure of the first rescue attempt and the 'fuss' in England. Nobody believed that it would be manned for more than three, or at most four, months. The Germans were trying to do the same thing, only still farther inland, because Greenland is wider to the north. Writing at a distance of thirty years, Scott lists Courtauld's motives as three: the job had to be done; as a self-sufficient individual he knew that he could do it; all the pundits had said that no man should remain alone in the Arctic and this presented an irresistible challenge. But 'I feel sure that there was no *conscious* idealism.' Chapman adds a comment on the self-sufficiency: 'He really enjoyed being alone. His greatest joy in England had been to push off in his boat alone and to eat when he felt hungry and sleep when he felt tired. He was a natural rebel against normal social conventions.'

On 15 November the temperature wavered between −20° and −32°, and Courtauld's diary records:

> Drifts very bad, sledges overturned every few yards. Freddie's sledge showed signs of breaking up, so we camped about 4. Decided to lighten his sledge and only take on enough food for one man (self) at Ice Cap. We shall therefore only take 4 instead of 14 ration boxes there. It looks as if the useful result of this journey will be small indeed. Had a tin of sardines for supper. V.G. Distance today 2 miles.

On the 16th they lay up all day and he read 'the whole of *King John*, sundry sonnets and the whole of *Alice in Wonderland*.' And so it went on. On the few fine days they began by digging everything out and finding that the dogs had chewed through their traces. Sledges kept overturning on a surface alternately 'knife-edge drifts as hard as concrete and soft snow.' At each overturn the framework of the sledges weakened further. They were plagued by frostbite, the chill of hoar frost and fine drift in the tents, dogs that ran away or pupped in the snow, the irritation of breaking traces. 'The continued effort at this height (6,000 or 7,000 feet) of struggling through the snow without snow-shoes (which the dogs have eaten), keeping the sledges upright, cursing one's dogs and continually restarting, tires one out almost beyond endurance' (21 Nov.). And they still had a long way to go.

On 30 November conditions improved and they allowed themselves full rations. By seven p.m. on the moonlit night of 2 December they felt themselves very near the station. Frantically they searched around, but could not find it. 'It was freezing over sixty degrees and the wind bit through our clothes as if we were naked.' At last they were forced to pitch tents and crawl into half-frozen sleeping-bags. They did not sleep. It was not until after dark on the next day, 3 December, in eighty degrees of frost, that Chapman spotted the Union Jack. With shouts of *'Evening Standard! Star* and *News!'* they clambered along the tunnel.

The reunion with Bingham and D'Aeth was warm, but the joy of it was sadly damped for Courtauld by intense pain in his fingers and toes from frostbite. On 4 December an enormous, premature Christmas dinner was held. That evening Bingham, the doctor, wrote in his diary: 'Courtauld wants to stay alone, but I have given a very decided opinion against it.' Thus, by the time he made his own diary entry, Augustine Courtauld knew very well that the doctor considered he was in for an unjustifiably tough ordeal:

> Doc and the others do not like the idea of my staying here alone, as it may be for three or four months, but short of abandoning the station there is no alternative, as there is only food for one man for that period.

This is a diary jotting; he goes on to describe the soreness of his fingers and toes from frostbite. Very different is Byrd's amplified assertion, written four years after the experience, that he wanted 'to be by himself for a while to taste peace and quiet and solitude long enough to find out how good they really are.' Courtauld was never explicit about his deeper motives.

On 5 December a gale blew and the return party was forced to lie up. Wager, who found himself in one of the snow-houses, commented, 'Courtauld seems quite cheerful about staying here for three months by himself'; also, that there was not enough food for two, though when

The British Arctic Air Route Expedition.

two whole boxes were found at the station he half expected and was prepared to be left as well. However, 'I don't think I should care for more than one month here by myself.' Courtauld was renowned for being invincible when once he had made up his mind. He must have put his arguments very cogently to overcome the doubts of the others and to win over Chapman, who wrote that evening:

'The Doctor and D'Aeth are dead against one man staying alone. They say they have experienced it and they know. However, Courtauld is determined to stay, and, eventually, we gave in. I must say it would be a thousand pities to abandon the station now, since it has been established and maintained with so much trouble. Courtauld is very keen to stay, and judging by Watkins' experience among the Labrador trappers it is not so bad as people make out.'

On the 6th, therefore, Courtauld said goodbye to the others, not knowing when he would see them again. Nor could he know how the same problem, the risk to human life set against the scientific programme to be carried out, was being faced further north by the Germans, whose attempt was to end disastrously with the loss of the leader and one Eskimo companion. As he saw his friends go he may have reflected again upon his own action, but the only reason he added, later in life, to those given in the diaries was that he had frostbitten toes and did not fancy the journey back. The British have a reputation for public understatement; this perhaps is particularly true of the between-wars generation. In that spirit of matter-of-fact, won't-show-my-heart resolution he returned to the tent.

I took a photo, and then with a 'Damma, damma, damma'[1] they were away down the trail. Although there was a feeble sun it was bitterly cold and I did not watch them long. Coming out again an hour later, I could just see them as a speck in the distance. Now I am quite alone. Not a dog or even a mosquito for company. However it is very comfortable, or will be when I have cleared up the mess a bit. The great problem at the moment is to get my things dry. My sleeping bag is full of ice and all my clothes except what I have got on are the same. Still my pipe tastes just as ever and the igloo is warm, so really there is nothing to complain of unless it be the curse of having to go out every three hours into the cold wind to observe the weather.

It is interesting to compare Byrd:

I stood at the trapdoor and watched the two Citroëns move away. . . . I went below, intending to busy myself with the wind-speed records; but the errand was a piece of self-deception which I could not quite bring off. For perhaps the only moment in my adult life I was conscious of being utterly at loose ends. The shack, which had seemed bright and cheery, now was neither. And, obeying an impulse which I had no time to be ashamed of, I rushed up the

1. Eskimo cry used for urging on dogs.

hatch ladder. Just why, I don't even know now; perhaps for a last look at something alive and moving. Although the cars were by then some distance away, I could still hear the *beep-beep* of the horns and the clatter of the treads, so clearly do sounds carry in that crystal air.[1]

The house in which Courtauld's next five months were to be passed consisted by now of an eight-foot snow wall circling the tent and snow-houses to make a courtyard; the tent itself was covered with a layer of snow so that the sound of blizzards was muted to a faint whispering down the ventilator. In the 'hut' formed by the snow-plastered tent were two raised 'divans' made from boxes. A skin covered the floor between, while primus stove and lamp were supported on a box. Often the lamp alone was sufficient to keep the hut warm and the primus could be turned off. The entrance was still through the tunnel, some five feet below floor-level. The tunnel, about twenty feet long, had side branches to the two snow-houses, which had been built from snow-blocks on the lines described by Vilhjalmur Stefansson, the great exponent of living off the country in the Arctic. These igloos, eight feet in diameter and four and a half or five feet high, were found hard to warm.

Byrd's home by contrast was luxurious: a shack having 800 cubic feet of space and weighing 1,500 lbs, brought in by tractor and plane, made of white pine, with cardboard and kapok for insulation, with ceiling and walls of bright aluminium, to reflect light and heat. The bunk had been fastened to one wall, six shelves to another, clothes hung from nails, stove and table gave a sense of comfort; weather instruments peeped out everywhere, tunnels led to the various stores. Compared with the American base now at the Pole it was a hovel, but beside Watkins' tent it would have seemed a palace. Being more spacious, however, it was also harder to keep warm. 'You'll freeze to death in this dungeon,' one of Byrd's companions remarked cheerfully, just before leaving. And the prophecy very nearly came true, for a reason different from those that anybody had imagined.

Courtauld knew something of the routine from Bingham and D'Aeth,

1. *Alone*, from which the other passages are taken.

who had spent nine weeks there. It was a simple one. They had exercised themselves on the igloos and in the courtyard, throwing snow out over the eight-foot wall. They had been for only one walk, to leave a message four miles away for the relief party. As Wager put it, 'there is no point in walking'. (Byrd would not have agreed. A naval man, he began to make the daily promenade a feature of his daily routine: so many steps this way, so many steps that, holding on to a line in case he should lose himself in the Antarctic night.) For Bingham and D'Aeth the three-hourly instrument check had provided the discipline. For the rest, they had smoked and played cards or chess, told all their stories and read all the books. They had found that they ate progressively less. For about a fortnight during the middle of their stay Bingham had found himself very out of breath, and used to wake in the night, sweating and panting. At the end neither had looked fit.

All this Courtauld knew when he waved goodbye to the others. He knew also that he would be very lonely – 'not a dog or even a mosquito for company.' 'No place can be lonelier than the Ice Cap,' Scott wrote. There is a 'vast aloofness' about it, as there is about Antarctica, which frightens a man until he can find the right spirit with which to meet it. At the same time it is hard to know exactly what is being met. Most of the hazards of civilised life are absent. You will never catch a cold, and are unlikely to break a leg, but you cannot do any of the 'normal' things, like sitting around outside, for the cold would numb you in a moment and the wind nip your fingers with frostbite. Perhaps it is no more than this sense of oppressive cold and size, which worries.

The instruments were only a few yards from the tunnel exit, but in a blizzard it would be easy for Courtauld to lose the way back. After that, there would be nothing between him and the sea. Besides the mental strain, there would be the physical strain of digging and keeping the tunnel clear, a job hitherto done by two men, of reading the instruments every three hours, of cooking and washing and mending and doing the household chores.

From the diary, glancing aside from time to time to see how Byrd fared when similarly placed, we shall see how Courtauld adapted himself. It is all, as Chapman had it, a question of 'the right attitude of mind.' And for both of them Chapman's favourite sentence from Shakespeare proved true: 'There is nothing either good or bad, but thinking makes it so.'

Courtauld's first diary entries after 6 December are almost conscientiously matter-of-fact:

December 9th, Tuesday. Nothing of note today except that I changed my underclothes as I had had itching for the last night or two. Found a good many bugs, much to my disgust, so put my clothes out in the snow in the pious hope that the cold would kill them. This is what comes of lending one's clothes to Eskimos.

December 10th, Wednesday. Did some tidying up. Lamp lit first time today instead of taking four hours as it did yesterday. No more sign of bugs.

When the wind blew and snow fell, the entrance to the tunnel drifted over and he had to dig his way out. Whenever the wind changed, the new exit would disappear and he might have to dig every three hours. 'Change of wind has completely drifted up the courtyard as well as the entrance to the house, so now one has to wade knee-deep in snow, after fighting one's way out of the tunnel, and then climb over a six-foot drift to get outside the walls. A further wade, tripping over ridges and falling into invisible holes in the diffused light, brings one to the instruments' (December 15). On the next day he recorded, unfortunately, in a laconic two lines, an experience which he shared with Byrd: 'Got lost getting to the instruments at 7, for drift was so thick.' Byrd once had the worse experience of being unable, when he returned, to open the trapdoor which would take him down into the shack. He panicked, crooked his arm through the grip, clawed and cursed. At the end of his strength he remembered a shovel left out a week before. By pushing it through the grip and working it upward with his shoulders as he lay on the ground, he managed at last to raise the trap and tumble in. His graphic description of the blizzard raging at that time applies as well to the Ice Cap as to the Ross Sea Barrier:

There is something extravagantly insensate about an Antarctic blizzard at night. Its vindictiveness cannot be measured on an anemometer sheet. It is more than just wind; it is a solid wall of snow moving at gale force, pounding like surf. The whole malevolent rush is concentrated upon you as upon a personal enemy. In the senseless explosion of sound you are reduced to a crawling thing on the margin of a disintegrating world; you can't see, you can't hear, you can hardly move. The lungs gasp after the air sucked out of them, and the brain is shaken. Nothing in the world will so quickly isolate a man.

Inside his smaller lodging Courtauld had his frostbite to worry about, just as Byrd was anxious about the shoulder wrenched while he was helping to unpack gear. Completing the entry for 16 December Courtauld wrote: 'Tonight unbandaged toes. Unpleasant sight. Left toenail came off. Other will soon, I expect.' Byrd, after the first few days alone, recorded: 'A fearful amount of lifting remains to be done. So far, I've managed with one hand by using my hip as a fulcrum.' Despite their disabilities both men had all the chores to do and some heavy manual work, and the temperature kept dropping. On the Ice Cap the sun had half gone, but there was still light. On the Ross Sea Barrier, of course, Antarctic night reigned.

As compensation for the pains and trials of solitude, the beauty of sky and snow should, one feels, grant that special insight into the nature of things which a man sometimes achieves when he is alone. On 21 December Courtauld wrote:

Aurora wonderful tonight, like purple smoke wreaths twisting and writhing all over the sky. At ten o'clock it was completely still. The silence was almost terrible. Nothing to hear but one's heart beating and the blood ticking in one's veins.[1]

Such moments are what all of us who leave the crowd hope to find: 'rare moments of intellectual ecstasy which occur perhaps on a mountain

1. The entry concludes: 'Other toenail came off tonight. Looks very nasty, all soft, dead and gooing.'

Augustine Courtauld
(*Scott Polar Research Institute*)

Courtauld on return to Base (*Scott Polar Research Institute*)

The Ice Cap Station, as found in May 1931 (*Scott Polar Research Institute*)

summit, perhaps on a glacier at dawn or in a lonely moonlit bivouac, and which appear to be the result of a happy coincidence in the rhythm of mind and scene'.[1] So Eric Shipton writes, the mountaineer and friend of Courtauld. Most of us hope to find such moments nearer home: on Snowdon or Ben Nevis, even on the Norfolk Broads. Some, however, need the extremes. Byrd, during his first two months at advance base, made use of the opportunity he had been given for thinking out a 'philosophy' which would make sense of his surroundings. This deserves a brief summary.

First, in the brilliant and orderly revolutions of the stars he seemed to sense, each night, a harmony or rhythm which accorded with some mood in himself. 'It was enough to watch that rhythm, momentarily to be myself part of it. In that instant I could feel no doubt of man's oneness with the universe. The conviction came that that rhythm was too orderly, too harmonious, too perfect to be a product of blind chance, that, therefore, there must be purpose in the whole and that man was part of that whole and not an accidental offshoot.'

His life during the first two months was a life of the mind. Solitude was almost a companion, enabling him to reflect as he had wished to. The regular processes of nature which he observed and which his instruments recorded made him 'know' inside himself, not only that 'blind chance' did not rule but that the evolution of the human race was as much a cosmic process as the aurora or the Ice Barrier. Psychological laws must ultimately aim at harmony, as do natural laws. The age-old convictions of right, sifted by time, would make for freedom and harmony, just as those things that man was slowly rejecting as 'wrong', brute force and selfishness, made for slavery. Peace or harmony was not static but moved as the stars move and required effort. When a man found harmony in himself, he was happy. A nation made up of such individuals was a happy nation. No man could achieve more than that on earth, any more than he could understand more than a tiny fragment of the universe around.

This was, Byrd recollected, how it had seemed to him; and it had seemed to him also that to come into contact with this reality of universal law was sufficient reason for spending months alone on the Barrier.

1. *Upon That Mountain.*

Edward Wilson, years earlier, had put rather the same thought in the more personal form of a relationship with God: 'Surely God means us to find out all we can of His works, and to work out our own salvation, realizing that all things that have to do with our spiritual development "are understood and clearly seen in things created"' (Letter to his wife). Byrd also recorded a curious experience that had a bearing on his conception of harmony. At 12.15 a.m. on 11 May he climbed out to see the aurora. The night was calm and clear, and he left the trapdoor open with a record of Beethoven's Fifth Symphony playing down below. 'Presently I began to have the illusion that what I was seeing was also what I was hearing, so perfectly did the music blend with what was in the sky.' The aurora itself seemed to pulsate and quicken, until music and night became one. 'I told myself that all beauty was akin and sprang from the same substance. I recalled a gallant, unselfish act that was of the same essence as the music and the aurora.'

Only once did Courtauld in his diary touch the same theme at any length or wrestle on paper with the eternal Why. This was much later, after three months at the station, when the paraffin was running low and he was lying half the time in darkness, with only hot porridge in the mornings to warm him.

Why is it men come to these places? So many reasons have been ascribed for it. In the old days it was thought to be lust for treasure, but the treasure is gone and still men wander. Then it was craving for adventure. There is precious little adventure in sledging or in sitting on an ice cap. Is it curiosity? A yearning to look behind the veil on to the mysteries and desolations of nature in her forlorn places? Perhaps, but that is not all. Why leave all whom we love, all good friends, all creature comforts, to collect a little academic knowledge about this queer old earth of ours? What do we gain? Do we in fact morally bury ourselves in fleeing from the world? Do we simply rot or grow rank like some plant thrown over the garden wall, or do we rather come nearer to reality, see more clearly the Great Purpose behind it all in stripping our souls of the protection of our friends and in putting from us the pleasures of the body? How little the worries of the World seem to be in such a situation as this; how grand and awful the things that are here, the things that grip the heart with fear, the forces that spin the Universe through Space.

In leaving behind the transitory hopes and fears of pathetic humanity, does one, perhaps, come closer to the things that abide, to the forces which endure?

So Courtauld in doubt, and it may be asked, since the two voluntary hermits are thus philosophising, why does the Satopanth hermit not join them here, instead of being relegated to Chapter Two? The answer is implicit in that chaper. The Satopanth hermit stood to one side of the path of experience that leads from Brown to Courtauld. His mind was passive, empty of personal purpose, of thoughts of work or of his own life and safety. Courtauld and Byrd were there because they had a job to do, because they did not want to let a side down, for motives that translate themselves easily for us. It has been remarked that if a mystic, and *pari passu* a *sadhu*, tried to turn his powers to practical ends, they would disappear. All the other survivors we have named were trying to do just that; the hermit was not – and we were right, therefore, to bid farewell to him early, and to all the ascetics who rise in shadowy ranks behind his fleshless figure.

Towards Christmas Courtauld found himself very much taken up with daydreams, both of last Christmas and of next. Thus on 23 December:

How jolly if I was at home or even at the Base. I suppose they will be having a blind and finishing the last of the ale. . . . If only I could put the clock on to next Christmas. How marvellous it will be to get back next summer. If plans go according to their appointed destinies – which they probably won't – I think I should like a small house in Suffolk between twenty and sixty miles from H. Should be near for trains and near the sea, preferably Pin Mill. No land except a garden and fewest possible servants. No waiting at table. If any money, would rather spend it on a boat than a house. Something like *Colona* would be V.G. though possibly a little small for long passages.

He wondered where in England they would land, where he could cruise conveniently, and in what sort of boat. However, his fantasies were interrupted by a nasty shock. The 'house' had creaked and groaned many times, but a little after seven a.m. on the morning of the 27th he heard 'a soft rumbling close to my head, which increased and ended in a dull crash. It flashed across my mind as it began that the weight of snow was too much and the whole house was going to come in on me.' Nothing further happened and he concluded soberly that some blocks of the wall must have given way, and hoped that nothing further would happen that night.

At 11.30 p.m. on 31 December he wrote:

New Year's Eve! It is certainly quiet. The last few days have been fine and cool with some magnificent aurorae. Expecting to see the sun again any day now. It is quite bright in the southern sky in the middle of the day. . . . Toes have been hurting considerably lately, so bathed and bandaged them. Did a bit of spring cleaning for the N.Y. Discovering lots of useful and amusing information in Whittaker. Shall make a list of books lately published therefrom.

N.Y. Resolutions
1. Mend moccasins and sleeping bag.
2. Get home and ask M. to marry me.
3. Find (a) a house (Suffolk, Sussex or Dorset); (b) a boat; (c) a job. (a) and (b) rather depend on condition of financial affairs when I get home.
4. Give up exploring.
5. Collect a library and study (a) English literature and poetry; (b) Music; (c) Polar exploration with a view possibly to try to write a book about it.

Wish I could send a wireless to M. Wonder how they are doing at Base; finishing up the last of the good eats and drinks, I suppose.

On 1 January he noted that the mean temperature for several days had been – 30° or – 35°, while in November it had dropped to – 50° or – 55°. These temperatures were not, of course, as low as those experienced by Byrd, but, to counterbalance that, the Ice Cap station was 8,000 feet higher than advance base and correspondingly less well supplied with oxygen. The entry for 1 January finished with a 'list of books worth reading taken from Ice Cap Library, 1 January'. Undoubtedly the most convenient escape, even easier than daydreams, lay through books. On the way up, hemmed by blizzards, Chapman had read aloud from *The Golden Treasury* as they lay shivering in frost-stiff bags. H. W. Tilman writes of the Himalayan mountaineer that his worst enemy is bedsores and his best friend the chest of books, and on an ice cap station a man would be equally lost without a library. Courtauld's comments on books have a fresh, rather immature seriousness about them:

Just finished *Vanity Fair*. Liked it well. There is something very satisfying in reading perfect English, whatever the story, and have now started de Quincey's *Opium Eater*, which seems very long-winded and pedantic, but again it is well worth reading for its style. . . .

Just finished Pepys. Wish it was continued further. What a hopeless fool Charles II seems to have been. Not only by his effeminacy and incompetence did he let down the country at the time, but he broke people's faith in kings for ever and sacrificed all their power and prerogatives for his successors. He deserved the block fully as much, if not more, than his father. . . .

Reading *Guy Mannering* (Scott). V.V.G. Descriptions of food make one writhe, worse than *Forsyte Saga*. But I like reading about it. The Potage à la Meg Merrilees sounds marvellous. . . .

January 4 he described as a 'frightful day'. A gale was blowing when he awoke and this meant that the tunnel would be snowed up. By the time he had dug himself out his clothes were full of snow, which got over everything. One piece dropped inside the lamp and broke the mantle. At eleven, one, and two-thirty he dug his way out again, the entrance being completely blocked each time and snow seeming to fill it as fast as he dug. 'By this time (2.30) the back of the tunnel was so full of snow caused by digging out the entrance that I could scarcely wriggle up it. At 2 the drift at the entrance was deeper than my height and I had some difficulty in getting out even when I had dug away the snow.' By three-thirty he could not push the snow back from the entrance, and the wind had turned into a blizzard which made it impossible to see outside. He retired indoors and lay up, letting the weather observations 'go hang'. 'Hope the air keeps breathable and the roof doesn't collapse. If (a) doesn't or (b) does, my end should be peaceful enough, and I have four slabs of chocolate to eat during it. Anyhow, it won't be attended by the fuss and frills one's pegging out at home would.'

On 5 January:

Came to the conclusion this morning that it was impossible to dig out the tunnel, so dug out the entrance of the starboard snow-house and cut a hole in the roof. Luckily it did not fall in and so I was able to get out. THANK GOD.

And on 6 January:

'Had a jump this evening. As I was in a sort of doze I heard M. call me twice, 'Aug, Aug'. The time was 11 p.m. G.M.T.

In Courtauld's case the physical deterioration which the doctor anticipated came gradually. He experienced no sudden crisis, as did Byrd.

January 16th, Friday. Felt rather faint yesterday at 4 p.m., probably as a consequence of turning on the blasted arse-warmer. Thought I should not be able to get back into house. However all was well, though heart beating very fast. Gave myself a rest for six hours, so missed the 7 p.m. obs.

To encourage him the sun came up that day and he remarked that 'it is grand to see it casting its rose-pink light along the snow, making dark shadows and bright places so that one's eyes blink.' To worry him, the house showed further signs of collapsing under the great weight of snow; he had only ten gallons of paraffin left; some of the tins, all laboriously to be dug out, he could not find as he had forgotten their position, and some leaked; he could not stay out for more than a few minutes, his feet froze up so quickly; he had dropped the barometer into the cooking pot and broken the maximum thermometer while cleaning it; there was no sign of the aeroplane which was to have come over. 'Probably it cannot take off, so I shall have to wait a few more months till someone can sledge here.' (January 28.)

On 1 February he was in pessimistic mood:

I wonder when, if ever, I shall get away from here. Not that I am bored, but I notice that my legs are getting very thin, partly from want of exercise and partly from lack of fresh food, I suppose. If I have to sledge back it will be pretty rotten unless the going is good enough to ride. These gales are nerve-racking things. I am daily expecting the house to fall in, for both the side snow-houses have partly done so. I wish there could be some decent weather. Whenever the sun is out and it is clear it is about 50 degrees below zero, and the rest of the time it blows blizzards so that one can see or do nothing on account of the drift.

Later in February he was experiencing serious difficulty in keeping the tunnels clear and digging out buried stores:

February 14th, Saturday. Have now been ten weeks alone. Weather this week has been damnable. First of all too cold to do any digging (90 degrees of frost) so that I am running short of rations because the others are buried about ten feet under snow. Then I left the opening of the snow-house roof unstopped one night and it came on to blow from the south-east and filled it up completely. With great difficulty I got it a bit clear and stopped it coming in from that direction, when last night it went back to the north-west and filled it up again. Now impossible to get out without letting all the snow down the tunnel, which is so small now that I can only just wriggle through it. Only one more day's food after today. Still blowing.

*February 17th, Tuesday. . . .*Could not get out this morning till ten o'clock, by which time it was calm. As the outside boxes seemed unobtainable and as I had run out of all the palatable rations I started work on the one buried in the snow-house. It was slow work digging away the concrete snow and filling it into biscuit-tins to empty outside. However, thank God, I have got something decent to eat at last. Came on to blow again this evening, barometer crashing. Hope to goodness the entrance doesn't come in again or I shall be snowed up for good. . . . Hope the chaps have not set out from the Base yet. This weather is impossible for sledging. As far as I can see six months at least of the expedition will be a complete waste of time. All the proposed long sledge journeys will go to pot.

At 5.30 p.m. on the 19th a further incident tautened his nerves. As he lay reading he heard a rushing sound from behind, ending in a sudden crash like the breaking of an avalanche. He thought that at last he was about to be overwhelmed, but nothing happened. When he climbed out at seven p.m. everything appeared normal. He concluded that some chasm had formed in the ice far below, as happens on glaciers.

On 25 February, Scott flew with Cozens from the base, intending to drop supplies, but they could see nothing at all of the station. Next evening Courtauld wrote:

At last the gales have died down and given way to clear cold weather, though still the north-west wind blows. The temperature has been down to $-60°$. Am getting thoroughly fed up with going out to the observations every three hours and getting all outer clothes covered with snow by having to wriggle through the tunnel. Am down to the last four gallons of paraffin now. If the others don't turn up in three or four weeks, I shall be reduced to cold and darkness. If ever I get back to the Base nothing will induce me to go on the Ice Cap again. When the others will come God knows. These gales will have made sledging impossible and have raised drifts like young hills even here. What it is like farther out Heavens knows. Judging by when we arrived, when the going here was good, I should think absolutely impossible.

Things looked black.

Upon Byrd, by contrast, the physical and nervous disability was to descend suddenly. This was not due in the first place to the cold, against which he was well equipped, or to lack of food or paraffin. He could keep clean and even enjoy a bath. He was knocked unconscious, while making radio contact with Little America on 31 May, by carbon monoxide fumes from the gasoline engine which generated power for the transmitter. On top of this he later blamed the leaky joints in the stove, which for weeks past had been causing nausea and headaches.

Byrd came nearer to dying than Courtauld; indeed, he thought that he was going to die, and for some days he divided his wakeful moments between doing very slowly and mechanically the routine jobs that must be done, and reproaching himself bitterly for letting down his wife, his family and the expedition. He records that on the evening of 1 June, after another bout of unconsciousness, 'I dropped into the chair, convinced that the end was near. Up till now I had been sustained by a conviction that the only way I could nullify my mistake and make reparation to my family was by transcending myself and surviving. But I had lost. I flung my arms across the table, and put my head down, spilling a cup of water I had in my hand. My bitterness evaporated, and the only resentment I felt was concentrated on myself. I lay there a long time, sobbing, "What a pity, what an infinite pity".'

He wrote a message to his wife, and could not help thinking of the famous last entry in Robert Falcon Scott's diary: 'For God's sake look after our people.' He even felt impelled to write out a summary of his reflections during April and May, beginning with his acknowledgment of an Intelligence in the universe that aims at harmony or peace. It ends:

The human race, then, is not alone in the universe. Though I am cut off from human beings, *I* am not alone.

For untold ages man has felt an awareness of that Intelligence.

Belief in it is the one point where all religions agree. It has been called by many names. Many call it God.

After these letters there came to him out of 'five everlasting, interminable days' the realisation that he need not die, which changed gradually into a conviction that he must not die or he would be letting down his own philosophy as well as everybody else. He then examined practical steps to avoid death: to husband strength, to force himself to eat, to use the stove sparingly and the gasoline pressure lantern not at all. Gradually, but very gradually, 'the melancholy began to lift'. The physical discomforts, however, caused by his resolution to do largely without heat, increased. The cold became intolerable to a body weakened by lack of food.

The pains of Byrd's next two months would take too long in the telling and are told in his own book. He bore one burden that Courtauld never had to shoulder, that of personal responsibility combined with the maintenance of the radio schedule with Little America. (Watkins' transmitter had never arrived at the station.) If Byrd once let on what had happened, his men would come through the Antarctic night to his rescue, and he was convinced that they would not survive this. The strain of making contact, much greater after a second attack of fumes, could not dispense him from listening to important expedition matters which needed decisions. 'These early morning schedules are killing,' he wrote, and succeeded in changing them to later in the day. On July 5, his problem was doubled by the breaking lug of the generator drive shaft. From then on he was forced to crank by hand, a toilsome business which left him sick with exhaustion.

Like Courtauld, Byrd was helped during these months by escapes into other worlds: through reading, through the gramophone (he had an advantage here), through daydreams. 'I surrounded myself with family and friends; I projected myself into the midst of green, growing things. I thought of all the things I would do when I got back.' He played patience. Though he would not have liked to think it, the radio schedules which he so hated may have saved him in the end. Sensing that something must be wrong, Charles Murphy, back at Little America, persuaded the others that the date of the relief party should be advanced,

SECTION

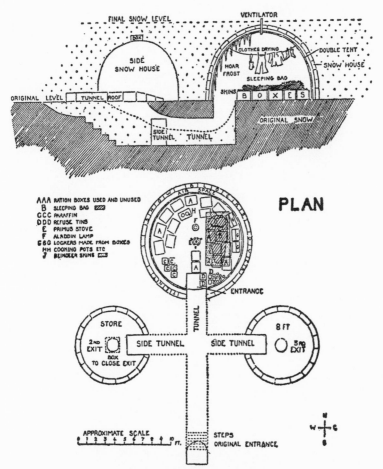

The Greenland Ice Cap Station

under the ingenious pretext that Dr Poulter, second-in-command, was anxious to observe meteors. Thus, despite false starts and an approach journey by tractor through crevasses in bitter weather at very low temperatures, Byrd was relieved much earlier than had been planned, on 11 August of 1934.

While Courtauld was writing his despondent entry of 26 February the first relief party was planning to set out from Watkins' base hut. Scott and Riley started on 1 March, but one sledge broke in half. After a second false start these two, with Martin Lindsay, got away on the 9th. They were soon in trouble. The season was very early for travel, but the aeroplane had failed to locate the station and Watkins was anxious to relieve Courtauld as soon as possible. Scott, Riley and Lindsay met the worst conditions they had known, conditions which, according to J. Gordon Hayes, 'approached the limits of human endurance.'[1] Courtauld feared these conditions on their account, and his anxieties, as well as his faith, begin to show more prominently, like the bones of a starving man, in the diary.

March 7th: One can only trust in God. If they do not arrive before the end of the month I shall be plunged in darkness and only have cold food. Weather now broken again.

March 15th: Less than two gallons of paraffin left now. Hope to goodness the others come before it runs out or I shall have nothing to drink. Have reduced food rations and am only eating under a pound a day. However, this is sufficient. It is boring sitting most of the day though. In short-lighted intervals am reading *Forsyte Saga* again. Extremely good.

March 22nd: As I expected, no sooner had I got the new entrance secure against the drift than it started to blow and continued until now there is such a weight of snow on top of it that I cannot now raise the box, so I am completely buried. Paraffin has very nearly run out and things generally are pretty dismal, especially as, as far as I can tell, it is bright fine weather outside now. Just been reading M.'s last letter. It is the only thing left to do that gives me real pleasure. However, God has kept me going so far, so perhaps He will see me the rest of the way. Wish I knew how everybody was at home.

1. *The Conquest of the North Pole.* In the context of weather, the 'limits of human endurance' seems a phrase without much meaning.

On the 25th he listed the pleasures he would 'like to have granted if wishing were any good.'

1. Sitting in an armchair before a roaring fire listening to M. playing and singing.

2. Eight a.m. on a fine summer morning at sea at the helm of a small boat, a fresh breeze blowing, all sail set with M. and a smell of breakfast coming up to say 'good morning'.

3. Just having got into bed with clean sheets and ditto pyjamas.

4. Bright autumn morning, eating an apple in the garden before breakfast (an enormous one): kippers, poached eggs, kidneys and mushrooms, cold partridge.

5. Getting into a hot bath.

... 'Oh for the wings of a Dove', or better still a peregrine falcon.

Meanwhile, the relief party, travelling along a line of latitude which should bring them to the station, was still among roaring gales. Thick drift denied visibility for observations. By Easter Sunday they had been on the look-out for the station for a week, and still it was not to be seen. They could not risk staying too long, or they too would be marooned without enough food. On that Easter Sunday, Courtauld wrote:

April 5th, Sunday. Now been here alone four months. No sign of relief. Only about a cupful of paraffin left and one or two candles. Have to lie in darkness almost all the time. Chocolate finished and tobacco almost (half a pouch left). What a change from last Easter at Falmouth or the one before at Abbotsbury! What wouldn't I give to be living either the one or the other again or to be with you, my dearest! But if it were not for having you to think about as I lie in the dark and cannot sleep, life would be intolerable. I wonder what you are doing. If I could be sure you were happy I would not mind. But I trust in God absolutely. I am sure He does not mean me to die alone here and never see you again. If I didn't I could not be singing your songs or keeping cheerful as I am. Oh, that fatal day 9 months ago [when the *Quest* sailed]. Why did I ever leave you?

On 10 April, after searching north and south, east and west for as long as they dared, Scott confessed, 'We have been beaten', and the party turned for base, hurrying so that the second relief party could set out as soon as possible.

The last entries in the diary deserve detailed quotation; most of them are quoted in *Portrait of an Ice Cap*. Even as one reads them it is difficult to appreciate that by now all was quite buried – 'house', courtyard, snow-houses, all but the Union Jack – under the winter snow; that Courtauld was lying in the dark, almost without fuel to make the liquid without which he could not live.

April 13th, Monday. Finished my last pipe of baccy today. There is now precious little left to live for. Can have light only for meals, which consist of porridge just warmed up, biscuit, cold pemmican and marg. This means that the house has got very cold and is covered with hoar frost up to the roof. Still impossible to get outside. Feet keep on freezing up and have to be always taking off socks and warming them with my hands. Hardly any paraffin left or candles. I suppose I shall soon be reduced to chewing snow. At present I am reduced to a pint of water a day and under a pound of food. I wonder if *Cariad* is cruising now. What wouldn't I give to be aboard her now and eating a beef and onion pudding! I would give an eye to be home now and with you, my own, and see yourself instead of only your poor old pipe for which I have no tobacco.

April 20th, Monday. Only one candle left. Hardly any paraffin. Lie in dark all day designing the ideal cruiser and the ideal meal. Left foot swelling up, hope it isn't scurvy.

April 26th, Sunday. Just six months since we left Base and started living on sledge rations. Been here about twenty weeks. Everything running out. Using last candle. Very little paraffin. What I shall do for drinking water I don't know. Only two more biscuits. In four days I officially run out of food but have a reserve, thank God, of pemmican and marg. Smoking tea as I have no fuel to cook it with.

May 1st, Friday. No sign of relief. Shall have to think of walking soon if I can get out. Biscuits finished, also candles. Am burning ski-wax for a light, but it makes mostly smoke. Have no sugar as the last tin is outside. Food has officially run out, but I still have a fair amount of essentials, though lemon juice is running low, which is pretty serious.

This is the last entry writt῀ while he was alone. The next, written on 6 May, reads:

Yesterday was the greatest day of my life. All Monday I kept on wondering what it was that May 5th should be famous for. I could not think of anybody's birthday or any event, so I decided it must be that the relief was going to arrive. Yesterday (May 5th) the primus gave its last gasp as I was melting water for the morning meal. I was lying in my bag after this so-called meal of a bit of pemmican and margarine and had just decided that I should have to start and walk back on June 1st if I could get out, when suddenly there was an appalling noise like a bus going by, followed by a confused yelling noise. I nearly jumped out of my skin. Was it the house falling in at last? A second later I realised the truth. It was somebody, some real human voice, calling down the ventilator. It was a wonderful moment. I could not think what to do or say. I yelled back some stuttering remarks that seemed quite futile for the occasion. 'Hooray,' they shouted. 'Are you all right?' 'Yes, thank God you've come. I am perfectly fit.' 'Thank God,' they said. It was Gino and Freddie; they were as relieved as I was. The whole world seemed turned inside out. At one moment I was lying in the dark wondering how ever I was going to see anybody again or ever get home, and, the next, home was in sight. . . .

Very soon Gino had smashed a hole in the roof and let in the blinding sunshine and blue sky, blinding even with dark snow-glasses on. The next moment they had dropped through the hole and we were grasping hands and thanking God that the job was done.

They pulled him out through the roof. Weak after nearly two months under the snow, he found that he could still ski halfway to the camp two miles away: a dry, warm tent, a roaring primus, food and light. Contrast, it has often been remarked, is a large ingredient of pleasure, but he found that he could eat very little, and did not try. Nor could he sleep at all that night, from excitement. Next morning after hot porridge they sledged back to the station to collect the valuables, and made a bonfire. 'To see them make a bonfire with a tin of paraffin – a tin I would have given a fortune for a day ago!' Then they started the journey home.

He made the diary entry for 6 May comfortably propped among sleeping bags as the sledge moved smoothly along. One man walked in front, and the last sledge took bearings, since all the flags had been buried. A level horizon circled them around: dazzling white snow beneath the burning blue sky. 'It is very like sailing across a dead white sea.' He exclaimed:

I was and still am unbelievably happy. – That my trust in God's goodness should have been so wonderfully justified and that now I could sledge comfortably back in the warm early summer and get back to good friends and food, friends whom I might never have seen again and then later in the summer to sail south and see M. again.

The journey back took five days and he was able to ride all the way, reading *The Count of Monte Cristo* in the sun. On 7 May a plane came over and dropped food, notes, sledging cases, 'almost on our unsuspecting heads'. These notes gave the first news of the alarm caused in England by the defeat of the first relief party and of the excitement aroused by the rescue expedition. It was a not unnatural alarm, but it was natural that he should pooh-pooh it:

Nothing the Base can do or say, or the Committee at home, can stop this absurd hysteria. However, now that they have seen us all coming out we hope that they will all go away. It really is too ridiculous when even the second relief only arrived five days late, and even then I had 30 lbs of food left which would have lasted another two months.

Perhaps he had forgotten in his relief how near to the edge he had gone. Certainly he recovered with remarkable speed. By the time they reached the base hut on the coast he was eating and sleeping normally, ready to enjoy social life. They tramped in at four a.m. on the 11th, Watkins shaved and carefully brushed as usual, to rouse the sleeping expedition mercilessly. The reunion was joyful. 'Then breakfast, hot porridge, real white bread and marmalade served by the [Eskimo] women' – how could one know that they taste so good? That same day, after he had been photographed and fed, had shaved and rested, Courtauld was out with Scott, scrambling on the mountainside of the rim, hunting ptarmigan for the pot.

But this was only a beginning. On 6 May he had written: 'Personally, once I get to Base I shall stay there. I have had enough of sledging, ice caps and boat journeys.' Yet in August we find him setting out, with Watkins and Lemon, on what proved an epic and hair-raising openboat journey of 600 miles, down the east coast and round the tip of Greenland. He reached England in November.

Byrd, after the relief of 11 August, 1934, stayed on at the shack with the relieving party, but in vastly altered circumstances: 'The two months that followed the tractor's coming were as pleasant as the others were miserable.' When he returned to Little America it was to find that, though he still commanded, there were now things that he could not do, which he was forced to entrust to men younger than himself. In his summing up he acknowledged that the polar station taught him two lessons: 'I did take away something that I had not fully possessed before: appreciation of the sheer beauty and miracle of being alive, and a humbler set of values. . . . So I say in conclusion: a man doesn't begin to attain wisdom until he recognises that he is no longer indispensable.'

Nobody can say what is the final impact of such experiences. Almost immediately other pictures obtrude on the mind, blurring the clear outline that had seemed to form itself 'out there'. We all know that 'if only I get out of here' feeling, and know too how vows made in time of stress are doomed by the nature of their making. Even the sense or hope of 'protection' which may cause non-praying people to pray and to draw strength, whether from above or from the hidden reservoir, can fade once the moment of crisis has passed. And even when the impact appears negative, we still do not know how personality would have developed, had no extremity arisen.

All we know is how people react *in* the ordeal. From what becomes of them afterwards we guess at the rest. It is not surprising that Augustine Courtauld accomplished his New Year resolutions of 31 December 1930. He married, happily. He bought the yacht *Duet*, of which he wrote later: 'She has proved, in the twenty-five years I have owned her, the perfect vessel.' He gave up large-scale exploration, but returned to the Greenland mountains with his wife in 1934. In the Second World War he found his most important job, with the Navy. His mind stayed young, he remained absurdly modest. Finally, throughout his life he held to those values which shine through the pages of the Ice Cap diary.

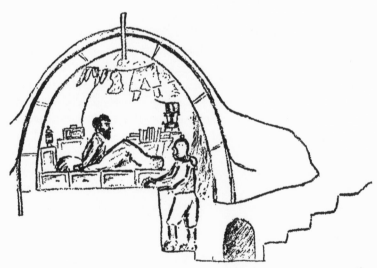

An Impression of Courtauld's Tent

7

Concentration Camp Ordeal: Maisie Renault

To survive any ordeal courage or 'guts' is the most obviously useful quality, but it has always been extremely hard to separate mental and physical resistance, courage of the mind and of the body. Tiira, some would say, needed physical courage to deal with sharks, mental courage to face an apparently endless succession of days alone. But the distinction blurs and becomes meaningless. Moral courage is perhaps more distinctive, if one uses the term in the sense of resistance to compulsions from other people. So far in this book the human forces have been, on the whole, on the side of the survivor; but at many periods in the history of nations men and women have had to face pressure on personality compared with which physical suffering took second place. Nowhere has the struggle of human beings to survive total destruction of their moral, mental and physical capacities been more starkly silhouetted than in the concentration camps of Nazi Germany, before and during the Second World War.

I am neither competent nor ambitious to write a history of the camps. Their literature is already vast, as any visitor to the Wiener Library in London will find. For the story of their structure and organisation one may go to books like *The Theory and Practice of Hell* by E. Kogon, or that amazing documentary, *Macht ohne Moral*.[1] I refer to the wider political and social implications of the camps, and to the make-up of the S.S., only in so far as they affect the survival problem, and particularly the survival of one victim. I would write more incisively if I had had the experience myself. Perhaps nobody has a right to generalize who has not. Yet it may be that the outsider is well placed to survey the whole scene from above, and to pounce on the significant details. These he will offer in a spirit of humility.

To generalise is dangerous. Each person who survived did so for a different reason, or rather complex of reasons. Broadly speaking, an inmate had to survive two types of pressure. First, obviously, comes extreme physical hardship and privation. On a diet almost devoid of calories one was expected to work for up to eighteen hours a day, to stand in rain or snow at roll-call without change of clothing, to sleep in sub-slum conditions, three or four in a bunk, and on top of this to endure beatings and whippings. Secondly, one had to withstand constant degradation at the hands of the S.S. In a grotesque and macabre way, many prisoners returned to the world of childhood. From the moment when, on entering, they were stripped naked for the showers, they were treated like dangerously irresponsible children. For this reason some preferred a beating to an ignominious slap on the face; others, on the other hand, were tempted to behave as they were treated. Moreover, the camps were a microcosm of Nazism in that they deliberately set out to destroy personality. To be a nonentity in a crowd gave one a chance of safety, and consequently every prisoner, at roll-call, would try to be in the centre and not at the edges of the parade. To be generous, to help others, was risky, because thereby one might draw down the wrath of the S.S. on a whole block. Men and women resigned themselves to being numbers, numbers attached to bodies disposable in life as in death.[2] The S.S. aimed to achieve disintegration of personality by torture, by the unpredictability of punishment, by deliberately

1. By Reimund Schnabel; a compilation of documents and photographs from S.S. and other official sources.

2. A German psychiatrist, Dr W. von Baeyer, observed at a recent conference that the hopelessness induced by becoming a nameless number affected prisoners more than hunger or torture, and that the results of this '*Herabwürdigung unter ein Niveau*' linger as a depressive factor in their personalities today.

fostering bad feeling among prisoners, by allowing no outlet for individual choice, by destroying the will to live. The 'Musulmen',[1] wandering hopeless and vacant round the camps until they died, were a symbol of Nazi victory.

Now, many people survived the physical stresses who did not survive the moral pressures. Indeed, they survived physically just because they made so great a compromise with conscience that in the end they were aping the very S.S. who were responsible for their plight. In his study of mass psychology, *The Informed Heart*, to which I have already referred, Bruno Bettelheim shows how, besides the *kapo* (prisoner in authority), who was usually a condemned criminal anyway, many others came to identify their interests with those of the Nazis and to accept Nazi standards. Taking it out on weaker prisoners, they ensured their own survival by ingratiating themselves, as they hoped, with their masters. The prisoner hierarchy could be helpful, and many were saved through the courage of its members, but it was a system that often demanded the death of conscience for the sake of life, and the accepters of that way out do not count as survivors in my sense. One part of them had died and could never be restored. A distinguished Resistance agent, who was himself a concentration camp inmate, put it that all survivors were not the heroes pictured in popular imagination, just *because* they survived. Good, bad and indifferent survived, and many of the indifferent had in the process become bad rather than good.

> And a thousand thousand slimy things
> Lived on; and so did I.

This may seem a harsh judgment, passed by one who had been through the mill himself, yet the point is valid. One could not get by without a certain minimal lowering of standards; indeed, that was part of the necessary process of adaptation. The mortality rate among new prisoners, many of whom could not adapt, was far higher than among the older inmates. One accepted fleas, was not choosy about

1. So called erroneously and callously because they seemed, like Muslims, resigned to their fate. They spent their last days in an almost serene state, among dreams and memories which no one could take from them.

food or friends, or squeamish over using fists to secure one's portion. The question which put itself was: need one lower standards the whole way? Bettelheim suggests that it was helpful to draw a line at the outset: 'Thus far I will go but no farther, or the life which I preserve will have lost its value'. This would mean that survivors who kept standards at a level fixed in their own minds 'survived' in a higher and quite different sense from those who adapted without reservations. Even among these 'good' survivors, of course, there were enormous differences of personality, since it is impossible to talk of any *general* standard. What was high for one would be low for another.

Is it possible then to find a person who survived physical and mental extremes and who came out with standards, which had been high before, maintained and perhaps even exalted? I believe so. I have chosen only one case out of several possibles even among my own acquaintance, because the canvas here will be more crowded than in earlier chapters; and I have chosen a woman, Maisie Renault, both because she has herself shown implicitly, in her story *La Grande Misère*[1], how moral fibre as well as body can survive, and because, being a woman and brutal behaviour by or towards women being especially repugnant, she the more poignantly underlines the twin problems of torment and temptation. She was a survivor in all senses.

We have seen that the survivor is not usually a type which would strike one in a crowd. Maisie Renault came of Breton stock, one of a large family of seven sisters (of whom the eldest died young) and three brothers. Being the eldest sister, she was the one who looked after the others, the one who, naturally, responded when an unpleasant job was going. In the summer of 1941 she quietly insisted on joining her brother 'Rémy's' underground network in Paris, where, as he records, she would sit typing the most dangerous letters as calmly as if they had been business missives. In his book *Courage and Fear* he tells the story of the arrest of Maisie and of Isabelle, at eighteen the youngest of all, on 13 June 1942. At Christmas 1943 five sisters, Madame Renault and

1. Published in France by Chavane, not available in English. I am also grateful for personal contact, and for the special help of her sister, Mrs R. F. Russell.

one of the brothers, Philippe, were all at Compiègne Prison. Later, Madame Renault, Hélène, Jacqueline and Madeleine were released, but Philippe was deported to the concentration camp of Neuengamme, and Maisie and Isabelle to Ravensbrück.

They had already been through two years of prison when on 14 August 1944 they had the shock of learning that they were to leave Romainville, whither they had been transferred, for Ravensbrück in Germany. The German warder, Kratz, walked up and down jangling his keys, announcing with joy, '*Nicht Messe, morgen. Alle mourir*' in a macabre mingling of languages. However, hopes were high, the Allies had already landed and were at Rambouillet, nobody believed that they would be away from home for long. Maisie, a devout Catholic, records how on that hot August afternoon, when they heard the news, a little Hungarian girl, pure of voice, burst into the *Ave Maria*. Moved to tears before the unknown, the women prayed together.

The trucks were crammed full. For six days and nights the train carried them like cattle through France, through Germany, to the little station of Fürstenberg which served Ravensbrück. On 21 August, 550 women, numb, dirty, dishevelled, breathed fresh air once more. Two hundred and fifty of these went on elsewhere. Of the remaining three hundred only seventeen were to survive to be liberated by the Swedish Red Cross. The prophecy of Kratz was largely to be fulfilled.

It was often by arbitrary, inconsequential frustrations that the S.S. started the break-up of personality, and they started even before the humiliating entry into camp life, which many found to be the most gruesome experience of all. Arriving at Fürstenberg at ten a.m., the prisoners had a long walk before they saw the camp before them. Inside the gate they waited, standing, as it were in the outer circle of Inferno, until their slight but precious baggage had arrived and was finally sorted. They waited on, for the promised showers, then, exhausted, they sat or lay on the black earth beside the ugly huts. At last they were told that it was too late to have showers that night, they must wait till morning, for until they were properly clean they could not have beds. The blankets came out, they huddled down and slept as well as they could on the churned ground in the glare of searchlights. Though it was summer, the night was cold.

They were roused by the routine siren at 3.30 a.m., the time when camp life started, the time when vitality is low. Anxious outsiders, they watched as S.S. and women guards moved about and the kitchen fatigue parties presented themselves. Then a whistle sounded the roll-call. In rows of five, perfectly ordered, the column of prisoners marched by from the direction of the Lagerstrasse, or Camp Street. This was the muster, whose purpose in theory was to decide the day's work. From the Punishment Block marched the ranks of the punished, compelled to sing German songs to cheerful airs, followed by ordinary prisoners in their striped dresses. After them Maisie made out 'columns of wretched creatures in rags, many of them barefoot, with spades or picks on their shoulders. The sick, haggard and stumbling, returned to their blocks supporting each other.' Last came the knitters (those not fit for anything else) and 'disposable' inmates. The women guards cracked their whips, blows rained and cries sounded from the laggards. Like Dante's chastised sinners, some were slow in entering Hell.

Maisie saw degradation and anticipated it for herself. A cart of sewage, pulled by women in traces, was being pushed by others from behind. When the sewage overspilled, those behind were covered with it. At last Maisie's group was allowed to pass to the showers, where they were stripped naked, examined – a searing humiliation – and passed to the 'hairdresser'. A Breton woman near them wept bitterly when her head was shaved; Maisie and Isabelle escaped this indignity.

The shower did them good, but after it they were told that their baggage would not be returned to them after all: another pinprick. Instead, an odd assortment of clothes was issued for the time being, their own being labelled and carefully put away. They tried to comfort poor old Madame B., who loudly bemoaned the loss of the Breton costume which she had worn all her life.

Now they filed off in rows of five, as prisoners. Again like Dante's Hell, Ravensbrück was entered by a not unpleasing limbo. The Lager-strasse had been nicely laid out and planted with flowers, a show-piece. But, penetrating beyond it, Maisie realised, aghast, the squalor that would be theirs. Here the flower-beds were choked with filth. In front of the dusty grey blocks, their windows broken and stuffed with cardboard, crowds of Russians and gypsies sat delousing themselves in the sun. In common with many new arrivals at the camps she found herself looking at the scene as if it were not real, as if she were spectator of a fantasy. Besides, hope vanquished premonition by assuring her that it would not be for long. At the showers, when they had been issued with a tiny piece of soap to last for two months, they had laughed. Were not the Allies at Rambouillet? Had they known it, by the end they would accept the filth as a commonplace.

In all her time at Ravensbrück, Maisie recalled later, she never saw birds fly over the camp.

Newcomers were held in quarantine for a week. This period was not too unpleasant, for the friends from the French Resistance network were together, forming the nucleus of a French group among other political prisoners, prostitutes, criminals; all jostling for the midday soup and eating it where they stood, while the sun blazed and coal-dust fluttered down into their bowls.

The dormitory looked clean, freshly scrubbed, with rows of beds divided by narrow alleys, but the bunks, in three tiers, measured less than three feet across, and there were only two among five. On the first day the friends were gathered on a bunk and chatting when they were interrupted by voices outside. Older inmates, friends from Romainville days, pressed against the window: a frightening procession of gaunt, grey faces, the eyes hollow and unnaturally large. Knowing how the new arrivals must have been robbed, they had brought little presents – a sweater, stockings, a pair of gloves – acquired at great cost. To a Frenchwoman the wardrobe is a symbol of self-expression; through it her personality shines out. By taking away their clothes the S.S. had already taken away something of their selves, as of course they intended. One recently married girl, robbed of her wedding ring, wound a thread of wool round her finger.

Small touches of individuality in clothes meant something in the fight to retain personality, yet at the same time, as has been emphasised, one of the defences of the prisoners was to lose themselves in the crowd, to be inconspicuous. There is a danger, Bettelheim puts it, that self-effacement may not only destroy the very self one wishes to preserve, but also remove the ability to take those quick decisions which from time to time are necessary to safety. Maisie soon learned the art of being inconspicuous, on the first morning of work when, without breakfast, they were marched outside camp to load waggons with sand. One did just enough to pass muster, without being conspicuous either for too much or too little zeal. One worked when somebody passed, otherwise leaned on a spade to conserve energy. The quick decision came later. In the afternoon, when she was trying to lose herself in a crowd of Russians to avoid another work party, she needed decisive strength to escape a woman guard who clutched at her in the mêlée by the hair.

On 4 September rumour ran that the French were to be transferred. All were ordered for inspection outside the Infirmary. There they were stripped and left to stand naked the whole morning. In such circumstances one either felt intensely humiliated and showed it, or succeeded in looking through the S.S. as if they did not exist. Maisie recalled how at Compiègne old Madame Tillion, having risen late and being clad only in a nightdress, was warned, 'But, Madame, the corporal will be coming!'

'My dear,' the reply came with the sweetest smile, 'for me a German is nothing more than a chair.'

The morning grew warm, they were tired. Bodies sagged, damp flesh against flesh. At last, one by one, they were passed into the next courtyard. Here the medical personnel, joking in their direction behind monocles, handed them on to nurses, who inspected hands and teeth. Next day they were submitted to a similar, but more intimate and distressing inspection.

After this inspection all the younger French girls, except for Maisie, Isabelle and Lotte von Zeissl, a Viennese, were transferred to Torgau. The names of Maisie and Isabelle had been spotted by a French friend in the Works Office as marked with the sinister red sign which meant 'Not to be let out of sight'. She had removed them from the transfer list with the intention of saving them.[1]

Those who went had to give up their few belongings, laboriously acquired by exchange of bread or other valuables. All these articles,

1. One instance of the usefulness of the camp hierarchy.

along with the baggage of newcomers, went to the 'shops' run by the prisoners, in which a continual barter took place. The manual workers had little to offer, but the cooks who kept something from the rations, those in the Works Office who could juggle with names, the nurses who could steal drugs – all these were buyers. Thus, beside the miserable ulcered bodies in rags could be seen plump, well fed women wearing silk frocks of elegant design. Maisie found one of these eating her soup with a crested silver spoon and drinking coffee in secret from a delicate porcelain cup.

After the transport had gone Maisie and the few remaining French were transferred to Block 23, far dirtier and even more crowded than Block 24. Nothing covered the rotting straw palliasses, three slept in each bunk and only manual workers were allowed blankets. The French found themselves submerged among Russians, Czechs, Poles. Dark figures roamed at night in search of loot. Even though one used bags and shoes as pillows, objects might slip through to the bunk below and be snapped up at once. One morning a girl who had gone to sleep with her hands clasped round her spoon woke to find the hands still clasped, but the spoon no longer there.

As if to make thieving simpler, dysentery was taking its toll. Visits had to be paid in the night to the primitive latrines. To reach them one walked on a carpet of slime, and, as shoes had also to be used for pillows, the stench at night pervaded air, clothes, everything. In the daytime the *Waschraum* (washroom) became a scene of confusion. Some inmates did not bother to remove fleas, and spread the vermin by piling their clothes indiscriminately. Towels had long since been stolen and soap had disappeared. Naked living bodies, pitted with flea-bites or ulcers, jostled above the dead, who lay at the side, splashed and ignored, waiting to be taken away.

During September the mornings became colder and it was now impossible to avoid 'Gracious', the Block Commander, so nicknamed for her whip and bullying ways. She it was who devised the special torture of shutting the block doors after morning roll-call, thus keeping the prisoners on their feet from five a.m. until midday. They could not now avoid the labour units: the useless, weary work with the sand went on. Maisie and Isabelle indulged continually in shared daydreams, one of the sure antidotes against reality. They made up menus, recipes, furnished a house from top to bottom. . . . At last the sun would pierce the chilling September mist, they were warm again and midday had drawn an hour nearer.

In the *Waschraum* Maisie and Isabelle met Madame Melot and her daughter Suzanne. They were inseparable, and the well-brought-up Suzanne did not hesitate to smack or punch in order to win her mother a stool, or to fight the camp police (themselves inmates) if this would get her off work. Bettelheim found that close intimacy was a dangerous defence in the camps, because prisoners had too much bile to be continuously good company as friends, and also because separation, if it came, was all the harder to bear. In this last respect Maisie and Isabelle were lucky. They stayed together, apart from one or two agonising moments, the whole time; for Maisie, the elder sister used to looking after the others, the need to protect formed a major incentive to survive. Isabelle would probably have been less affected had they been separated. On the other hand, the case of the Melots underlines Bettelheim's point, as we shall see.

Twice in one week Maisie fainted at roll-call. On the insistence of Isabelle her temperature was taken, and was thought sufficiently high for her to be admitted to the Infirmary with acute dysentery and fever. Nobody took notice of her on the first day; on the second she received a dose of tannin.[1] Isabelle succeeded in visiting her window daily.

The first night Maisie heard screams, which she was told came from the lunatics. She saw them next day: grotesque forms in single cotton garments, skeleton-thin, heads shaven, continually fighting. Then one night she heard an unaccustomed noise outside. A shutter had been left open, and by the light of the moon, just then piercing the clouds, she saw a lorry standing parked in the roadway. Suddenly a door opened, and the mad women, shivering in their single garments, terrified by the dogs and by the massive silhouettes of the S.S., were hounded into the waiting lorry. With their whips and black hoods the women guards looked like Angels of Death. Above the din rose the

1. A very poor remedy, as a doctor comments, which one would not expect to receive outside a concentration camp.

scream of one old woman: 'I'm not mad! I'm not mad!' But she too was borne off, and silence followed. The places of these were soon taken by others.

Like Suzanne Melot, Maisie was intensely, fundamentally devout; yet, if she had turned the other cheek and accepted the blows that rained, she would have died. 'Maisie is a fighter,' her sister Elisabeth once said, and she needed her pugnacity in the days that followed, when after a short stay she was discharged, the fever having gone but the dysentery remaining. She knew that she was too weak to work and might become more seriously ill if she did. With Isabelle she dodged from block to block as work contingents were collected, often having to fight to escape. 'We became past mistresses in the arts of kicking and punching.' Then came an even sterner struggle. Three hundred women from the death camp of Auschwitz were announced: there they were, one evening, a wave held from breaking only by the outstretched arms of the Block Commander. She lowered her arms. There was a single rush, the battle for berths was joined. 'They leaped upon us. Kicking, striking, pulling hair, they tried to throw us out. We defended ourselves with the energy of despair.' Then the lights went out. To cries of 'Help!' or 'Save me!' the battle continued in the dark.

'At Auschwitz,' one of the new arrivals explained coolly, 'we never knew whether we'd be alive the next day. We're going to sleep tonight. We may have to kill someone, but we're going to sleep.'

The fighters were women, many of them mothers. Some of the older Frenchwomen gave up the struggle and lay on the floor. Later, it was found that some women had died, strangled by the invaders.

'*Achtung!*' It was 'Gracious', and she had come to search. Every small, secretly treasured object was hastily hidden. The search was conducted, and 'Gracious' left.

'*Achtung!*' There she was again, only a moment later. Everything that had been hidden had now been replaced, an easy prey. Soon she had taken everything. In a few minutes she was back again.

'Achtung!'

These pinpricks, irrational and unexpected, wore upon the nerves of prisoners, as was intended. They were all desperately tired and in October the elder Frenchwomen of Maisie's acquaintance were already beginning to die. Madame Elbard died during roll-call, then Madame Boulloch. Mademoiselle Vachon, suffering from dysentery, was not admitted into the Infirmary because of her age. Her palliasse had been removed because she fouled it, and she was denied water. She died quietly in the night.

'Il faut s'entr'aider, c'est la loi de nature.' So sang La Fontaine, though he cannot have envisaged either the snow basin of Haramosh or the Infirmary of Ravensbrück. One evening Maisie and Isabelle risked everything to visit their friend Denise Fournaise, who was not strong and who had been taken ill. She was so desperate, crying 'Don't leave me!' when time was up, that they took even greater risks the next evening, climbing over the sill to come right to her bed. She was a little better, having had an injection at last, but the day after, to their horror, she had disappeared. Only later they learned that she had been moved to the Camp Hospital Block.

Sympathy here proved stronger than the urge towards self-survival. As on K2, on Haramosh, the two ran counter to each other, yet the former strengthened the latter. The few words of comfort to Denise seemed worth the risk. And by a curious accident this fellow-feeling, which might have destroyed them, saved their lives later. When the Torgau transfer returned, much better fed and looked after than the Ravensbrück inmates, they immediately volunteered for another transfer. Maisie and Isabelle would have volunteered too, but stayed, to be near Denise. As things turned out, the next transfer, to Klein Königsberg, was a death-trap from which few returned.

October dragged to a close; with the cold the elderly died apace. This was no world for them, yet it tore the heart to see them go. Poor Madame Raspilaire, who took a certain number of turns round the court each day to keep in form for her son, a great walker, found that she had to cheat on the last turn, shortening it a little. Then she weakened to immobility and died. The fires of the crematorium rose higher as the weeks went by.

One of the defence mechanisms of prisoners was to take a pride in working hard, thus re-establishing dignity for themselves and also, secretly, feeling a sense of superiority over the idle S.S. The Polish women, '*d'une force herculéenne*', were of this order. The objection to that solution was that it often meant working well at jobs which helped the Nazi war effort. When, therefore, at the end of October Maisie and Isabelle found themselves unwilling members of a work shift engaged on extracting pine-roots from the ground, they felt no scruple at taking things as easily as possible. Thanks to Hilde, a francophile *kapo* imprisoned for being mistress to a Frenchman, they were kept warned of the approach of guards. They received extra midday soup and in the evening sausage, with which Suzanne, forced at last to work, could feed her mother. The great pine-woods hinted at freedom and beauty, in contrast to the camp.[1] The friends were together. When the sun rose and the cold left them, they spoke of music, books, and always of food, concocting delicious recipes. In the evenings they would bring back sprigs for those confined to the knitting room.

These were their happiest days, but they came to an end when Hilde was betrayed and dismissed, and the informer took her place. The rain beat down and they took the midday soup standing in a derelict hut, shivering in clammy clothes which they had no hope of changing. In these conditions, given the will, antibodies seem to multiply indefinitely; the pneumonia which they had expected passed them by.

Meanwhile, the flirtatious S.S. having gone, the women guards, prowling with dogs, made it impossible to shirk the heavy work of hoisting, without ropes, great roots from holes six feet deep. On 10 November the first snow fell. Clogs had been issued, and they had to stamp them every few steps to shake off the clinging masses of snow. The pines rose mournful and oppressive in their white coats. While the prisoners shivered, the guards toasted bread at huge fires and heaped it high with butter. At evening the columns would stagger back along the road, carrying the heavy soup tureens, passed by lorries that were empty. Useless effort, useless torment, and, when they were back, an ice-cold, overcrowded dungeon.

1. A strong feeling for beautiful things was an asset in that it gave an incentive to live, to enjoy them again; but ugliness was correspondingly more repulsive.

One evening they were ordered to a new block, which turned out to be even colder and dirtier than the others. All the panes were missing; some frames were stuffed with cardboard, some were not. Only a few beds near the windows remained empty, and those had no palliasses. Looking for a berth in the interior, Maisie asked a woman lying there if she could help. No answer. Then a voice from alongside:

'Can't you see she's dead? They'll take her away by tomorrow evening.'

That night they hardly slept, lying near the windows in their wet clothes.

It has been said already that to be too intimate with another was not necessarily a help. Even between the sisters there were periods of estrangement. One suffered from cystitis, an inflammation of the bladder, the other from dysentery, and in the night each was in the way of the other. Isabelle was becoming restless at the constant solicitude of Maisie, and clearly irritated, one night, when in climbing down from their bunk Maisie dropped a shoe, which was immediately stolen. Next morning she had to go to work with one bare foot.

Maisie was painfully conscious that she was responsible for their presence here. On the day of their departure from Romainville the French Commandant had told her that, if she asked it, she and Isabelle could stay in France. She had refused, because she had felt that her job was to help the older women who were going. Therefore Isabelle was here because of her. And now, as dysentery and the cold drained her strength, she was frightened to think that she would become a burden. Isabelle had the right to be irritated.

Straight brutality was easier to bear than mistrust. One day a new woman guard decided to halt the column on the march and search everybody. She found a handsome S.S. shirt on Maisie, bought at the shop against bread. (By Maisie's standard to take an S.S. shirt was permissible, to take another prisoner's would not have been.) The guard lost her temper, punched the face in front of her until blood poured from the mouth. Obstinacy, pride, scorn, what is it that holds back the

Concentration camp inmates

Maisie Renault,
photographed in
Sweden shortly
after Ravensbrück

Maisie Renault in
1948

tears which might double the blows rained down? Stripped half-naked in the snow, Maisie was threatened with the dreaded 'Bunker', death-hole of punishment – a threat which, fortunately, nobody troubled to follow up.

Sometimes they noticed – 28° or – 30° Centigrade on the ther-mometer of the main gate. The women guards were cold despite their fires; to keep warm they prowled round the prisoners, who needed no whip but the cold to keep them working. During each midday halt the ground which they had dug froze again. Suzanne Melot, separated in the daytime from her mother by the change of blocks, looked grey and haggard, with great purple patches under the eyes. Isabelle had become desperately thin, but once, seeing that Maisie had not the strength to wield her pick, took it from her and broke the iced ground. In this small act they rediscovered their affection, and for the moment forgot the cold.

It was at night, at the hour of the first siren, that the cold struck worst, when they were snatched back from oblivion into the horror of living and scrambled pell-mell through the doors, a human sea, to regroup at the appointed place, each trying to be somewhere in the centre of the crowd, away from the exposed edges. As they waited, numb and swaying, through the icy hours of the dreary roll-call, Suzanne would whisper Mass, while Isabelle gave the responses and Maisie said *Ave Marias* for each of her family who had died. After roll-call came the work, more loathsome each day. Once Maisie slipped on ice and knocked herself out, but the whip brought her round and she struggled up to collect her faggots.

Now that parcels were arriving occasionally, one could see friendship in operation. Maisie received none, but Denise, now recovered, shared hers, and Isabelle too. Apart from these, the receivers of parcels usually formed cliques of the fortunate, sworn to give nothing to those who had nothing.

As truly as of Ensio Tiira it can be said that these women should have died long ago. Many did die, and often they were the strong ones, like '*la grande* Jeanne', who had worked with them in the forest. Denise seemed at the end of her strength and likewise Madame Melot, only able now to see her daughter in the evenings. Mlle Talet, a saintly woman loved by them all, died without the sacrament for which she had longed. A whole block was set aside for typhus cases, now numerous, and they all died. Prisoners loaded the shrivelled corpses, each numbered in violet ink on the breast, into the waiting lorries, where they lay in fantastic poses.

One day a decision had to be made. Many were giving up the cold, body-breaking work in the forest for a comfortable place in the big machine factory of Siemens near by. Because they were declining so fast, Maisie suggested that to survive they should do the same. Isabelle revolted.

'If we were put there, it would be different. But to volunteer for a war factory – I couldn't!'

The elder sister in France has authority. Maisie used it, pointing out what a grief it would be to their mother if they did not return, how they could sabotage the work once inside. Isabelle acquiesced, but only in order to stay with her. Next day they placed themselves at the spot where they could be picked up for factory transport. At the last minute, before the lorries appeared, Maisie whispered, 'What are we doing here? Let's hide!'

The thought that they would be making V-1 bombs for the Nazis had overpowered her.

The year was near its end. To a Catholic especially, Christmas is a time of church service, of communal prayer, of festal adornment. The S.S. too loved Christmas, and saw nothing incongruous in rigging and decorating an enormous tree in the middle of a concentration camp. The year before, Maisie was told, all the prisoners had had to stand the whole day in front of it without food. This year one or two tiny trees smuggled in from the forest, the odd parcel, a relaxation of vigilance because the guards were enjoying themselves, made it a more tolerable Christmas. They exchanged seasonal wishes and sat nibbling fragments of biscuit, a shared parcel, but the suicide of a Pole, who hanged herself from homesickness, and the news of German advances in the west formed a sombre backcloth to their day. The outward festivity of Christmas seemed a mockery.

The year 1944 went out like a bad candle.

The survival situation catches us with our defences down. We have seen how many of those whom the psychologists might have pronounced good survivors go under, while other, unlikely, candidates shine out with a new light. Three strands formed the life-line for Maisie Renault. The first, religious faith, does not necessarily point the way to survival. If you view the next world as a better place, then there is some reason for going there as soon as possible. Faith might not help you to survive, but it helped you to live with dignity. By giving comfort, through the release and repose of one part of the mind, it could in some people create a strength which prolonged life. It could equally well promote a willingness to die, and to die well, as in the case of the nun who substituted herself for a prisoner walking to the gas chamber. The second strand was an obstinate hope that, whatever the appearances, the Allies would come through and the camps be broken up in the end. With this strand went the 'fighting spirit' already noted in Maisie. The third strand was woven of her rediscovered relation with Isabelle, and the elder sister's need to look after and protect the younger. For others, too, she was 'the leader' (a characteristic inherited from her mother). A leader looks after others and has no time to worry about herself. A leader does not die, unless murdered.

1945. They exchanged greetings, but in their hearts many did not expect to see the end of it. However, on 12 January, Maisie and Isabelle found themselves again assigned to Block 15, the French block, cleaner than the rest. '*Nous nous sentons en famille.*' A friend had bought them nightdresses at the market, and for the first time since entering Ravensbrück they changed for the night. They were even spoiled with sleeping sacks and a blanket. Only Suzanne, her head now shaven because she no longer had the strength to fight the vermin, had a hard time. On the first night Maisie found her in the *Waschraum*, on a stool. Her bedfellows, finding her verminous, had thrown her out. By dint of blows Maisie succeeded in reinstating her to cries of indignation and 'Ssh!' Some minutes later there were more cries. Suzanne had been expelled again, her belongings scattered and lost. She begged to be allowed to stay in the *Waschraum*, and passed the rest of the night there on two stools. Leaving her, Maisie could see that she was praying.

It was all like a nightmare return to school. Sometimes the whole block was punished for the fault of one; no midday soup or a full day's work on Sunday. Soon the easier time in Block 15 ended, and they were transferred to the hideous Block 27. Suzanne, now a walking dummy, lost the last shred of interest in life around when she learned that her mother was to be transferred to the *Jugendlager*, or 'Youth Camp', ironic name for the separate quarters of those doomed on account of their age. In effect these two died when they parted, with heart-breaking tears, on the morning of 29 January. They had been too close to one another to survive separation. Madame Melot died that very evening, on the way to the showers. Her daughter, ignorant of this, lingered a little longer, eyes red with tears. From now on she became a 'Musulman', wandering about, not bothering to wipe the blood off her face if she fell, or her nose when it dripped. Even Maisie had to master a strong feeling of repugnance. Suzanne's one flicker of pleasure came when she heard from a nurse the pious lie that the *Jugendlager* was a place of rest and comfort for the aged, but she cannot really have believed it. She walked a few days more and then, having long refused food, was admitted to the Infirmary and died on 7 February. Maisie realised how near she herself might be to the same fate when one evening, much later, Isabelle was not called into the block with the others. She felt her mind beginning to crack under the anxiety. Suddenly the door opened and there was Isabelle. Somebody had forgotten her number, it was as simple as that. But the moral was plain: it is dangerous to survival to be dependent.

Air-raid warnings multiplied, yet to those who had not lost the conviction of Allied victory their inconvenience was welcome. During alarms the 'guinea pigs', usually pretty young Polish girls selected for vivisection experiments, used to escape and hide. In the daytime they were seen about, hobbling on crutches. Time and use harden an outer crust; Maisie became accustomed even to the sight of these most pitiful of all Nazi victims.

Now the food became scarcer than ever; *ersatz* coffee was substituted for soup in the evenings and the bread did not arrive until late at night. Once, going to barter milk against bread for the sick friend of a friend, Maisie was almost defeated by temptation. Why not take the smallest sip on the way back – a little commission? She did not know the woman, after all. She told herself that if the passageway was free, she would not drink; if it was full, she would. It turned out to be conveniently full, but she reached the dormitory without having touched the milk.

Intimate friends would quarrel over a bone, while behind them the prostitute Hélène sat eating succulent slices of roast meat.

The survivors of Klein Königsberg had now returned, and were lodged in even worse conditions, under squares of canvas stretched between blocks, with almost no food. They told a story of killing work on ice-bound, gluey plains exposed to the winds. Many had died by the time the rumour of approaching Russians put the camp in consternation and sent the S.S. flying. Immediately there was a raid on stores, which some French P.O.W.s from near by joined, but the rumour proved to be false and the S.S. returned to interrupt the orgy. The men were shot, the terrified women flogged and driven back to Ravensbrück, many dying on the way.

'I demand a prayer for the extermination of the German race,' one of the listeners said.

The others agreed. They had lost the power to pardon.

On 13 February, quite unexpectedly, a large convoy was chosen and, after a day of anxious waiting, bundled into trains at Fürstenberg. They passed a night of crowded confusion, unable to move yet forced to do so by their ailments, which drove them to the closets. They had received an extra bread ration, but Maisie was too thirsty to eat. In the dark, unable to get back to her place, she found herself among Russians and a bitter fight followed for the bread. At last, in the morning, they arrived. To their disgust they were only thirty miles from Ravensbrück, at Rechling. However, everybody said that this was a very agreeable small camp, that the Commandant was horrified at their appearance and determined to look after them well.

During the first day they were left alone, and things seemed none too bad. Then they were set to work on a trench and the groups were again split up so that the French were no longer together. They had a taste of things to come when, at midnight, the hour of deepest sleep, the whole camp was startled out of bed with the bellowed order of 'Showers! Showers!' Whipped out into the night, they were marched at quick pace for over a mile, kept waiting in the darkness, then led to showers hardly tepid with no towels provided. Their group was forced to wait again outside, cold and wet and convulsively shivering in the dark, until the next had finished. When they arrived back, some of Maisie's things, left under her palliasse, had been stolen. Isabelle's, which she had taken to the showers, had already disappeared.

This arbitrary and pointless operation gave the lie to the benevolent nature of the Commandant. Next morning the five French found themselves marched off on a work detail, to dig a hole supposedly to lodge an aeroplane. (Holes would be abandoned the next day, and others started. This seemed to worry nobody so long as prisoners were unpleasantly occupied.) The hours dragged wearily, backs and arms ached, minds fixed themselves upon the vision of rest and soup. Midday came at last, the sirens sounded, they laid down their spades with relief, but the S.S. pounced upon them: '*Los! Los!*' At this camp, they learned, the 'midday' soup was not distributed till four p.m., when they returned. The siren was for the luncheon of the S.S., eaten near by and smelling delicious.

Anything to pass four hours! They talked of travel, of home, boats, little thatched cottages by the sea with flowering gardens. They chose and furnished a house, spoke of the friends they would invite, of the menus they would give. At long last the final whistle sounded, and a cold barrack and a washroom in which the water refused to flow welcomed them. The fleas were worse than at Ravensbrück.

An interest in others, whether of an objective or sympathetic sort, helped one to forget one's own plight. Isabelle undertook to look after the ageing Jeannot, while Maisie cared for Denise, who was by now very frail. The work had now changed to gardening, since the Commandant had decided to have a fine garden round his house. Denise's thin fingers could hardly carry the great lumps of turf from field to house.

It was unsafe to shirk jobs, since the many gypsies at Rechling were always ready to turn informer. They also stole, and a stolen bowl meant no soup. Sometimes they upset the tureen fighting for more. And the soup, now given to the Hungarian Jews to distribute, was so thin that the Ravensbrück food seemed by comparison ample. This was starvation level.

It is comparatively easy to live on very little, but not to do hard work on very little. For a fortnight they marched seven miles out each day, to collect and carry back on their shoulders four-foot sections of young pine trees. Prisoners fought for the thinner sections and they arrived back after dark, arms and shoulders numb, tired beyond caring. As the work advanced the logs became thicker, until it took two to carry them. Pairs were arranged irrespective of height. If one slipped, she lay unable to rise until beaten into it. Denise tired, sickened, and was sent to the Infirmary. Isabelle, hardly able to walk, made plans for next Christmas as they staggered along, escaping the present. Maisie, excused work because of a temperature, was still unable to give up for fear that this would separate them for ever. Fear ruled them: fear of separation, of theft, of violence. Maisie fought a Russian *kapo*, who tried to delouse her naked in the *Waschraum*, and on another occasion fainted from a kick on the head by a Pole annoyed at the conversation below her bunk.

One day Denise departed smiling on a lorry, bound, as she was told, for hospital treatment at Ravensbrück. Hope seldom learns. Nobody ever discovered what became of the lorry and its load.

Not the least danger to the prisoners came from their own side's air attacks. On one occasion Allied planes made a fierce dive-bombing attack on the air field. As they took shelter, Maisie noted that she did not feel any fear, only intense joy at the noise and smell of burning. Some prisoners and guards were killed. Arriving back at the camp, exhausted, they had hardly lain down before they were hustled back to the airstrip to fill in the craters. They were back again at dawn the next day.

On 13 April, after two more days of harassing work on the airstrip, it was suddenly announced that Rechling was to be evacuated. Rumour had it that the French prisoners would be released. They returned in lorries to Ravensbrück, and though a characteristic reception did not seem to augur well, the evacuation saved their lives. In a few days more at Rechling they would have died.

These were the days of the final breakdown of German resistance to incessant bombing and the movement of Allied armies from west and east. Everybody knew that peace was now a matter of days or weeks. Count Bernadotte of Sweden was already busy arranging the repatriation of prisoners through the Red Cross. Because they might thereby ease their own predicament later, the German authorities were proving amenable to these advances, despite the complications and risks. This explained why, on the morning of the 24th, the Commandant himself and a whole staff of medical officers appeared at the showers and set about inspecting each woman. Those who passed, so the rumour ran, would be released.

Waiting in their lines, they wondered who would be rejected. Disease cases? Shaven heads? Maisie and Isabelle were all right on that score. One sick woman in front of them was rejected. Jeannot, Isabelle, Lucienne Dixon, the American, all passed. Maisie, trying to look well and cheerful, made to follow. A hand seized her, pushed up her chin and revealed the swollen, ravaged face. Rejected. Isabelle, finding an empty space beside her, turned round and tried to go back, but was thrust away. Maisie had time to call, 'Kiss Mother for me!' then she too was pulled back in the opposite direction.

The officials at the showers continued their inspection, unmoved. Maisie and the ten other rejects dragged themselves slowly across the square, conscious that they had heard their death sentence. On the way they met Lotte von Zeissl from the Works Office.

'Where are the others?' Lotte asked.

'They're over there. We've been separated. I'm to go to the Infirmary.'

Lotte winced. 'Risk anything, but don't go there!' She spoke quickly, fearfully, then was gone.

There remained only one possible way of avoiding the gas chamber. Maisie turned slowly and approached the massive backs of the inspecting officers, still intent on their work. She prayed, 'God! Don't let them turn round!' A glance to both sides, a few swift steps, and she was among the ranks of those who had been passed. 'Isabelle, it's me!' Isabelle turned, saw her, burst into tears.

Had she been spotted, she would have been shot outright. There is a lot of luck in survival.

In the showers, where they were kept waiting, they were able for the first time to meet old friends, who were horrified at the blackened faces and wild, feverish eyes of those who had come from Rechling. The talk flowed all day until, in the evening, they were told that they would not be leaving until tomorrow. In the block, packed in a bunk with Lucienne, Maisie and Isabelle made plans and resolutions, like children. 'We shall never quarrel again. . . . We shall make pilgrimages. . . . We shall devote our lives to the happiness of others.'

Next morning, however, a new list awaited them and these three found themselves eliminated after all, Lucienne as an American, Maisie and Isabelle by special order from Berlin. Disappointment overwhelmed their resistance, which had been stretched tight in the last days. They had no strength or will to do more than lie, in a block of kindly Poles who looked after them. Lucienne and Maisie, both suffering from unsteady heart, were lucky to be supplied, through a friend, with cardiasol. Isabelle's throat tormented her, so that she could hardly swallow. A Canadian food parcel had been given to them, but the rich food aggravated their dysentery. Everyone knew that the Allied armies must now be near, but that did nothing to ease their fevered anxiety. Might not the S.S. exterminate them all, just to stop them from talking?

April 22. 'All Frenchwomen to the Lagerstrasse. General departure.' This was it! They were formed into a column and rapidly marched to the main square. As they drew near, Isabelle whispered, 'They've got lists again!' Officers read out the names, no longer numbers, of those rejected. Sure enough, they heard their own names, and were pushed aside once more. They drew back, now in the deepest despair.

Isabelle whispered, 'Let's get back in the ranks! We haven't got our numbers any more, they can't recognise us.'

Maisie, conscience-torn, objected, 'There can only be a certain number of places in each car. We'll be pushing off the last two. You go if you like.'

'If you stay I stay. But we're wrong.'

Isabelle looked really ill. Though they did not know it, she was suffering from diphtheria.

The Commandant explained politely that they were being kept as hostages, and ordered another food parcel to be given to them, but they were past caring for food. It did not help to hear from Lotte that several lorries had gone off with empty places, when those chosen failed to take them. Maisie's sacrifice of them both had been in vain. In the *Waschraum*, among the mud and water, Maisie noticed something glittering. It was a medallion of the Virgin. For the first and only time she burst into tears.

April 23. Throughout the camp there was great agitation, as the women guards wandered here and there, disorientated. The Allies, it was said, had reached Berlin. Through an interpreter the hostages were asked if they would answer for the Commandant's past behaviour when the time came for them to be questioned by the Allies. They refused, but, reckoning that their refusal was dangerous, decided to slip into any lorry that they saw going out. The first lorry, full of Jewesses, seemed too risky. At about three o'clock in the afternoon the hostages were told to present themselves once more at the showers. Here they again waited a long time. At last two officers appeared, one of them, they noted with dismay, the brutal Pflaum, the officer responsible for the choice of work units. Still in prison clothes they passed the great gate and were led down the road along the lakeside. To the left lay the gas chambers that had claimed so many victims already. To the right they could see a large group of people on the skyline.

Where the roads parted, they were halted. The interpreter waved towards the right.

'You are free.'

.   .   .   .   .

Over an 'immense picnic' their freedom was underlined by the behaviour of the dreaded women guards, now wandering aimlessly from group to group. 'You will tell them, won't you, that we didn't treat you too badly?' they pleaded.

Soon the smart lorries arrived and an officer descended, to be greeted by a transport of gratitude.[1] They set off on the drive across a Germany still fraught with danger from Allied bombardment, and reached the frontier of Denmark. Everywhere delighted welcome, fresh bread, hot coffee, real milk.

Not until they sailed from Copenhagen were they truly free, for the first time in nearly three years. Isabelle, to Maisie's intense relief, had been pronounced out of danger from her diphtheria. Installed comfortably at the Musée de Malmö in Stockholm, they rested and at last, after a period of quarantine and careful diet, they were allowed by the doctors to eat to their hearts' content. Isabelle once disposed of fourteen cream cakes in a row.

Like John Brown, many prisoners died after rescue. Maisie Renault, after seeming to be fully recovered, fell ill with a virulent form of typhus and came very near death. Two operations were brilliantly performed in Sweden, and the second was successful beyond all expectation. Before it, she had received the last sacrament.

As Maisie recovered slowly, the pain of disease was replaced by a gnawing anxiety about the fate of her brother Philippe, at Neuengamme. Confusedly at first, then more clearly, the story came through that three troopships full of prisoners had been warned by the British, who believed them full of troops, to put back to Lübeck. One had returned, the others had not. The British had opened fire and sunk both ships. Philippe was on one of those which were sunk. For Maisie the return home was clouded by a sadness that need not have been.

Why did Maisie survive?

I remember an inmate of one of the eastern camps telling me of his mother, an elderly lady with a great concern for her ailments, who

1. Human nature is such that one of the younger girls could not help exclaiming, at sight of a handsome Swede, 'There's a *man* for you!'

visited spas and seldom rose before midday. But she had a mind of her own, and from the moment she found herself inside a camp never suffered a day's illness. She walked long distances daily to and from work, drank her soup, quarrelled and suffered with the rest. 'It was action and reaction,' he said. 'As simple as that. They wanted her to go one way, so she went the opposite. She was an obstinate old woman and she was damned if she was going to let the Nazis do her in.'

In some degree that obstinacy was shared by Maisie. Whether it be hate or faith, or both together, strong feeling fortifies: an *actively* strong feeling, something to oppose to the dead weight of persecution. Those who were resigned and charitable in an other-worldly way as Mlle Talet and the good nun whom Maisie lamented and admired, died. Their death was more beautiful than most lives, but they are dead.

Prayer, too, worked to her good. She seldom prayed directly for help; she prayed in the deeper sense of seeking communion with what is outside, with what beckons us – Christians and Communists, yes, and agnostics too – out of ourselves into other people, and from them towards the 'eternal mode' beyond. Sympathy with others, particularly – and here she was lucky – with her sister, persuaded her to the effort of survival. She endured, as did Marceline, in order not to let others die through her defection.

What other threads from earlier chapters here join in the strand? Discipline certainly, in that finer sense of self-discipline. Maisie refused to drink the milk she was carrying for an invalid, or to take two places in the lorry to safety when it meant depriving two others. Both these decisions were wrong in the short run, but they reinforced an emotional stability which in the long term won through. Character, too, hard to define: self-respect combined with humility, the positive component set against the negative hatred of the Nazis. Lastly, sheer courage, both the hard, uphill grit which faces cancer and the gallantry which shines in a moment of danger, when many are cowed. All these, and luck. 'He was lucky to have survived.' True, but we know that all who survive are lucky.

.   .   .   .   .

Maisie Renault concluded her book, *La Grande Misère*, with the words: 'Let the memory [of those who died] help us to drive out all hatred and to understand that the only happiness in life consists in spreading happiness.'

8

'*And Found No End . . .*'

WHAT DOES IT ADD UP TO? MUCH MORE, CLEARLY, THAN I suspected on that March afternoon when the Agadir earthquake set me thinking. The simple question of why some people survive ordeals which kill others has taken us near fields of physiology and psychology, medicine and theology, in which it is dangerously easy for the amateur to talk nonsense. What can one undedicated layman offer as his contribution?

In a discussion of the Hunterian Society on 'The Limits of Human Endurance' in December of 1958,[1] Dr O. G. Edholm pointed out that there are, obviously, physical limits, even if we cannot define them. The human body will never be able to high-jump twelve feet or swim the Atlantic. Physiology can explore these limits, investigate the physical qualities needed to reach them, and by testing discover those best fitted to make the attempt. Endurance, we have seen, involves far more than physical strength; if it did not, Tiira would have gone

---

1. *Hunterian Society Transactions*, vol. XVII. Sir Vivian Fuchs' observations on personnel in *The Crossing of Antarctica* should be read alongside his part in this discussion.

under and Ericsson would have survived. More subtle factors are in question, of which more will be known as the years pass. One person is well adjusted; another, though apparently tough, is not. Here the blood-sugar level, cell pattern, oxygen-intake capacity and the rest play their part.

In the same discussion it was observed that the body adapts itself slowly to conditions which would kill the unadapted. The climber who goes up by gradual stages can operate comfortably at 26,000 feet, a height at which the unacclimatised, dropped from an aeroplane, would die. Similarly the Channel-swimmer is able to immerse himself for longer and longer periods, the skin of the Antarctic explorer's fingers hardens until he can handle metals at −40°, and so on. Different bodies seem to accustom themselves best to different conditions. I am lucky in acclimatising quickly to height, but I cannot imagine any amount of immersion fitting me for long periods in the water. At home I feel the damp chill and used to suffer chilblains, but I have not been worried by the dry cold of the Himalaya.

Turning to the mind, we have remarked here also an ability to adapt to new environment. This, along with the courage it demands, would seem to be the one quality common to all our survivors, and because by its very nature it is unpredictable it fits well with Bettelheim's assertion that it is environment that makes the man. Whether you are trapped in a coal-mine or beset by disease, lost at sea on a raft or avalanched down an ice-slope, whether you volunteer to sit for months under the snow or are faced with the unlooked-for horror of a concentration camp, you will survive according to your ability to adapt to conditions as they arise. According as you adapt, you become the new unit, climber-and-mountain or sailor-and-sea, with greater possibilities of endurance than climber or sailor alone.

This does not mean that you cannot be prepared, in some degree, by advice and by similar experience. Tiira's wandering life accustomed him to face new situations and undoubtedly helped him. Travel and purposeful testing of one's physical limits are a good practical preparation for the survival situation. The ordeal of K2 equipped Streather for Haramosh. Or take another mountaineering example from recent history. In August 1961 four young Frenchmen joined with three

Italians in an attempt on the Central Pillar of Fresney on Mont Blanc, one of the great Alpine 'plums.'[1] Below the crux, at a height of some 14,800 feet, they were trapped by a thunderstorm, which held them bound on a ledge for three days. Then the party struggled down. One of the young Frenchmen, who wore an aid for deafness, had already been hit by lightning and been affected in his mind. Walter Bonatti, veteran of many first ascents and of arduous Karakoram climbs, led them, '*à pas de géant*' as Pierre Mazeaud put it. Four men (three French and one Italian), superbly fit and as accomplished on rock as anyone climbing, died on the way. They were very young. Bonatti, the veteran, survived and was soon back on the mountains.

Because of their greater experience and hence endurance Sir Vivian Fuchs said in the discussion that he tended to choose men of between thirty and thirty-five for Antarctic expeditions. Speaking of the qualities for which an Antarctic leader looks, he cited 'emotional stability', which makes a man refuse either to be put out by failure or made rash by hope of success. (In the survival situation success usually equals escape.) This stability may be equated with the self-discipline which we have already observed, the man who controls his emotions being the man least affected by the vagaries of his environment. Partly this stability comes through experience, partly it is a matter of temperament. Of all the survivor's equipment it is perhaps the most susceptible to the microscope of the psychoanalyst.

It has been said that the instinct of self-preservation ingrained in all of us explains any remarkable case of survival. But that is not nearly enough. That instinct we share with animals, but all the situations of this book have been survived by virtue of qualities far beyond those that any animal could bring into play. These situations sometimes accentuated characteristics already obvious, like the obstinacy of Brown or the loyalty of Maisie Renault; but sometimes they lit up new facets of personality, the adaptable in Tiira, the enduring in Courtauld and, most obviously, the religious in the Catholic convert. Moreover, we have seen at least one case where the instinct of self-preservation was overridden by a sense of community with other

1. The first ascent was made not long after by D. Whillans and C. J. S. Bonington.

people which, while strengthening the will to survive, drastically cut down the chances of survival. That is why, though at first sight it seems paradoxical, a sense of self in community runs through these stories, and one reflection which they induce is upon the value of co-operation and tolerance and trust. No man is an island, no man can survive utterly alone unless it be the Satopanth hermit, who, I have said, stands aside from the living stream. Even John Brown, gas-choked and chilled below tons of rock, was cheered by the dim sound of his rescuers at work. Those whom we have considered survived through the help and encouragement of others. Of all the trials prolonged and hopeless solitude must have been the hardest to bear,[1] but even Burney was helped by clandestine communication with other prisoners, and was buoyed by the lively hope that others were working for his release.

If one is alone, or feels alone, in certain circumstances, another 'presence' may be felt. Small children have no difficulty in believing in the 'familiar'. They talk to him or her, go visiting, buy presents, know the likes and dislikes of 'the friend'. Their elders are more wary. Some believe that the 'second self' (not the same as, but stemming out of, the subconscious self) is susceptible to scientific demonstration, but for most it is an apparition born of inner stress or exaltation. The simpler sense of duality is very common. I have had it on very high mountains in a way similar to, though less marked than, John Emery's experience on Haramosh. I was two people, the upper self remaining calm and quite unaffected by the efforts of the panting lower. Under a different type of stress, that of being arrested by Franco's men, Arthur Koestler wrote of 'a dreamlike, dazed self-estrangement, which separated the conscious self from the acting self, the former becoming a detached observer'.[2] But stress is not necessarily the prompter. I know a woman who, at a performance of the Emperor Concerto by a certain player, 'felt as if one half of me was just above my body and quite disembodied

1. Odette Hallowes, in conversation, said that she did not mind solitary confinement in the dark. This happened to suit her; she felt free and not worried by the blackness because she had once lost her sight for a time as a child. The S.S. had misjudged her – understandably.
2. *The Invisible Writing.*

and listening with an intensity of enjoyment I have never experienced before or since. At the same time I was fully conscious of my usual self sitting in the seat and listening in my normal way below.'[1] She heard the same performer and the same concerto again later, but the experience was not repeated.

In Alphonse Daudet's case 'this terrible second me' appeared at his brother's death, mocking the first self's grief. But I am being led outside my field into that of the psychoanalysts, to whom the second, or even third, personality is a familiar figure. In times of stress, with which we are concerned, the second self sometimes puts on the clothing of another human. Quoted almost *ad nauseam* is the classic case of Frank Smythe, who, alone at 28,000 feet on Everest, turned round and handed a piece of mint-cake to his imagined companion. Before Ericsson died, Tiira had already sensed a third person in the raft. When he was alone, the feeling became much stronger and only disappeared when he finally gave up conscious hope of living. When Shackleton, Crean and Worsley made their 36-hour crossing of South Georgia, at the end of their strength and held together by their common aim and the need to bring help to those they had left behind, a fourth walked beside them; the feeling that they were four and not three was experienced and recorded separately by each member of the party.[2] There may even be more than three. Eric Shipton (who accompanied Smythe beyond Camp 6 in 1933) tells me that he has had this experience regularly on arduous mountain journeys: there has often been one more member of the party.

Sometimes the experience goes one stage further, and the 'person' takes an active part, as happened to Joshua Slocum on his lone voyage round the world;[3] or even becomes God, as when the extraordinary Fred Rebell, sailing alone from Australia to Los Angeles, was given specific instructions by an authoritative male voice at his ear.[4] Even among our small group of survivors several had the 'second self' experience and one or two connected it with a power outside them-

1. From a letter.
2. *South* by Sir Ernest Shackleton.
3. *Sailing Alone Around the World* by Joshua Slocum.
4. *Escape to the Sea* by Fred Rebell.

selves, not necessarily with the God of a particular creed (Tiira said the Lord's Prayer, but that was because it was the only prayer he knew from beginning to end), but with a power which seemed, in Streather's phrase, to be pulling on the rope.

At this point it would be very easy to stop, to say that I have produced a small case-book of survival stories, that these show certain lines which the would-be survivor might profitably cultivate but that various interpretations can be put upon the fundamental factors making for effective survival. Let each take his pick.

Such a conclusion would be pleasant but cowardly. I must risk going a little further.

The clue is given, I think, by the two threads that have been running through these stories. First, the importance of hormones in our temperamental make-up and the increasingly close connection which is being discovered between the material cells of our bodies and the processes which we like to term spiritual.[1] The distinction between mind and body, horse and rider as they used to be, is becoming ever more blurred, for all that our conscious selves may believe and continue to believe that 'I am the master of my fate: I am the captain of my soul.' A future of discovery lies with the physiologists, the endocrinologists and the biochemists.

This future may reveal the causation of what we have called the 'second self'. As long ago as the last century it was predicted that levitation and thought-transference would one day submit to natural laws. So also, perhaps, will the 'familiar', who plays so curious a role, under different guises, in extreme situations. Whatever his biological origins, he fulfils a fundamental need at certain moments in the lives of some people.

The answer to what this need is may lie in the direction of prayer or 'prayerful communion'. I am the last person to write a treatise on prayer, and I am trying now to stand outside Christian terminology.

1. 'Feelings of divine possession and subsequent conversion to a religious faith can be helped on by the use of many types of physiological stimuli' etc. W. Sargant, op. cit.

In extreme situations a need is felt to pray, as Houston prayed above House's Chimney, as Courtauld prayed when buried under the snow. In a tricky position on a mountain I have felt a prayer rising in my throat and had to beat it down, because I felt that it was a request rather than a communion and that it made nonsense to ask for things in a crisis unless one's whole life was of a pattern into which such a prayer naturally fitted. But the urge was a normal and reasonable one. Those who have that type of faith believe that they are saved *because of* their prayer. I am thinking of two very fine men. One was strung upside down by the Japanese for three days during the Burma campaign; the other, when his ship was sunk by enemy action, survived thirty-six hours in the water with a broken arm. Both prayed and came through. Whether their prayer was 'answered' in the literal sense we are not discussing here. The point is that, as I believe, 'energy which but for prayer would be bound is by prayer set free and operates in some part, be it objective or subjective, of the world of facts.'[1]

I quote from William James, and shall lean on him a good deal from this point. Wisdom is not unwise for not being new, and I have nowhere, now that our fashions of thought have parcelled the field too neatly for generalisation, seen the same truths more tenderly and understandingly put than in the conclusion to *The Varieties of Religious Experience*. If you add to James the further dimension of the interdependence of mind and matter which we have noted, you may reach a conclusion something like the following:

'It is agreed that the subliminal self is far larger than appears, submerged like the lower part of an iceberg below our conscious personality. In the excavation of that lower part Freud, Adler, Jung and many more have done miracles, while the physiologists and biochemists are establishing a closer and closer relation between it and our bodies. What is still not clear is the link between those icebergs on their very farthest side, both with each other and with something else beyond.'

F. W. H. Myers wrote: 'The Self manifests through the organism; but there is always some part of the Self unmanifested; and always, as

1. Houston's prayer is the clearest case quoted in this book. Relevant is Robin Hodgkin's remark and that of Alain, quoted in the footnote on page 107.

it seems, some power of organic expression in abeyance or reserve.'[1]
Much of that unmanifested self James wrote off as insignificant, a
collection of 'silly jingles' and 'inhibitive timidities'; psychoanalysis
today attaches an importance to these which he could not foresee. He
admitted that from it came performances of genius. But, also, the
farther side of our subliminal self seems to continue into something
beyond.

Let me then propose, as an hypothesis, that whatever it may be
on its *farther* side, the 'more' with which in religious experience we
feel ourselves connected is on its *hither* side the subconscious con-
tinuation of our conscious life. Starting thus with a recognised psychological fact as our basis, we seem to preserve a contact with 'science'
which the ordinary theologian lacks. At the same time the theologian's contention that the religious man is moved by an external
power is vindicated, for it is one of the peculiarities of invasions
from the subconscious region to take on objective appearances, and
to suggest to the Subject an external control. In the religious life
the control is felt as 'higher'; but since on our hypothesis it is prim-
arily the higher faculties of our own hidden mind which are con-
trolling, the sense of union with the power beyond us is a sense of
something, not merely apparently, but literally true.[2]

This much is a doorway, as James describes it, after entering which
each person adds his or her own overbeliefs. It is so elastic that some
have said that it does not matter to what 'higher' presence you pray,
so long as you pray; so wide that others call it a gateway to the obvious.
The important point is that 'the conscious person is continuous with
a wider self through which saving experiences come'. To this I will
add briefly my own overbelief, so far as it concerns survival. It differs
in some points from that of William James, and brings us back once
more to the 'second self'.

1. *Proceedings of the Society for Psychical Research*, vol. VIII. The scientologist
of today goes much further: 'The concept of the "unconscious" is re-evaluated
in Dianoetics by the discovery that the unconscious mind is the *only* mind which is
always conscious.' *The Science of Survival*, Publisher's Introduction.

2. William James, op. cit.

It is a known fact that in stress of brainwashing and torture those prisoners are likely to last longest who can successfully turn their thoughts to something quite outside, as did Col. R. H. Stevens when chained by the Gestapo to a wall for two years (told in a B.B.C. broadcast, 1947). We have already noticed the part played by daydreams of home and friends in the survival situation, and of outside interest in the sick person. A sense of humour, too, is of help because it implies detachment from the situation. Detachment brings repose.

The second self and the repose brought by prayer both seem to be a further answer to an organic need, as food is the answer to hunger; as if the teeming cells of which we are composed sent an S.O.S. into the farthest interior and beyond. Obviously, as Marceline had it, one immediate effect of prayer is to quieten the worried or pained part of us by submitting it to 'another', as the child does when it confides in its parent. This 'other' could be part of our own wider personality, called in to fill the need, sometimes, in Mrs G. and Tiira for instance, called in even when the conscious personality has given up hope.

It is called from our remoter self, but also (and this is no more than my own belief) from the shores of others' extended selves. When we are alone or in difficulty it can appear as a personification, though dim, of what we need in order to escape our isolation or helplessness. Because of human association and past experience stored in subconscious memory, it takes the form of another person. I believe that it may indeed *be* another person, summoned from the deep in which, unknown to conscious mind, we are joined with those others who provided that association and that experience.

In me, labouring over the Geneva Spur of Everest without oxygen (in which I put more faith than I need have done), it was only semi-detached, if I may use that word, an admirably calm, unruffled, lordly being which looked with pitying sympathy on the labours of the under-me. Its presence was one stage more manifest in John Emery's case, where the stress was greater. To Tiira, to Hermann Buhl when he climbed alone to the summit of Nanga Parbat, to Shackleton, to Slocum in his small boat, to Smythe particularly, it seemed a friendly, helpful presence. Smythe records having experienced a feeling almost of disappointment when he came in sight of Camp 6, where Shipton was, and the link snapped. As of the traveller on the road to Emmaus, we ask the question phrased by T. S. Eliot in *The Waste Land*:

> Who is the third who walks always beside you?
> When I count, there are only you and I together
> But when I look ahead up the white road
> There is always another one walking beside you
> Gliding wrapped in a brown mantle, hooded
> I do not know whether a man or a woman
> – But who is that on the other side of you?

This figure vanishes when 'normal' human contact is restored, or, as in Tiira's case, when the sufferer has gone beyond even its helping presence.

With the identification of this other personality with a God in the accepted sense I am not, mercifully, here concerned, but I come back for my conclusion to William James, and, substituting 'second self' for his 'prayerful communion', state as a lowest common denominator of belief that 'the appearance is that in this phenomenon something ideal, which in one sense is part of ourselves and in another sense is not ourselves, actually exerts an influence, raises our centre of personal energy, and produces regenerative effects unattainable in other ways'. It is as if, in ceasing for a moment the agonising struggle to be a perfect self, one became an imperfect part of a far greater self.

The survival situation struck a spark which in many lay unsuspected or dormant. This spark seems to me to have some essential connection with other people. Even the one-year-old baby which survives may have been affected by the *ambience* of the efforts being made to help it. The recent case of Terry Jo Duperrault is harder to account for. Terry Jo, an eleven-year-old girl, survived the murder of her parents and brother and sister on a ketch off the Bahamas, launched herself in a cork raft after the mad skipper had sailed off in the dinghy, and survived three and a half days of rough seas when there was every reason for her to die. To her, as to Tiira, a strong instinct of self-preservation, a youthful love of life, must be ascribed. Usually, however, faith in the co-operative powers of others working to our good is a major factor making for survival. I cannot imagine a murderer surviving easily, for the sense of sympathy is a quality of ordinary human beings, and 'ordinary persons have much greater powers of adaptation to circumstance than most eccentrics or psychotics.'[1] I doubt, too, whether a thorough-going miser would survive – unless, of course, like Harpagon, he succeeded in personifying his *cassette* until it became another person.

Faith in others demands courage, and courage is the conquest of fear. In the wider context of the survival of the human race under threat of the Bomb, fear, as Bertrand Russell has been underlining lately, is the root of our trouble. We need courage even more than good intentions, of which there are plenty. We have not a sufficiently courageous faith that the common cause of our humanity is strong enough to break down the fears by which our separate selves are hedged. For the individual, as for the state, the way to survival lies through trust, through the strengthening of those subtle ties which link each iceberg to each, underneath, and through a co-operation in which the individual can join without losing his individuality. Few would quarrel with Byrd's conviction that we are part of that larger whole, whether we like it or not, and that the processes which we recognise in ourselves have some counterpart in those of the universe around us.

This courage can be shown in the recognition that our similarities are stronger than our barriers, and that survival lies in the cultivation, whether we are Christian or Hindu or agnostic, of sympathy with others, of an adaptability to their needs which will enable us to adapt to our own when occasion demands. Such courage can be gained by submitting ourselves to experiences likely to call for it and by accepting with goodwill tasks of collaboration which 'reason' at first sight refuses. Thus may be born, perhaps, that 'energy' which we so badly need.

What is the ultimate *reason* for survival, what is the 'transcendental focus'[2] or Omega which is and will be when this fragment of a star has cooled into disintegration – there I stop, having already, like Milton's fallen angels, strayed too far 'and found no end, in wandering mazes lost'.

1. William Sargant, op. cit.
2. Father Teilhard de Chardin's phrase.

Bibliography

A list of books to which reference is made. Many more have, of course, influenced me indirectly.

Alain, (Emile Chartier). *Minerve ou de la Sagesse*. Paris: Paul Hartmann, 1939.

Barker, R. *The Last Blue Mountain*. London: Chatto and Windus, 1959. New York: Doubleday, 1960.

Beau, G. *Le Cancer*. Paris: Editions du Seuil, 1961.

Bettelheim, B. *The Informed Heart*. London: Thames and Hudson, 1961. Chicago: The Free Press of Glencoe, 1960.

Blake, G. *The Ben Line*. London: Nelson, 1956.

Bombard, A. *The Bombard Story*. London: André Deutsch, 1953. New York: Simon and Schuster, 1954.

Burney, C. *Solitary Confinement*. London: Macmillan, 1952. New York: St. Martin's Press, 1961.

Byrd, R. *Alone*. London: Putnam, 1938. New York: G. P. Putnam's Sons, 1938.

Cameron, D. R. G. *A Saharan Venture*. London: Arnold, 1928.

Chapman, F. Spencer. *Watkins' Last Expedition*. London: Chatto and Windus, 1934. *The Jungle is Neutral*. London: Chatto and Windus, 1949.

Cooke, K. *What Cares the Sea?* London: Hutchinson, 1960. New York: McGraw-Hill, 1960.

Eliot, T. S. *Collected Poems*. London: Faber and Faber, 1936. New York: Harcourt, Brace and World, 1936.

Evans-Wentz, W. Y. *Tibet's Great Yogi Milarepa*. London: Oxford University Press, 1928.

Fisher, H. A. L. *Our New Religion*. London: Watts, 1933.

Frazer, Sir James. *The Golden Bough*. London: Macmillan, 1891.

Fuchs, Sir Vivian. *The Crossing of Antarctica*. London: Cassell, 1959. New York: Little, Brown, 1959. Remarks, *The Hunterian Society Transactions, vol. XVII.*

Geikie, Sir Archibald. *Geological Sketches*. London: Macmillan, 1882.

Hayes, J. G. *The Conquest of the North Pole*. London: Butterworth, 1932. New York: Macmillan, 1933.

Hedin, S. *Through Asia*. London: Methuen, 1898. New York: Harper & Brothers, 1899.

Hession, B. *Determined to Live*. London: Peter Davies, 1956.

Hill, A. Memoir of Dailly Parish in *The Statistical Account of Scotland, vol. V.* London: Blackwood, 1845.

Houston, C. S., and Bates, R. H. *K2: The Savage Mountain*. London: Collins, 1955. New York: McGraw-Hill, 1954.

Howarth, D. *We Die Alone*. London: Collins, 1955. New York: Macmillan, 1955.

Hubbard, L. Ron. *The Science of Survival*. The Hubbard Association of Scientologists International, 1959.

Hutchinson, R. C. *Food for Survival*. Melbourne University Press, 1959. (There are very many manuals, like *Survival: Land, Sea, Jungle, Arctic*, published by the *Infantry Journal*, Washington, D.C., 1944, and *Survival Training in the U.S.A.F.*, but space forbids a long list.)

Huxley, Aldous. *The Doors of Perception*. London: Chatto and Windus, 1954. New York: Harper & Brothers, 1954.

Innes-Taylor, A. *Arctic Survival Guide*. Scandinavian Airlines System, 1957.

James, M. *Born of the Desert*. London: Collins, 1945.

James, William. *The Varieties of Religious Experience*. London: Longmans, Green, 1902.

Kirwan, L. P. *The White Road*. London: Hollis and Carter, 1959. New York: W. W. Norton, 1960.

Koestler, Arthur. *The Invisible Writing*. London: Collins, 1954. New York: Beacon, 1955.

Kogon, E. *The Theory and Practice of Hell*. London: Secker and Warburg, 1950. New York: Farrar, Strauss, 1950.

Lewis, C. S. *The Problem of Pain*. London: Bles, 1940.

Maraini, F. *Secret Tibet*. London: Hutchinson, 1954.

Mason, P. (*nom de plume* Philip Woodruff). *Whatever Dies*. London: Cape, 1948.

Nesbitt, P. H., Pond, A. W., and Allen, W. H. *The Survival Book*. New York: Van Nostrand, 1959.

Nicholl, G. W. R. *Survival at Sea*. London: Adlard Coles, 1960. New York: DeGraff, 1960.

Pallis, M. *Peaks and Lamas*. London: Cassell, 1939. New York: Alfred A. Knopf, 1949.

Powell, T. *The Long Rescue*. London: W. H. Allen, 1961. New York: Doubleday, 1960.

Rebell, F. *Escape to the Sea*. London: Murray, 1939. New York: Dodd, Mead, 1939.

Rémy, (Gilbert Renault-Roulier). *Courage and Fear*. London: Barker, 1950.

Renault, M. *La Grande Misère*. Paris: Chavane, 1948.

Sargant, W. *Battle for the Mind*. London: Heinemann, 1957 (Rev. 1959). New York: Doubleday, 1957.

Schnabel, R. *Macht ohne Moral*. Frankfurt: Röderberg, 1957.

Scott, Ernest. *Australian Discovery by Sea* and *Australian Discovery by Land*. London: Dent, 1929. New York: Dutton, 1929.

Scott, J. M. *Portrait of an Ice Cap*. London: Chatto and Windus, 1953.

Scott, R. F. *Scott's Last Expedition*. London: Smith, Elder, 1912. New York: Dodd, Mead, 1913.

Shackleton, Sir Ernest. *South*. London: Heinemann, 1919.

Shipton, E. E. *Upon that Mountain*. London: Hodder and Stoughton, 1943.

Slocum, J. *Sailing Alone Around the World*. London: Sampson Lowe, 1900. New York: Century, 1911.

Stefansson, V. Various writings on living off the land in the Arctic.

Bibliography

Teilhard de Chardin, Father P. *The Phenomenon of Man*. London: Collins, 1959. New York: Harper, 1959.

Tiira, E. *Raft of Despair*. London: Hutchinson, 1954. New York: Dutton, 1954.

Wechsberg, J. *Avalanche!* London: Kimber, 1960. New York: Alfred A. Knopf, 1958.

West, F. *Lifeboat Number Seven*. London: Weidenfeld, 1958.

Williams, C. *The Descent of the Dove*. London: Longmans, Green, 1939. New York: Oxford University Press, 1940.